RADIANT MIND

RADIANT
MIND

Awakening
Unconditioned
Awareness

PETER FENNER, PH.D.

SOUNDS TRUE
Boulder, Colorado

Sounds True, Inc., Boulder, CO 80306
© 2007 Peter Fenner

Book designed by Karen Polaski

Published 2007
Printed in Canada

ISBN 978-1-59179-577-3

Library of Congress Cataloging-in-Publication Data

Fenner, Peter G., 1949-
  Radiant mind : awakening unconditioned awareness / Peter Fenner.
    p. cm.
  ISBN 978-1-59179-577-3 (hardcover)
  1. Spiritual life. 2. Awareness--Religious aspects. I. Title.

BL629.5.A82F46 2007
204'.4--dc22
                              2007004308

Dedication

I dedicate this work to my main teachers.

Lama Yeshe for giving me his boundless love and showing me his truly expanded vision.

Sri Satya Sai Baba—I don't know who I'm thanking when I thank you, but I know you've been guiding me in recent years.

My daughters Tahli, Yeshe, and Brooke—thank you from my heart for making me more real and for your sound counsel.

My Timeless Wisdom students—thank you for becoming my guru and for letting me find you wherever I go.

As a conduit for these beautiful forces and influences I dedicate this book to the radiant awakening of all beings everywhere.

Contents

Acknowledgments

In 1975, the late Lama Thubten Yeshe asked me to teach the dharma. Lama's boundless love and wisdom gave me everything I needed as he set my roots firmly in the Mahayana path. The radical way in which he made Tibetan Buddhist relevant and alive for his Western students continues to be a constant source of inspiration. *Radiant Mind* is a humble attempt to fulfill my guru's wishes. I thank the many Tibetan teachers with whom I've been privileged to study and practice over many years. Lama Zopa Rinpoche in particular has helped keep me connected with Lama Yeshe's vision and intention. I especially thank Sogyal Rinpoche who helped me through the difficult transition phase from monk to post-monastic.

I am forever grateful to the blessing field of Sri Sathya Sai Baba. My relationship with Sathya Sai is a complete mystery to me, but it has been instrumental in the development of the Radiant Mind program. Various sections of this book were written in the mandir at his Prasanthi Nilayam ashram in Puttaparthi. His invisible influence brought coherence to my thinking and greatly increased the efficiency of my writing. I'd also like to thank Dr. Fernando Flores for supporting my own training in his "ontological paradigm" and for his coaching and conversations.

I owe a great depth of gratitude to Tami Simon, the President of Sounds True, for accepting my work in the list of esteemed publications and productions for which Sounds True is renowned. I thank my editor and producer at Sounds True, Randy Roark, for his supportive, inspired, and enthusiastic guidance throughout the editorial process. Stephan Bodian provided his super-efficient editing and astute comments on the entire manuscript. I give very special thanks to Shayla Wright who stepped in when critical deadlines were looming. Shayla let me throw notes at her at all hours of the day and night and returned them clean and coherent the next day. I thank Jasmyne Boswell for help in assembling material drawn from my teachings. I give special thanks to Brigitte Auloy who stood behind me during the initial creation of the Radiant Mind program. She helped me with background research and her enthusiasm often helped invigorate my weary mind.

I give special thanks to my very dear friends Margo King and John Steiner who have given me so much at every level. Their support has given me the time, resources, and teaching opportunities to develop and refine the Radiant Mind approach. I similarly thank Melissa and Terry Stuart for their generous and comprehensive support of this work. I also thank my spiritual brother, Dr. Jean-Marc Mantel, for his multi-functional support.

Finally I thank my wife Marie for her companionship and enthusiastic support of the Radiant Mind initiative, particularly as it transforms into a community endeavor and expands in Europe and elsewhere.

UNCONDITIONED AWARENESS
The Ultimate Goal of All Human Endeavors

As the darkness of the night,
even were it to last a thousand years,
could not conceal the rising sun,
so countless ages of conflict and suffering
cannot conceal the innate radiance of Mind.
TILOPA (10TH CENTURY), *SONG TO NAROPA*[1]

R*adiant Mind* is designed to teach you how to access and deepen the highest possible spiritual experience—and how to share this experience with others. This state—which I am calling "unconditioned awareness"—has been known by many terms in many different traditions over the ages, including enlightenment, egolessness, pure awareness, and perfect wisdom. Most people have enjoyed spiritual experiences of one kind or another, either in the context of a particular practice or arising spontaneously without any apparent cause, including experiences that can arise through meditation and in the presence of powerful spiritual teachers; but the experience of unconditioned awareness is quite unique and identifiable—it is a level of consciousness that hundreds of thousands of practitioners in various spiritual traditions over the centuries have contemplated, meditated on, inquired into, and experienced. In fact, Eastern efforts to develop expertise in accessing this liberating state of awareness have paralleled the pursuit of scientific expertise in the West, and the inner knowledge and experience they have accumulated over the centuries parallels the more obvious accomplishments of the outer sciences.

Radiant Mind focuses on unconditioned awareness because it's the ultimate goal of all human endeavors. Everything we do in every field of activity—religious, scientific, political, economic, and artistic—aims at achieving a state where all needs and desires are realized. As the Dalai Lama often says, all beings are seeking the same happiness and fulfillment. But if all our needs haven't been fulfilled, we haven't reached our final goal. Conditioned mind tells us we still have further to go!

As humans, we explore myriad ways of achieving this fulfillment, but the only experience that can satisfy all our needs is unconditioned awareness. Why? Because when we rest in unconditioned awareness, we don't need anything. We're complete and fulfilled exactly as we are. We don't have to get rid of certain thoughts or emotions or change our circumstances in any way. Thoughts, feelings, and perceptions arise, but they no longer condition us. As extraordinary as unconditioned awareness may sound, it isn't distant from our everyday life; it's always readily available to us. Through the experience of unconditioned awareness, we can discover total fulfillment in the midst of our conditioned existence.

In this book, we're approaching our concern for deep fulfillment from a nondual perspective. What does this mean? It means that freedom or liberation isn't a state that exists in contrast to feeling stuck or in any way imprisoned in our life. In fact, it doesn't exist in contrast to anything. It's a level of experience that coexists with everything. The nondual state of unconditioned awareness can't exclude thoughts, feelings, and perceptions, because it includes all that is, and so isn't separate from our everyday dualistic existence. But it's not here in the same way that sensory objects or feelings in a body are, nor is it somewhere else.

The material presented in this book is firmly based on the wisdom contained in nondual traditions, such as the Perfect Wisdom (Prajnaparamita), Zen, Middle Way (Madhyamaka), Universal Embrace (Mahamudra), and Complete Fulfillment (Dzogchen), yet with a fresh and contemporary flavor. From time to time, I may make some connections between what we're "doing" and these traditions, but such comparisons are of secondary importance. Our central task is to gain easier and easier access to unconditioned awareness, and learn how to integrate this experience into the totality of our life. Our aim is to produce and integrate a transformation of our minds so that we are less susceptible to suffering and more confident in living the joy, love, and freedom that can make every moment of our existence meaningful and precious.

Radiant Mind will take you inside your own mind and the minds of teachers whose work is inspired by unconditioned awareness. To a certain extent, it will also take you inside the minds of nondual spiritual masters: Zen roshis, Advaita gurus, Dzogchen lamas. By entering their being-state, you'll discover what it's like inside them, how they experience others, and how you might experience the inner structure of nondual work as they experience it. These practices are available to anyone who wants to take charge of their own psychological and spiritual evolution.

The nondual work presented in this book is open and at the same time precise. This book introduces you to the experience of unconditioned awareness with as much economy of effort and time as possible. In order to do this, we need to be equipped with a set of skills.

The practices taught in *Radiant Mind* include:

- Developing and expanding your contemplative practice
- Gaining skills in observing and dissolving fixations
- Exploring living in the here and now and finding a foundation for being and action that transcends your desires and preferences
- Learning how to listen and speak from a space of pure openness
- Learning how to communicate more effectively so you can be complete, moment by moment
- Increasing your capacity for nonaction, for not needing to know who or even where you are
- Refining your ability to act with precision and clarity in the world while still being rooted in the experiences of noncompulsive action and not knowing
- Learning how to produce deep and conscious transformation during the periods of silence that can arise in nondual teaching
- The capacity to accept and integrate the experience of discomfort and heightened pleasure
- The capacity to rest comfortably in unconditioned awareness when relating with others

- The ability to observe people's predispositions and biases and share them in such a way that people can recognize them
- Discovering how to bring your attention to what is happening in the here and now
- Using deconstructive conversations to dismantle fixed ideas and rigid interpretations
- Learning how to manage silent conversations
- Learning how to use natural koans to enter unconditioned awareness
- Learning how to dance in the paradoxes of nondual awareness

THE INSPIRATION BEHIND THIS APPROACH TO UNCONDITIONED AWARENESS

From an evolutionary point of view, the most remarkable event in the history of humanity is the phenomenon of people dissolving their identifications with the prevailing systems of thought, beliefs, rituals, and practices, and entering an experience of unconditioned awareness, which is identical for everyone. Here, we transcend space and time and become participants in the shared birthright of all conscious beings. In centuries to come, when humans are living on the farther reaches of our galaxy—at which time they may look quite unlike humans of the 21st century—there will no doubt be individuals who, through their sincere inquiry into questions such as "Who am I?" and "What is this?" will break through to the very same experience.

As I've already mentioned, the nondual approach has been inspired by the examples of masters and sages from the nondual spiritual traditions of Asia. The most illustrious of these masters include Buddha, Lao Tzu, Garab Dorje, Nagarjuna, Bodhidharma, Hui-neng, Saraha, Tilopa, Padmasambhava, Atisha, Shankara, Milarepa, Longchenpa, and many others. But there are also tens of thousands of masters about whom we know nothing, some of whom spent their lives as "realized governors," "enlightened mothers," "illumined farmers," and "awakened artists." Though they differ enormously in their personalities and influence, these masters all share an identical experience of unconditioned awareness.

Nondual traditions have applied various terms to the experience that marks the full evolution of consciousness: self-knowledge, witness consciousness, no-mind, primordial mind, reality, openness, pure awareness, buddha-nature. The great Dzogchen master Longchenpa listed an extensive set of terms that refer to this unconditioned reality (Thurman 1996):

> *This reality has names of many different kinds.*
> *It is "the realm" that transcends life and liberation.*
> *The primally present "natural spontaneity."*
> *The "essential realm" obscured by defilement.*
> *The "ultimate truth," the condition of reality.*
> *The originally pure "stainless translucency."*
> *The "central reality" that dispels extremisms.*
> *The "transcendent wisdom" beyond fabrications.*
> *The "indivisible reality" clear-void-purity.*
> *And the "Suchness" reality free of death transitions.*
> *Such names are accepted by the clear-seeing wise.*[2]

I will generally use the term "unconditioned awareness" in this book, but I could just as well use any of the other terms listed above.

THE AIM OF NONDUAL TEACHING

The primary intention of nondual teaching is to introduce people to the unconditioned dimension of their existence, and then to deepen and stabilize the experience. This simple intention is identical with Garab Dorje's quintessential summation of the nondual Dzogchen tradition. According to Garab Dorje (Reynolds 1996), the function of Dzogchen can be described through three key aspects:

- Direct introduction to one's own real nature
- Clearly recognizing this unique state
- Continuing to abide confidently in this state of freedom[3]

Following Garab Dorje's model, the material in this book has three key functions:

- To introduce you to a space of contentless awareness in which nothing needs to be done and nothing needs to be thought about or understood

- To help you identify this state when it's present by demonstrating that there is nothing to do or to know, nothing that can be enhanced or degraded, and so forth. The authenticity of this state can be determined through questions that reveal whether you're resting in a structured or unstructured state
- To assist you in remaining in this experience by observing how you move out of it by making it into "something"—anything—which can then be lost and gained. This "making it into something" can occur in a number of ways, for example, by trying to figure out what it is or by wondering how to maintain or discover it in future situations

More simply, the aim of nondual work is to:

- Eliminate the fixations and habitual patterns that cause suffering
- Gradually transform our life into a source of joy and inspiration for ourselves and others
- Ultimately, saturate our existence with the bliss and clarity of unconditioned awareness

This final aim may sound ambitious or excessive, but why not! As one of my main teachers, Lama Thubten Yeshe, often said, "Think big, act big, without getting caught in the magical, superstitious mind." That is, don't get caught in the mind that fantasizes about our spiritual progress and anticipates our imminent enlightenment!

Radiant Mind focuses on giving you access to unconditioned awareness in the midst of your conditioned existence, without needing to drastically change your personality or lifestyle. Through a variety of exercises and techniques, this book will help you to make the transition from being preoccupied with getting what you want and avoiding what you don't want, to experiencing life free from the constraints of habitual behaviors and limited preferences.

My presentation of this material dispenses with the doctrines and complex rituals that can attach to spiritual traditions, and goes to the heart of their liberating intention. In this way, it mirrors the direct and unencumbered teachings of the greatest masters and sages, including the historical Buddha, who transcended the religious structures in which they were immersed, and spoke directly to the hearts and minds of their disciples. You don't have to adopt a foreign set of beliefs, customs, or practices to benefit from this work or to learn to rest in unconditioned awareness. The nondual state of consciousness is your natural state, your birthright, and each of us has the opportunity to cultivate direct access to it.

In this book, we will focus solely on the result of these practices — the experience of the unconditioned. Our ideal is to do nothing more and nothing less than what is needed to awaken the experience in the here and now. And when this experience is not possible for us in the present moment, then we will at least be preparing our minds for future moments when we will be able to have this experience.

The Paradoxical Nature of Unconditioned Awareness

U nconditioned awareness is a state of consciousness that contains, yet goes beyond, all forms or structures of experience. It's sometimes also called the "source consciousness" because it's *that* which everything appears to arise from and return to. When we rest in unconditioned awareness, we don't need anything; there's nowhere further to go. In unconditioned awareness, there are no problems or solutions because nothing is missing. It can't get any better because there's no better or worse. There's no attachment nor aversion—nor our natural tendency to grasp on to pleasure and resist pain—because we are no longer attached to or repelled from whatever arises in our experience.

To provide a clearer description of unconditioned awareness, it can be helpful to contrast it with conditioned mind. Of course, in identifying unconditioned awareness in this way, we also need to realize that we aren't identifying unconditioned awareness as any thing. Contrasts and comparisons exist only in conditioned mind. Unconditioned awareness can't be compared with anything, which is what makes it unique. If you can accept how an attempt to come to know unconditioned awareness in this way doesn't make logical sense, then you have a sense of unconditioned awareness.

Most of us operate from our conditioned minds most, if not all, of the time. It's the mind that feels that something is missing and seeks solutions, remedies, and strategies to solve its problems. Conditioned mind operates entirely on the basis of preferences, likes, and dislikes; it seeks to avoid pain and maximize pleasure. Conditioned mind tries to hold on to experiences we judge as "good" and reject experiences we judge as "bad," and believes that happiness is a product of aligning our experiences with our preferences. When our experiences and preferences are misaligned, we experience it as a problem, which conditioned mind tries to solve by formulating a strategy to solve the problem. This usually involves changing our situation, our way of thinking, our feelings, our relationships, or our material circumstances. We then experience a period of relief from the problem, but the practice of judging our experiences according to our preferences is so habitual that we soon find ourselves with another problem to solve. In this way, what I've just written and what you're reading are products of conditioned mind! In fact, it is conditioned mind that led you to buy this book.

Unconditioned awareness is a nondual state of consciousness, which means that it includes all phenomena and experiences, with nothing left out. If any experiences are excluded or resisted in any way, the state is, by definition, dualistic rather than nondual. This nondual quality inevitably embraces paradox—that is, the possibility that something can be both true and false, good and bad, present and absent. Contrary to the experience of conditioned mind, unconditioned awareness allows us to remain peaceful and undisturbed in the midst of paradox and ambiguity. Our usual preferences for order, structure, categories, and concepts don't exist when we rest in this nondual awareness.

In the West, if we find that our thoughts contradict themselves, we become embarrassed or concerned that we lack clarity or rationality. In the East, paradox is welcomed because it shows the mind its own limits, which opens us to the possibility of experience that lies beyond our conventional mind-stream. The Eastern mystical paths move fluidly in this paradoxical domain without any embarrassment or distress. Experience tells them that unconditioned awareness can be described only through paradox and contradiction, so you can expect to encounter paradox again and again in any discussion about unconditioned awareness. (For more on paradox, see Chapter Two.)

When we're resting in unconditioned awareness, our conditioning—our age, sex, history, education, physical condition, and financial situation—no longer limits us. We find ourselves intimately connected with everything within and around us, yet we're beyond being disturbed in any way. We transcend suffering, not because our problems are solved, but because we experience a level of consciousness in which nothing is missing, a way of being that doesn't depend on the conditions of our mind, body, and life situation.

The experience of unconditioned awareness takes us outside the cycle of reactive responses and emotions by connecting us with the nature of our mind as pure, contentless, unstructured awareness. We're at home with ourselves in a totally natural and uncontrived way. In the Vajrayana tradition of Buddhism, this experience is called invincibility or indestructibility. While fully accepting our finite and conditioned existence, we rest in a level of consciousness that can't be damaged or degraded by the presence of any thought, feeling, or sensation.

Just as the experience of unconditioned awareness is the ultimate goal of all human endeavors, it's also the ultimate fruition of the spiritual path. When there's nothing further to realize or attain, nothing missing from our experience right now, no attachment or aversion, no desire for circumstances to be different from the way they are, we have achieved the fulfillment described by the great masters and sages when they talk about self-knowledge, egolessness, pure awareness, or perfect wisdom. Our experience is identical with theirs—and we can know this with absolute certainty because the experience is precise and identifiable. It's the only experience that's completely open, unstructured, and without content, which is why it's sometimes called "contentless wisdom."

For me, perhaps the most remarkable thing about this experience is the certainty with which we can identify it. While transcending culture or location, it also links people across time and space and from one generation to another. It's the whispered lineage of Dzogchen, the special transmission beyond texts of Zen, and the contentless transmission of the Prajnaparamita in Mahayana Buddhism. What's unique about all these forms of transmission is that they have no content. They are the direct transmission or transfer of the experience of unconditioned awareness from one mind-stream to another.

Many times I'll use the term "experience" or "state" when I'm talking about unconditioned awareness. I'm using these terms in the same way that others talk about the experience of nirvana or enlightenment, or the experience of no-mind. But please don't get hung up on these terms. Unconditioned awareness isn't an experience that happens to someone. It's also not a state of consciousness, because it's not something that can be contrasted with anything else. It's not a biological state. This is why I will often return to saying it's "nothing." But, of course, it's not nothing either.

UNCONDITIONED AWARENESS AND RADIANT MIND

Radiant mind arises when we rest in unconditioned awareness and allow it to radiate through the totality of our conditioned existence, bringing peace, wisdom, and love to everything we experience. Radiant mind is the integration of unconditioned awareness into the conditioned body-mind, gradually transforming the body-mind in the process. When the unconditioned refracts through and perfumes the flavor and quality of our everyday existence, we experience radiant mind. In the Dzogchen tradition, the experience of radiance is likened to transparent light (the unconditioned) refracting through a prism (the radiant mind), bringing forth and illuminating the infinite richness and diversity of the conditioned or manifest universe. When you live in radiant mind, you experience yourself as a unique human being, and at the same time you rest in a unified expanse of unconditioned-bliss-awareness.

DEEPENING AND EXPANDING THE EXPERIENCE OF UNCONDITIONED AWARENESS

The nondual experience can be spoken about in terms of three parameters: purity, depth, and duration. By purity, I mean the absence of conditioned structures of understanding and interpretation. By depth, I mean the extent to which the unconditioned pervades or infuses our conditioned existence. By duration, I mean the length of time we can rest in this state.

Paradoxically, when we're actually resting in the experience of unconditioned awareness, none of these parameters make any sense. In fact, they simply don't apply. The experience of unconditioned awareness can't be pure or impure, because it has no structure. It can't be deep or shallow, because it isn't like the ocean—it's more like pure space, without a reference point. And it can't be spoken of in terms of duration, because it doesn't arise or dissipate. Since it isn't a thing, it can't come into being, nor can it be said to exist or not exist.

But at the level where it seems there's something we need to do—which is the level where most of us find ourselves most of the time—we can sensibly talk about purifying, deepening, and expanding the experience of unconditioned awareness. The path to full enlightenment generally proceeds from a heavily conditioned state of consciousness, in which attachment and aversion rule our behavior, through an initial glimpse of unconditioned awareness, to repeated peak experiences of unconditioned awareness that increasingly infuse our conditioned existence. This path ultimately culminates in complete freedom from conditioned patterns and an unbroken resting in the nondual state of consciousness.

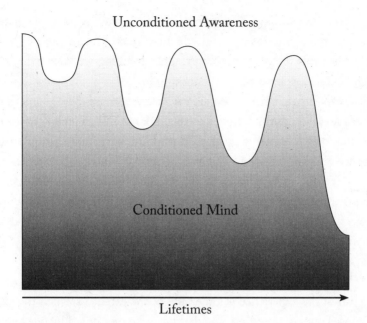

Unconditioned Awareness

Conditioned Mind

Lifetimes

The graph above illustrates this progression. The white scalloped dips at the top represent the experience of unconditioned awareness becoming longer and penetrating more deeply into our conditioned experience.

PURITY

Purity signifies the extent to which our experience is free of structures, by which I mean feelings, thoughts, cognitions, and interpretations. Most ordinary states of mind are heavily structured, bearing a thick overlay of ideas, beliefs, and emotions that obscure a clear, direct experience of what's occurring from moment to moment. Other states of mind are more lightly structured, in the sense that the overlay or veil is subtler and more translucent. Most spiritual experiences belong in this category: they're generally lightly structured by feelings of calm or bliss, ideas of transcendence, or insights into the nature of reality. But they're structured nonetheless.

By contrast, unconditioned awareness has no structure—it's pure, unfabricated, unmanipulated, contentless awareness within which everything arises just as it does. In our work, we need to be able to distinguish between structured and unstructured experience. Otherwise, we may think we're experiencing unconditioned awareness when, in fact, we're experiencing a lightly structured state of mind in which we're still identified with certain spiritual thoughts or feelings—for example, thinking we know what's happening, or enjoying a feeling of openness or joy.

If an experience is structured, we can lose it because there's something to lose—an idea, an interpretation, a feeling. For example, a feeling of joy or an awakening insight may come and go. But we can never lose the unstructured experience of unconditioned awareness, because it's empty of content. Strictly speaking, it's not an experience at all, but the ground or space in which all experiences come and go. When we're truly resting in pure unconditioned awareness, we can't be disturbed by any experience, no matter how difficult or painful.

DEPTH

The depth of the experience is a measure of the extent to which the experience infuses our conditioning. The depth can be monitored by our tendency to move out of the experience of unconditioned awareness and return to the state of conditioned awareness. When we're resting in the experience, we have a certain composure or equanimity, in that we're not trying to push away or hold on to anything. Nevertheless, at some point, a trigger of some kind moves us out of the experience. Generally, a move away from the experience gets triggered when something happens that we think shouldn't be happening.

If we have a preference for accessing this state through silence or meditation, we may be triggered when someone speaks, walks into the room, or gets up from their chair. Or we may simply think, "This is great!" and immediately we're locked into a structure or fixated on the experience itself. We've then moved away from unconditioned awareness.

If we're attached to the experience of unconditioned awareness, we might try to avoid painful or challenging experiences that could trigger a reaction that this shouldn't be happening. But such avoidance or resistance immediately degrades the experience, because we can't simultaneously avoid our conditioning *and* be present in the state of nondual awareness. It's natural to move in and out of the experience of unconditioned awareness. By noticing the triggers that can take us out of the state—by recognizing them without judgment or disdain—we can often immediately return to the experience.

As we become progressively more familiar with the experience of unconditioned awareness, we find that we can be present to events that would previously have moved us out of the experience. Those who preferred meditation can increase their capacity to be present to conversation or activity without thinking that those events should or shouldn't be happening. When someone enters the room or does or says something, it doesn't disrupt or disturb us in the slightest. As the experience of unconditioned awareness deepens and stabilizes, previously challenging events gradually become pervaded by the equanimity and imperturbability that characterize this state.

Initially, we might enjoy the experience of unconditioned awareness for a few minutes at a time. As we become more familiar with the experience and find it easier to access, we gradually come to enjoy it for longer and longer periods of time. Complete enlightenment is the permanent, unbroken experience of unconditioned awareness at the utmost possible depth. No conceivable event could cause us to think, "This should or shouldn't be happening." However, complete enlightenment is an ideal, and fixating on it as a goal merely causes us to struggle for something apart from our present experience, which paradoxically undermines the experience of unconditioned awareness.

The approach I recommend is to cultivate this state of consciousness without trying to control or strive for it. When we let unconditioned awareness do its work, in its own subtle way, we find it infuses the various layers of our conditioning. The more familiar we become with unconditioned awareness, the more readily it pervades our experience, without requiring any work on our part.

DURATION

This is the easiest dimension to understand. Duration simply means the amount of time we spend resting in unconditioned awareness. This might be just a few seconds initially, increasing to several minutes, and then to an hour or more. Sometimes people also have a real breakthrough experience, like a satori event, where they can rest in no-mind for some days or even a few weeks. In general, it's best not to give too much attention to how long we spend in unconditioned awareness. But, if we apply ourselves to this type of work, we can notice that as the years progress, we're able to spend more time resting and functioning from radiant mind.

DEVELOPING A HOMING INSTINCT: BECOMING MORE FAMILIAR WITH UNCONDITIONED AWARENESS

The more time we spend resting in and enjoying our ultimate nature, the more deeply we appreciate and treasure the experience, and the more naturally and spontaneously we gravitate back to it. In other words, we develop a homing instinct. When opportunities arise to let go of our preoccupations and daily concerns, we find ourselves moving effortlessly and without resistance into a more open, unstructured, accepting way of being. Because we value the deep peace and spiritual nutrition we gain from abiding in unconditioned awareness, we don't waste time in petty distractions or superficial intellectualizations. Our values and priorities naturally change, and we grow in our capacity to accept more freedom, love, and happiness in our life.

NONDUAL WORK AND UNCONDITIONED AWARENESS

As I mentioned earlier, another term that has been used to refer to unconditioned awareness is "nondual experience." Nonduality is the experience that we — as finite, individual selves — are, at our deepest essence, indivisible from an infinite expanse of unconditioned consciousness and bliss.

Nondual teaching has, in fact, been practiced in Asia for over three thousand years. It has often been revered as the pinnacle of Asian spirituality and was considered by many masters and sages to be the most effective method for transforming the mind into a continuous source of wisdom, love, and joy. These ancient masters and yogis applied a variety of spiritual methods based on the nondual approach designed to purify the body, mind, and soul, and lead people to their highest potential.

In India, China, and Tibet, many different forms of nondual instruction are practiced. Some are designed to be used privately as self-learning, without the hands-on guidance of a teacher. Others are practiced in group settings or under the direct and immediate guidance of a master. The private inner work generally uses subtle meditation methods to dissolve people's limiting concepts and disturbing emotions. The interactive work often takes the form of dialogues between teacher and student. All these approaches share the same goal — the removal of suffering and the cultivation of love by accepting and transcending our conditioned mode of existence. I will be introducing methods that can be used as "inner work" and others that can be used with partners, friends, and colleagues.

THE HEALING POWER OF UNCONDITIONED AWARENESS

In Buddhism, the experience of unconditioned awareness is called the "ultimate medicine." Other types of medicine—that is, other types of healing—have limitations. They work for some people and not for others, and even then, only some of the time. Universally, the ultimate medicine is healing. Every mind touched by the experience of its unconditioned nature moves closer to the experience of genuine freedom, which is, after all, the ultimate healing.

Unconditioned awareness heals in different ways. When we rest in unconditioned awareness, we're already healed, in the sense that we're incapable of worrying about our problems, no matter how apparently serious. This doesn't mean that we don't take appropriate action to cure an illness or resolve a financial difficulty. But when we rest in unconditioned awareness, we're free of the habitual tendency to construe that something is wrong or missing. We're satisfied with the way things are. Rather than needing our circumstances to be different to feel happy and fulfilled, we're already happy and fulfilled in this moment. At this level, unconditioned awareness acts as a healing force, because it penetrates and dissolves the basis of all illness, namely, the story that we're ill. We may still have a diseased body or bad credit, but we're no longer battling our condition. No matter what our physical and mental conditions might be, we can no longer experience ourselves as damaged or limited in any way. We're not in a state of denial; if anything, we're more aware of our circumstances. But we don't relate to them as if they shouldn't be happening. When we rest in unconditioned awareness, we're at home with ourselves and our world in an effortless and uncontrived way.

In nondual work, people arrive at a point where there's nothing left to do—not because they've reached the limit of their teacher's competence or exhausted the capacity of a therapeutic method, but simply because they find it impossible to construct a problem. They have no energy or interest in creating limitation or deficiency. Even the belief that they may suffer in the future has no meaning, because, in nondual awareness, future suffering is simply experienced for what it is—a thought.

The experience of unconditioned awareness also heals by percolating through the layers of our habitual conditioning and changing its structure, dissolving fixations and attachments, and possibly even producing a radical reorientation of our experience of reality. We become clearer, more open, and less reactive and defensive—and hence better able to release our fears and insecurities.

The Yoga tradition of Buddhism describes this process as the "transformation (*paravrtti*) of the structural foundations of our being (*asraya*)." Through contact with the pure, unconditioned dimension of existence, the energies and mechanisms that condition our life lose their power to distort our experience and cause us suffering. Other nondual traditions describe how the experience of unconditioned awareness infuses conditioned mind like a sweet perfume or a soothing breeze.

We can't predict in advance how this deconditioning will unfold. It occurs at its own pace and rhythm. Sometimes it's smooth and gentle; at other times, rough or abrupt. At times we may even have the impression that we're moving backward to an earlier stage of our development that we thought we had completed. Each of us is infinitely complex, and our path to full evolution is unique and often mysterious.

EMBODIED TRANSCENDENCE: AN INTEGRATED APPROACH

This approach to healing is closely aligned with the sutric lineage of the Dzogchen and Mahamudra traditions of Buddhism, in which unconditioned awareness is cultivated in the midst of our everyday existence. This approach stands in contrast with other lineages and traditions, where the experience of unconditioned awareness is pursued by taking time out from worldly commitments and going into long-term retreat.

In nondual teaching, the conditioned and unconditioned dimensions of being are integrated throughout. We will be cultivating unconditioned awareness while remaining fully engaged with the complexities of our work, relationships, and lifestyle commitments. The very structure of our personality will become the pathway for revealing the transpersonal nature of being itself. Every pattern of our behavior, every nuance in our thought, is a window that can reveal unconditioned awareness. In Zen, they say that unconditioned awareness is entered through a gateless gateway. The gateway is gateless, not only because there's no gate, but also because the gateway is always exactly where we are. In the nondual approach, there's absolutely no effort, struggle, or need to escape from who we are. In fact, any attempt to resist or escape our conditioning blocks us from experiencing our unconditioned nature. Every aspect and dimension of our experience is revealed to be an exquisite expression of freedom and transcendence.

INTRODUCTION TO THE PARTNER EXERCISES

Throughout this book, you will find exercises you can do with a partner. You can choose anyone you like to work on these exercises with you—a friend, colleague, partner, or spouse. When you read through an exercise, you might get an idea of someone with whom you'd like to practice it. It can even be someone who doesn't live near you—many of these partner exercises can be done over the phone. The most important thing is to choose someone you feel comfortable with, and someone who is interested in this kind of work.

The best way to find out is to just ask. You could say something like, "I'm reading a book about radiant mind—the healing power of our unconditional presence. There's an exercise I'd like to try with you. I wonder if you'd like to hear about it." As you talk to them about it, be sure to make it clear that this is not about having to believe something or go along with any kind of dogma. It's just about discovering for yourself what is happening right now. There is no right or wrong way to do these exercises.

When you engage in the actual exercise with your partner, be sensitive about what is happening for them. Allow them to take their own time and express things in their own way. Don't put any kind of pressure on them or on yourself. Welcome your "don't know" mind. That is your greatest friend and support in these exercises.

See how much you can appreciate your partner for being exactly the way they are. Be ready to discover something totally new about someone you may think you know quite well. And the same thing applies to yourself!

Enjoy! You can engage wholeheartedly in these exercises without taking them too seriously.

CHAPTER ONE EXERCISES

The main focus of this first set of exercises is to:
- Develop a profile of your experience of, and relationship to, unconditioned awareness
- Reflect on your expectations of your work with this material—what you want to get out of it

YOUR UNDERSTANDING OF UNCONDITIONED AWARENESS
- What terms or concepts do you tend to use when thinking and talking about what we are calling here "unconditioned awareness"?
- What is unconditioned awareness for you?

DEVELOPING A PROFILE OF YOUR EXPERIENCE
Generally, unconditioned awareness is an experience that you:
- Haven't yet heard or thought about
- Have heard or read about but haven't experienced
- Have experienced perhaps once or twice in your life, and you look back with a longing to reexperience it
- Are familiar with and which you enjoy quite frequently, in meditation, during nondual teachings, and in special moments with other people

NOW THINK ABOUT THE FOLLOWING QUESTIONS
- If you do enjoy experiences of unconditioned awareness, how do you know they are experiences of unconditioned awareness?
- If you feel that you haven't experienced unconditioned awareness, how do you know that you haven't?
- Do these last two questions make you rethink the category to which you belong?

In this chapter, I wrote about three different parameters through which we can understand a person's experience of unconditioned awareness: the purity, depth, and duration of the experience. Everyone has a different relationship to unconditioned awareness. Some people, for example, can have very pure experiences, but they are quite fragile. Others have a more stable experience, but it may not be as pure.

. Write a few lines describing your experience of unconditioned awareness in terms of purity, depth, and duration.

CHAPTER TWO

PHASES OF GROWTH
Understanding Your Conditioned Experience

In the last chapter, you developed a profile of your experience of unconditioned awareness. The importance of developing a profile of your
conditioned experience is that it tells you where you may need to change your
life at the practical level of relationships, career, health, etc., in order to create
a solid foundation for accessing unconditioned awareness, and thereby realizing the ultimate state of radiant mind.

In this chapter, I will describe a number of phases in the evolution to
the state of radiant mind—the experience where unconditioned awareness
refracts and radiates through every aspect of our finite, embodied existence.
Each phase I will describe corresponds to a different way that we interpret
our experience on a daily basis. These different phases represent different degrees or levels of resolution of conflicting beliefs. As our conflicting thoughts
and feelings are harmonized, we move progressively through the phases. Each
phase corresponds to a movement in which conflict and stress caused by inner
conflicting beliefs return to an experience of nondual awareness.

Phase one, called *disconnection,* indicates a fundamental irresolution
of conflicting beliefs, and the final phase, *radiant mind,* signifies the full
harmonization of all dualities. It represents a state in which conflict is simply
no longer possible, because we're no longer fixated on preserving or rejecting any belief system, feeling, or experience. In fact, at this level, there is no
experience of me in here, and the world out there, that's threatening or supporting me. Instead, we exist as an infinite field of stabilized unstructured
awareness that's indistinguishable from the constantly moving flux of sensations and thoughts.

Each phase describes a different orientation and approach to living.
Each phase has its own outlook, feelings, emotions, and moods. Each phase

also presents us with different sets of challenges and opportunities. Also, we are at different phases in different areas of our life. For example, we might have achieved a real level of harmony and coexistence in our closest relationships (with our partner and family) while we are still uncomfortable or in conflict with the work that we do for a living. Conversely, we might have everything we need at a material level while still struggling to find or create a fulfilling relationship.

In the sections that follow, I will try to give you the flavor of each phase. At the end of this chapter, I will give you an opportunity to profile where you are in different areas of your life. With this information, you'll know where to direct your attention at the level of daily practicalities and responsibilities.

THE HARMONIZATION OF CONFLICT AND PROGRESS THROUGH THE PHASES

There is no strict order to how we traverse these phases, though there is an overall sense of direction. They can represent a general pattern of growth over several years or even a lifetime. We are also prone to jump from one phase to another in response to the people, moods, opinions, and situations in which we find ourselves. In fact, usually we experience all of them in the course of a day, as we negotiate our way through the demands of our relationships, bodily needs, work, finances, leisure pursuits, spiritual practices, and so on.

PHASES OF GROWTH

PHASE 1: DISCONNECTION

The first phase, which I call "disconnection," rests on a powerful belief in a fundamental separation between us and the world. If we believe that we are separate from the world, we can become disconnected from the world and also disconnected from ourselves.

Disconnection is based on fear. Disconnection is driven by fear—either fear of ourselves or fear of the world. When we fear ourselves, we are thrown into the world in order to lose ourselves. When we fear the world, we retreat into ourselves in order to avoid the world. We tend to become totally preoccupied—either with ourselves or with the world. The bottom line in both styles of disconnection is to avoid anything sharp or painful, or even remotely uncomfortable, touching us—be it negative thoughts or other people.

Disconnection from the world. When we are disconnected from the world, other people show up as threats to our autonomy and integrity. We will hide out from other people—sometimes quite literally. We may go to great lengths to avoid specific people or situations.

We view the world as hostile and threatening. We live our life as though we are open to constant contamination. We live in a hostile environment that continually threatens us. We are always looking over our shoulder—on the lookout because we sense that some threat is just around the corner. Consequently, we are grossly constricted in the relationships we can form.

The people we do attract aren't attracted for their own worth and humanness but only for their role in confirming and validating our own limited identity. We aren't really interested in other people, though from time to time, we need to announce to people who we are and what we stand for.

When we live at this phase, we are predisposed to moods of paranoia, desperation, isolation, and claustrophobia, because we're driven by the fear that if we don't continually protect ourselves, we will disappear.

We might surround ourselves with our own familiar thoughts—the memorabilia of our dank, dark, and oh-so-familiar world. Or we might become immersed in self-improvement programs, commit ourselves to long-term therapy, or struggle to achieve spiritual purity.

We become preoccupied with ourselves. In this style of disconnection, we become so preoccupied with ourselves, so immersed in the exploration and experience of who we are, that we are effectively paralyzed—and no longer able to act powerfully and competently. We struggle to either stay the same or totally transform ourselves. But either way, there is no acceptance of who we are and how we are changing (or not changing).

We try to protect our beliefs. We will go to any lengths to keep our beliefs safe and secure. We refuse to test them in the world, and we actively insulate our beliefs from alternative viewpoints. If, for example, we believe that we are honest and trustworthy, we refuse to listen to any suggestion that we could be untrustworthy. We refuse to hear an alternative point of view. We simple won't have anything to do with people who threaten our autonomy—for us, they don't exist.

In this phase, we seek pure experiences: pure pleasure, absolute perfection, pure power, complete independence, absolute moral goodness, total health, etc., uncontaminated by the slightest trace of the opposite. We figure that in order to be good, we mustn't be bad—not even slightly. We look for the smallest injustice in order to invalidate other people or hold on to a single evil thought in order to destroy our own self-worth. We will destroy our own pleasures because they have been contaminated or interrupted by some small external interference.

Disconnection from ourselves. The other style of disconnection is disconnection from ourselves. We disconnect from ourselves by getting caught up in the world. The fear of being with ourselves drives us into the world—we lose ourselves by getting immersed in the world.

We lose ourselves in our work. We lose ourselves in our work, having to be always in action. Our behavior is erratic, incoherent, and inconsistent, because we have lost contact with who we are. We tend to jump from project to project. We work and keep busy in order to stay disconnected from who we are. It's like we throw ourselves totally into the world.

At work, we may only know how to bust our guts or collapse in a heap on the floor through exhaustion. There is no time to be with ourselves. The only choice is to be totally distracted or unconscious. There is no sense of balance or grace in how we manage our affairs.

We pursue impossible dreams. This style of disconnection is also characterized by narrow-minded pursuits. However, we only seek external achievements. For example, we may vow to become a millionaire before the year's end, or indulge ourselves totally in physical pleasures. Or we might simply try to be the perfect parent—every single moment of the day. It doesn't particularly matter whether we are being pure or indulgent; we are trapped and blinded by our single-minded pursuit of an external, impossible goal.

Internal disconnection. This phase is also marked by an internal disconnection—a dismemberment of our personality. Our feelings are disconnected from our thinking. Our behavior is disconnected from who we really are. We may be unable to say what we feel at any moment. Our feelings are just one big blur. We are either totally in our heads and disconnected from our feelings, or so immersed in, and overpowered by, our feelings that perhaps we cannot even talk.

Time feels solid. In this phase, time feels solid. A day is lived as a "block of time." We may wake up in a particular mood and carry it with us throughout the day until we go to sleep at night. If we have time to "fill in," it is a break-down. We don't know what to do. Likewise, if we find ourselves overwhelmed, it is a catastrophe. We don't know how to reschedule an appointment—it doesn't even occur to us as a possibility that we could rearrange our commit-ments. We are disconnected from time—it is something out there, and it runs its own course independently of us.

PHASE 2: CONFLICT

At some point during the phase of disconnection, we begin to acknowledge and feel the fear that drives our disconnection. We allow ourselves to be vul-nerable. If we have contracted into our inner world, we will begin to look outside. We transcend the fear of being with others and renounce our privacy. If we have become lost in the worlds of other people, we take stock and begin to gain a sense of who we are. These movements signal a new pull toward expansion—an evolutionary growth, in terms of either new relationships or a deeper understanding of ourselves.

Although this phase is evolutionary, it is a highly conflictual state because we are still living out of our old style of contraction. The two forces of expan-sion and contraction produce stress and conflict. We begin to expand our horizons but still feel a need to protect ourselves. Part of us would dearly love to stay in our shell, in our comfortable cocoon, but we feel an urge to grow. We can no longer ignore that there are points of view different from our own. It is clear that wherever we go, the shadow of conflicting opinions follows.

This phase has a rough and aggressive quality about it, as we brush up against circumstances and people who are seen as a hindrance and threat to our security and way of life. Our hope for complete autonomy or oblivion-in-the-world is now constantly challenged, and as the challenges intensify, we find ourselves forced to respond. Ordinarily, we would have some choice. We could take flight and retreat (disconnect), move forward by modifying our objectives and forming alliances (codependence), or stand our ground and fight.

We fight for what we believe in. However, in the midst of this phase, we have no choice but to fight for our beliefs. The only way we know how to deal with something different is to locate an opponent and fight it. At this point, we have no choice but to attempt to destroy it while surviving ourselves.

We find fault in others. Consequently, we may find constant fault in others. We make them wrong in order for us to be right, or we make others right in order to invalidate ourselves. At the very least, we struggle to avoid associating with people who stimulate conflicting thoughts or feelings in us.

We may constantly judge ourselves. The other option is to fight the battle internally—within our own world of thoughts and feelings. In this case, we torment ourselves by continually dissecting our thoughts, feelings, and behavior—judging whether they are good or bad, right or wrong.

The habits of our style of disconnection also follow us into this phase. If we are prone to disconnect from ourselves, then conflict may take the form of sacrificing ourselves by fighting for some cause—be it a team, a company, a religion, or a nation. If we are predisposed to disconnect from the world, the point comes where we can no longer ignore the world. We are impelled to fight for the survival of our opinions, values, and finally for our selves. We may forsake our marriage in order to pursue a private life, or give up our job in order to retire to the country.

Being and doing. This phase is also marked by a conflict between the internal and external styles of living. The conflict is a tension between being and doing. When we are in action in the world, we wish we could retreat inside. Then when we are with ourselves, all we can do is think about what we should do next.

If we are, by nature, introspective and self-satisfied, the fear is still there that we will lose our footing if we throw ourselves into relationships and projects. We will make forays into the world but rush back to the still point within for nourishment. We can't see how we could be nourished by our work.

Conversely, if, by nature, we are extroverted, then in this phase, we begin to seek refuge from the complex and consuming relationships or the overly ambitious projects that punctuate our life. However, try as we might to nourish ourselves through therapy, meditation, or just taking "time for ourselves," we are magnetically drawn back into external concerns. We are thrown from one extreme to the other. The only choice is to try to be composed and quiet, savoring the essence of our being, or else be caught up in the lives and work of others. There is no middle ground.

In this phase, it doesn't matter what we do. We are continually plagued by the thought that "this isn't what I'm meant to be doing."

Time is an enemy. In this phase, time is also an enemy. We construct time as an obstacle, a barrier that constrains us and which we have to break through. We will find ourselves under- or overscheduling commitments. We are caught between having too much or too little time.

Similarly, space is experienced as a commodity. We want either more space or less space. Space either constrains us—we feel hemmed in—or is a barrier to be overcome. People are either too close or too distant.

PHASE 3: CODEPENDENCE

Transition into this phase occurs as a response to the aggression and exhaustion that characterize the conflictual phase. Rather than fight a fabricated enemy, we now change tack and decide to adjust our identity in ways that will allow us to live in a world of different values, beliefs, and opinions. We give up fighting and fall into codependency.

In this way, codependence is also a reaction to disconnection. From the phase of conflict, we could retreat into isolation (disconnection), but the memories of that phase still persist, so we shift our stance and begin to resolve our conflicts by adjusting to accommodate the conflicts. However, the difference between disconnection and codependence is significant. If, for example, in the phase of disconnection, we seek refuge by retreating from the world, then in the codependent phase, our isolation and loneliness depends on having people around to actively ignore us.

We need others for our pleasure and pain. Though this phase begins with the simple adjustment of our beliefs in order to accommodate conflict and difference, before long, our beliefs become entwined in a constricting and limiting way. We begin to depend on others for our pleasure and pain. Our well-being and sense of self cannot occur independently of others. We learn to dance so well with our partners that we get trapped and blinded by our own skill. Ultimately, the survival of our identity depends on our interactions with other people. We experience the "disease of lost selfhood." In the midst of this phase, we focus exclusively outside ourselves for our experience of self-worth (be that positive or negative), and for our values, beliefs, and needs.

We seek external approval. We constantly seek approval from others for who we are. We use others to inflict the pain and suffering that we "deserve" per our own beliefs about our guilt and lack of self-worth. Whatever it is that we need, we get others to do it to us—be it to hate us, love us, dominate us, or ignore us. We might surround ourselves with people who are weak and pathetic, in order to confirm our own power and domination. Or we might throw ourselves into relationships with people who are cruel and insensitive, in order to confirm our kindness and sensitivity.

There is no room for individual change. We find that we are caught in a job or cannot extricate ourselves from dysfunctional relationships, because they precisely and accurately serve the needs on which we are dependent. Our relationships seem to fit like a glove to the point that there is no room for individual change or growth. If we grow, it is a breakdown, a catastrophe, for those around us. If they grow, it is a problem for us.

Internal codependence. This phase also manifests internally as an inability to separate our thoughts and feelings. We may find that we can't think and speak clearly in the face of powerful emotions. Our thinking is so dependent on our moods and feelings that if we are feeling excited, our thinking is necessarily scattered and all over the place. If we are feeling threatened, we have no choice but to be tongue-tied. We cannot disconnect our thinking from our feelings.

From the other angle, if we are in a racy conversation, we have no choice but to get swept up in the mood of excitement. We cannot both participate in the conversation and remain centered. Our moods and emotions can't function independently of each other. We may have to induce a mood of panic before we can move into action. Or we may need to get angry before we can be intimate with someone. The expression of each mood depends on expressing other moods.

Time controls us. In this phase, we also become dependent on time and space. We can become tied to time in a way that leaves little room for impulse and spontaneity. Time controls us and distance is always a limiting factor. Perhaps everything has to be organized weeks, even months, in advance. Our movements always need to be the most economical. We might begin to behave like the famous 18th-century German philosopher, Immanuel Kant, who never ventured more than a few kilometers from the place of his birth, and who followed a life of such extreme regularity that the people of his village would set their clocks by his daily constitutional walk. Though he lived alone, he was wedded to time and tied to his physical surroundings.

PHASE 4: COEXISTENCE

At some point during the previous phase, we see the compromising nature of codependence. We recognize the distortion of our personality that has been caused by accommodating the needs and concerns of other people. We also see the possibility of living in respectful and mutually empowering relationships. This signals entry into the phase called coexistence.

Coexistence is a wonderful phase of personal development, for it bridges all levels of coping. It begins at the point where we can adequately cope with ourselves, our work, and our relationships, and moves through to very elegant, empowering, and socially rewarding ways of participating in and contributing to life.

We fine-tune our judgments. Progress through this phase is measured by an increasing acceptance of the circumstances in which we find ourselves, and a growing capacity to fine-tune the judgments we make about ourselves and the world.

In this phase, we no longer make global judgments. We no longer think about ourselves or respond to others in simplistic, black-and-white categories. People, groups, professions, races, etc., are no longer just good or bad. Our judgments gain more and more texture to them. We distinguish and discriminate how and when we are being responsible or irresponsible, caring or indifferent, competent or incompetent.

We still keep an eye on the ball. Throughout this phase, however, there is still a sense of needing to manage the whole affair. At the beginning, there is a strong sense of having to work at it in order to manage our work and relationships, but even when we reach the level of being a master, there is a sense of effort and application. We may design and orchestrate our life in a masterful and elegant way, but we still have to constantly work at it—making evaluations, formulating plans, designing actions, correcting and adjusting, dealing with breakdowns, etc. Others may see our work and relationships as smooth, easy, and rewarding, but from the inside, we are still planning, calculating, anticipating, and living in terms of a game plan or strategy. We still feel a need to keep an eye on the ball. Our competence is tied to the acquisition of relevant skills—skills in managing our moods, our relationships, our career, negotiating mutually satisfactory outcomes, etc. We can even learn to design our moods to assist our thinking and use our thoughts to modify our feelings and emotions, but still our competence and ease of living is a function of learning. To do better, we need to know more, and then have more practice. Even so, this phase can bring us to the very brink of living a satisfying and rewarding life.

PHASE 5: PARADOX

This next phase can begin gently as a feeling of perplexity or mild confusion and uncertainty, or dramatically as the culmination of an emotional or intellectual crisis. It can occur in the midst of a mid-life crisis, or as little more than an intellectual quandary. Similarly, this phase can be experienced as a drawn-out emotional struggle for meaning and solidity, or as the final residue of an intellectual search for clarity and certainty. A point is reached on the path of self-development where we begin to lose our sense of progress and direction. It could be that things are being managed so easily and automatically that we begin to wonder who is doing this, or whether we need to be doing anything at all. We are not sure whether we are at work or on a permanent holiday.

We question who we really are. This phase could also begin with the realization that we are somewhere totally different from where we thought we were. We might wake up one day and find ourselves in a thoroughly boring job or relationship that just yesterday had captured all our passion and energy. We begin to question who we are and what we are doing at a very fundamental level. The very notion of making progress seems elusive. What would constitute progress, and where are we going anyway? We may question, "Am I going forward, backward, or standing still?" and have no real way of telling in which direction we are going. We may well want to retreat backward or go forward, but we also sense that such moments could take us anywhere—or nowhere. We find ourselves wanting to hold on and let go at the same time.

In this phase, our feelings can become so bare and open that we can't tell what we are feeling—our sensitivity is so acute that at the very same time and place we feel love, there is hatred. It is as though our sensitivity and openness includes yet transcends love and hatred.

This sensitivity extends to the environment. We might begin to notice that every time we register pleasure, there is a sense of hurt or damage and pain. This is particularly apparent if we are attached to the pleasure, in that the fear of a pleasurable experience ending can produce pain. At the same time, pain can have a desirable, even enjoyable, quality to it.

What is real or illusion? This phase can be accompanied by a whole range of moods and emotions. It can be perplexing and disconcerting, because we don't know what it is we are getting or what it is we are losing in every situation. Are they the same thing or different? The more we find ourselves being infused with a new energy and insight, the more we are at a loss to say what it is we are really gaining. Our awareness seems to expand to the point that it completely disappears. Perhaps what we are gaining is nothing! Every experience is deeply profound yet totally meaningless. We are not sure if this is the most real thing we have every experienced or if it is a total illusion. The *Lankavatara Sutra* expresses this dilemma this way: "Reality is not as it seems and nor is it otherwise."

As our sense of awareness increases, we also find ourselves losing every thought and conception we ever had about the goals we have been seeking. This experience can be exhilarating and unnerving at the same time, for as we continue to lose hope of ever finding our most cherished goals, we seem to be gaining everything we could ever want.

We also notice that if we try to make "letting go" of our hope and ambitions a method to produce or maintain this experience, we begin to lose what we already have. We might find ourselves in the double bind of wanting to let go of all our desires and trying to let go of any effort. We are not sure if it is anything we are doing or not doing that is behind the experience of pure awareness. All our efforts to "figure it out," to understand what is happening, are fruitless. On the one hand, our experience seems to be related to what we are thinking, but we also sense that it has nothing to do with what we are thinking or feeling. It is not clear if we are producing this experience or if it is just happening to us.

We get the feeling that we are not going to ever have this ultimate experience. We sense that we won't get it while we are self-identified as a particular personality. This could be the biggest disappointment of our entire life. Just when we are on the verge of getting it—that final insight, that ultimate goal—we go out to lunch! Is this a cosmic joke?

We finally realize that there is nowhere to go—nowhere to retreat to or move forward into. There is nowhere to be other than where we are. There is no one to be except the person we are. We come home to who we are and where we have always been. This moment—which requires no effort, change, or movement— signals the transition to the final phase. It is a letting go and acceptance of what has always been.

This transition may or may not occur. There is no way of telling whether or not it will happen, since there is nothing we can do to make it happen, or stop it from happening. Doing anything to make it happen—including doing nothing—is quite immaterial to the emergence of the final phase.

PHASE 6: RADIANT MIND

We cannot be specific about the final phase, called "radiant mind," because language falls away as an adequate instrument for describing it. Intriguingly, throughout the ages, thousands of people have spent millions of words trying to describe the state of nondual presence. Some have used words in an effort to say *nothing* about this state of existence. Others have remained silent as a way of trying to say *something* about it. However, what they have said or not said neither adds to nor subtracts from our understanding of this state. In fact, we can't understand this phase because it's not a state of understanding. That's why it's called "nonconceptual realization," or even an experience of "no-thing" or "no mind." As you'll discover in the next chapter, the attempt to "understand" unconditioned awareness or radiant mind is an obstacle to experiencing it.

Unconditioned bliss. The other phases we've described are characterized by different moods, emotions, and feeling states. In some ways, the experience of radiant mind has a certain feeling-tone to it; it's as though we can feel its presence. Yet, if we ask the question "What does this feel like?" when we're resting in the experience of radiance, we can't articulate it. We might ask ourselves, "Is this in any way painful or uncomfortable?" Clearly, it isn't. "Is it pleasurable?" Well, no, actually it's not. It's not an experience of pleasure, at least in the usual sense. Yet, there does seem to be a particular, ineffable quality to it. Asian mystics use the words *ananda* and *sukha* to describe this ineffable feeling-tone. In English, these Sanskrit words are usually translated as "bliss." But if we try to locate where the bliss is happening, we can't. It seems to be happening everywhere. And similarly, we can't find a source for the bliss either. So I like to describe it as unconditioned bliss.

Personal and transpersonal experience. This experience of radiant mind is and isn't a personal experience. In one sense, it's very clearly a personal experience because it arises in a stream of experience that we call an individual. When the Buddha became enlightened under the bodhi tree in India, the experience happened to him, and for him. But on the other hand, through the very nature of his realization, he discovered that there was no real self, no Buddha, no one to experience his awakening. Moreover, he discovered that he couldn't find the very experience of awakening that had arisen within him. When we glimpse or rest in the experience of unconditioned awareness for a few minutes or an hour, we, too, see that there's no you or me that has this experience, and that the experience itself is so unstructured that we can't say what it is, or where it is. We can't even say that it exists. Yet, it's you, or me, or someone else, who experiences this!

CHAPTER TWO EXERCISES

1. PROFILING YOUR CONDITIONED EXISTENCE

This exercise is designed to give you an opportunity to determine the predominant phases through which you experience different areas of your life. It will help you identify areas where you're already developed, and areas that are recurrently problematic for you. This is important information if you're wanting to cultivate the experience of unconditioned awareness, because the areas where you're undeveloped need to be handled in order to find the mental, emotional, and physical space necessary to discover and deepen the experience of unconditioned awareness.

For example, if you're struggling to pay the rent (assuming you're not living in a cave), then it's difficult to find the time and space to sit quietly and ponder the question "Where do my thoughts come from?" If you're upset year-in-and-year-out in your intimate relationships, forever trying to work out if you should stay or leave, it's difficult to merge at the level of unbounded consciousness with everyone around you. If you're letting your body go to rack and ruin, it becomes difficult to nourish your nervous system with the bliss of pure awareness.

If you're habituated to a particular spiritual practice, fearful of letting go, it's impossible to move into the free space of unconstrained, natural meditation. In order to work effectively with the material offered in this book, especially if you're doing this in a systematic way over a number of months, you need the time and leisure to do this, and periods of relative freedom from the demands of daily life.

Some "Western nonduals" argue that it's wrong to give any thought at all to our conditioned existence. They say that *any* attention we give to our livelihood, health, relationships, etc., only fortifies the ego, prolongs our suffering, and delays our final liberation. Nondualists are right to continue to bring this to our attention, because one of our main difficulties is that we're already consumed by the dictates of our desires.

But, for me, it's a question of balance. Certainly, it's very easy for us to become preoccupied, even totally consumed, by the need for financial security, the ultimate sexual pleasures, the perfect relationship, or the best spiritual teaching. But if we don't give appropriate attention to the areas of our life that throw us into states of denial, conflict, and confusion, reality can come knocking on the door in very abrupt and draining ways, which can unnecessarily side-track us. Of course, ultimately, there is no path and no goal, but it can be difficult to really experience this when we're struggling to maintain or achieve a particular lifestyle.

So we'll begin by helping you develop a profile of your conditioned existence. In this exercise, we will distinguish between nine different domains or areas of living:

Intimate relationship(s)	Sex and intimacy	Health
Family	Friendships	Career
Money	Spirituality	Body

I'd like you to handwrite your responses to this exercise on a letter-sized pad of writing paper rather than type them on your word processor. It's easy to get hung up on spelling, formatting, etc., with a word processor. Here, the task is to just get the words out. On a separate sheet each, write the titles of the above areas of living. Now I'd like you to spend five minutes writing about your typical experiences in each area. Write "automatically"—don't stop to think first; simply write what you're thinking and feeling. Don't sanitize your writing. This exercise is for your benefit. If you forget what you're writing about, look at the heading at the top of the page again. Just don't stop the contact between your pen and the paper. If you can't think of what to say, write that: "Can't think. Don't know. This is difficult. Nothing. Nothing . . . It pisses me off when . . ." If there are no thoughts, write, "No thoughts." Don't stop until the five minutes is up. This can be quite an intense exercise, so you might like to break it down into two or three sessions. Alternatively, it might be really easy for you.

TYPICAL CONVERSATIONS IN EACH PHASE OF GROWTH

In order to help you identify a phase within your responses to the above exercise, the table below describes some of the typical conversations that occur in each phase. When I say "conversation," I'm mainly talking about the story we tell ourselves, the commentary that goes on in our thoughts about what's happening to us. It's a conversation that we're having with ourselves.

Now go back and read what you've written, and try to identify the phase or phases that seem to come through your writing. You might like to have a highlighting pen at hand. Try to do your analysis objectively, as though someone else had written what you're reading. Make some notes similar to the following examples as you're doing this.

PHASE / EMOTIONS	GENERIC CONVERSATIONS
Disconnection	
Isolation	What's the point in this?
Rejection	I give up.
Fear	This is ridiculous.
Distraction	I'm nervous.
Separation	This is dangerous.
	S/he has no idea who I am.
	S/he has no idea how I'm feeling.
	I don't care about ...
	I don't care about how s/he is seeing me.
	It is no business of theirs how I'm feeling.
Conflict	
Anger	I'm pissed off.
Vindictiveness	It's their fault.
Blame	I'll get back at them.
	S/he is trying to make it difficult for me.
Codependence	
Dependence	I have to please X.
Neediness	I can't do this without X.
Boredom	What will X think if I ...
	I'll ask X if I can do this.
Coexistence	
Vigilance	I'm getting better at this
Application	I can see what I need to change.
Ambition	That didn't work so I'll change it.
Learning	I'm feeling better.
	I'm making progress.
	I'm getting closer.
	I'm learning how to do this.
	What else can I change?

PHASE / EMOTIONS	GENERIC CONVERSATIONS
Paradox	
Confusion	I don't know if I'm making any progress with this
Laughter	or not.
Perplexity	Should I keep doing this the same way or do
	something different?
	This is absurd.
	There is nothing to do!
	What am I supposed to do?
	I'm totally lost.
	This is it—isn't it?
	Should I continue or stop?
	I can't stop—I can't continue!
Radiant Mind	
Gentle awareness	Nothing.
Alertness	No difference.
Relaxation	
Full openness	
Presence	
Unconditioned bliss	

2. ESTABLISHING A NETWORK OF SUPPORT

You can't do everything via the exercises in this book. My focus here is to help you access and deepen the ultimate experience of unconditioned awareness. If you're aware of areas in your life that really aren't working for you, I encourage you to seek out the support you need by establishing a "network of support." Your network of support will include all the people (friends, advisors, coaches, therapists, teachers) and other resources (books, courses, the internet, etc.) that support you in gaining the life skills needed to become more skillful and competent in every area of your life.

I'd now like you to spend some time going through each area of your life, and begin to define a possible network of support. In particular, think about whom you can ask for help or hire to support you. Start with the areas that need the most attention. In parallel with the ideas and exercises I'm offering you in this book, I also invite you to continue the work that I'm sure you're already doing at the pragmatic levels of money, intimacy, and so on.

CHAPTER THREE

Obstacles to Experiencing Unconditioned Awareness

The noble way of Mahamudra never engages in the drama of
imprisonment and release. The sage of Mahamudra has absolutely
no distractions, because no war against distractions has ever been
declared. This nobility and gentleness alone, this non-violence of
thought and action, is the traceless path of all Buddhas.
To walk this all-embracing way is the bliss of Buddhahood.
TILOPA (10TH CENTURY), *SONG TO NAROPA*[1]

When we're deeply identified with our conditioned way of being—our beliefs, values, and preferences, and their related
emotions—we may have some initial difficulty accessing unconditioned
awareness. Common psychological phenomena that hinder access to the unconditioned include:

- Attachment to suffering
- The habitual need to be doing something
- The need to know what is happening and where we are
- The need to create meaning
- Fearful projections about unconditioned awareness
- The tendency to make unconditioned awareness
  into something

In this chapter, we'll explore what hinders our access to unconditioned awareness, and we'll become a skillful observer of how we create and recreate fixed

points of reference. In the process, we'll have an opportunity to experience living from a more open and fluid identity.

ATTACHMENT TO SUFFERING

When our experience falls outside narrowly defined parameters, we suffer. For example, we may need just the right level of mental stimulation. If the content and density of our thinking fall outside our ideal range, we become uncomfortable. If there's too much stimulation or the content isn't to our liking, we crave peace and quiet. If we feel understimulated, we seek entertainment. We're rarely satisfied. At some level, we're usually suffering.

It may sound strange to suggest that we're attached to our pain and problems, particularly given the amount of time and energy we spend complaining about our circumstances and dreaming about a "better life." But if we were so averse to suffering and committed to avoiding it at all costs, why would it continue to plague us, year after year? Why would so many people be unable to produce, in the course of an entire lifetime, any major reduction in the overall level of their suffering?

To the contrary, we seem to feel quite at home with our worries and concerns. Much of the time, we find it easier to soak in our miserable stories about how unloved and unappreciated we are, and to retreat into complaining, blaming, and feeling sorry for ourselves, than to live in a space where praise and blame, loss and gain, don't affect us. Even psychotherapy—the discipline meant to free us from our problems—may oblige us to have problems, by superimposing a familiar model of problems and resolutions rather than initiating conversations that open us to the possibility of being problem-free. By contrast, nondual practices aim to reveal our attachment to our problems and, through awareness, to offer the option of releasing those attachments.

No matter how spiritual they consider themselves to be, people who are strongly attached to their beliefs and opinions and deeply immersed in their stories often find it difficult to let go and become open to what arises in the present moment. Even people who believe they're open to experiencing nondual awareness and increasing the depth and duration of their experience commonly create some kind of problem along the way. For example, people who prefer using meditation to access natural presence may be irritated by noise or interruptions. Other people may become fixated on achieving full enlightenment and so find themselves striving to experience long, uninterrupted periods of unconditioned awareness. Still others may become bored during long periods of silence and believe they need more intellectual stimulation to help them access unconditioned awareness. By fixating on one particular idea or way of doing things, these people create obstacles to resting in nondual awareness.

HOLDING "HAVING PROBLEMS" AS A PROBLEM

We compound our problems when we become fixated on the need to be free of problems. When a problem arises, we may struggle to get rid of it. When a problematic thought enters our awareness, we may try to remove or reject it. By pushing the problem away in an attempt to access or maintain an experience of nondual awareness, we immediately undermine the experience. After all, "nondual" means that nothing is excluded or left out.

Inevitably, problems arise; only a fully enlightened individual ceases to create problems. As long as we believe that we shouldn't be creating problems, we prevent ourselves from experiencing the nondual state of mind for more than a short period of time.

HOLDING "HAVING NO PROBLEMS" AS A PROBLEM

We can even turn the experience of being "free of problems" into a problem by thinking, "What will I do if I have nothing to work on? Will my life become meaningless?" Voilà, we're back on familiar ground—we have a problem again. Most forms of psychotherapy subtly encourage us to hold on to our problems by focusing on them in order to process or solve them.

Nondual practices tend to reveal our attachment to having problems—our need to have something to keep us occupied and busy. They also reveal how we are limited and restricted in our capacity to be free of problems and concerns. These limitations reveal themselves as we become more and more aware of our desires and preferences.

THE HABITUAL NEED TO BE DOING SOMETHING

One of the characteristics of contemporary Western culture is a need to be active and busy. Out of boredom, restlessness, discomfort, guilt, or merely habit, we're continually creating projects: material projects, relationship projects, self-improvement projects, and, of course, the big one—the enlightenment project! There are strong cultural disincentives to simply being—in relaxed, unproductive fulfillment!

If we're troubled by our feelings or life circumstances—at work, with our partner or family, and so on—we're conditioned to respond by immediately attempting to do something about the situation. Our actions don't even need to be productive. Sometimes just anything will do—anything that keeps us distracted from our thoughts and feelings. In the absence of interesting stimuli, we doodle, sleep, have sex, watch TV, take in a movie, follow our breath, even trace hairline cracks on a wall with our eyes just to keep busy.

Obsessive busyness is an obstacle to unconditioned awareness—which needs nothing and is already fulfilled—because it's always focused on achieving some future outcome. Nondual practice invites us to let go of all effort and struggle, and experience unsurpassable peace in this very moment. As Longchenpa, the great Dzogchen yogi, wrote:

> *Since effort—which creates causes and effects, whether positive or negative—is unnecessary, immerse yourself in genuine being, resting naturally with nothing needing to be done. The expanse of spontaneous presence entails no deliberate effort, no acceptance or rejection. From now on make no effort, since phenomena already are what they are. Even the enlightenment of all victorious ones of the three times is spontaneously present as a supremely blissful state of natural rest.* [2]

But the opposite of not needing to do anything isn't doing nothing at all. We don't need to freeze up and become inactive, resisting the impulse to pick up the phone and communicate with others, or insisting on sitting passively at home when we could invigorate ourselves with some fresh air. "Doing nothing" means that we're free of all compulsion; there's nothing we need to do or not do. In nondual therapy, we reveal our habitual tendency to do, and open up the possibility of simply being present to what is, without needing to move incessantly toward a self-prescribed goal.

THE NEED TO KNOW

The need to know is endemic in our culture. We need to be able to say who we are, what we do, and what we stand for. If we can't, people may view us as vague, spaced-out, ungrounded, and incompetent. Without a well-defined story and a well-crafted identity, we may feel marginalized and vulnerable. The preeminence given to intellectual education makes us blind to the fact that knowledge gives us only half the resources available to us. Very few people explore what Alan Watts called the "wisdom of not knowing."

It's important to recognize that there are different types of not knowing. These different types of not knowing have different effects on our body and mind. At the level of our conditioned existence, there are many (perhaps an infinite number of) things that we don't know, yet which can be known, for example, a foreign language, tai chi, or auto mechanics. If the knowledge is important to us, we may feel frustrated and inadequate for not having it, and we may go to great lengths to acquire it—taking classes, reading books, and so forth.

At the conditioned level of our existence, we also cannot know the future, and this can be frustrating if we don't accept that. We can, and do, anticipate the future, but we cannot know it in the same way that we know where we are sitting at the moment, or what we did yesterday. Our knowledge of the future is, at best, fragmented and uncertain. Try as we might to predict the future, we very often get it completely wrong. Most significant, we don't know when we will die, or even if we will be alive tomorrow. If we don't accept that we cannot know the future with any real degree of certainty, we create the conditions for upset and disappointment.

Finally, there is the experience of not knowing at the unconditioned level. Here, we don't know because we're in a space where there's nothing to know, or we could say we know "nothing." This type of not knowing, also known as unconditioned awareness, is invariably liberating because it frees us from the need to know anything more or less than we already do.

We need to be careful to distinguish between these types of not knowing. Otherwise, we may make ourselves miserable by thinking we need to know the unknowable. In the not knowing of unconditioned awareness, there is simply nothing we need to work out, think through, or act upon. We're fulfilled, integrated, and complete without a need to know anything. Yet everything we do know remains immediately accessible.

"Dear friends, you cannot understand because there is absolutely nothing finite to understand," said Subhuti, the primary protagonist of the Perfect

Wisdom (Prajnaparamita) literature (Hixon 1993). "You are not lacking in refinement of intellect. There is simply nothing separate or substantial in Prajnaparamita to which the intellect can be applied, because perfect wisdom does not present any graspable or thinkable doctrine and offers no describable method of contemplation."[3]

As Subhuti makes clear, no one has ever known the unknowable, because it simply can't be an object of knowledge. No matter how much mental effort or philosophical skill we apply to the task, we can never understand or interpret the experience of unstructured awareness.

Of course, conditioned mind is tenacious, and even when we're told that unconditioned awareness can't be known, we don't give up. We immediately want to know what this "no mind" means, how we can acquire it, and how we'll know when we have it. This obsessive desire to know what can't be known is a common obstacle to resting in unconditioned awareness.

THE NEED TO CREATE MEANING

Closely related to the need to know is the construction of meaning. Most people are spring-loaded to construct stories and interpretations, and the slightest encouragement may trigger a well-honed, multichaptered life story or a virtual dissertation on spiritual metaphysics. Often our friends support our stories by expressing interest in them and reframing them in an attempt to help us create a more wholesome or enlightened story. But they're still just superimposing one story on another.

In nondual practices, the creation of meaning is just one possibility. We aren't compelled to make everything meaningful. It's also possible to just be with "what is," without needing to understand it, interpret it, or make it significant. Nondual practices such as "just listening" explicitly open up this possibility by giving us less encouragement to think and interpret. Just listening offers the listener few, if any, guidelines about what to say or do, which leaves us in the unknown; we may feel uncertain or even insecure. In such instances, rather than superimposing some meaning fabricated by our minds, we can just continue to listen.

When we just listen, without embellishing or reframing what people say with our own interpretation or desire to understand, people sense that we aren't colluding with their construction of meaning or encouraging any further storytelling. Often, at this point, people don't know how to proceed—they don't know what is expected of them, precisely because nothing is being expected of them. Within this not-knowing lies the possibility of experiencing unconditioned awareness.

FEARFUL PROJECTIONS ABOUT UNCONDITIONED AWARENESS

The concept of unconditioned awareness can elicit both positive and negative associations. In many ways, it's attractive as a concept because it comes bundled with ideas of freedom and liberation. But it can also trigger fearful projections.

When some people first encounter the idea of unconditioned awareness, they may think that it's black, like a vacuum where nothing is happening, like the dissolution of the universe, or like death. They may think that by cultivating unconditioned awareness, they'll lose interest and connection with their physical existence. These fears are familiar to many seekers, and it's important that they be acknowledged and contained within the path that cultivates unconditioned awareness.

For example, some people may think that they'll lose touch with the real world and become less capable of fulfilling their daily commitments. If they transcend their needs and desires and just accept "what is," they fear life might become bland, boring, and uninteresting. They might even lose their desire to act in any way, and end up starving to death! Other people may think that because unconditioned awareness is described as being empty of structure and content, it must resemble a vast, barren expanse of darkness empty of life or humanity. Clearly, there's a tendency for people to develop an automatic aversion to an experience like that. As psychotherapist Jennifer Welwood (2003) writes, "Rather than recognizing emptiness as our own nature, we see it as an enemy that we have to avoid or defeat." [4]

These projections have nothing to do with the experience of unconditioned awareness. In unconditioned awareness, nothing changes. At the empirical level, nothing drops out of our experience and nothing unusual enters it. We continue to think, feel, see, and touch. In fact, all the senses are as active as they've ever been. Yet everything is totally different. The unconditioned is not what we think!

MAKING UNCONDITIONED AWARENESS
INTO SOMETHING

When experiencing nondual consciousness, or unconditioned awareness, for the first time, people often ask, "What is this?" The most accurate response we can give is to say that it's nothing, or that it isn't anything. There's nothing here. Everything is here, but there's also the experience of nothing.

Conditioned mind can tend to conceptualize the nondual experience, labeling it as incomprehensible, boring, or too easy or simple. If this occurs, we can just gently note that we have moved out of the structureless state and are now trying to impose a structure on our experience. Having met with thousands of people who are knowledgeable in the areas of psychology and spirituality, I've found that they tend to begin constructing definitions and interpretations on the basis of very little evidence or experience.

Some people who are familiar with unconditioned awareness are uncomfortable describing it as "nothing." They feel that people might interpret this nihilistically and find it uninteresting. They are concerned that people will, in fact, become frightened about the possibility of access-ing and becoming familiar with the nondual experience if it is a state of nothing—without any structure or content. Still, I find the term "nothing" useful because it can correct our tendency to construct meaning, by which the experience is obscured.

THERE ARE NO OBSTACLES!

Up to this point, we have been speaking about various types of obstacles that can obstruct a clean and clear experience of unconditioned awareness. These obstacles are phenomena that can arise in our mind and body, and seem to distract us from experiencing the pure, open expanse of unstructured aware-ness. But if we look at the concept of an obstacle more carefully, we can see that in relationship to the unconditioned, there are no obstacles. Why? Be-cause the unconditioned isn't the type of thing that can be obstructed.

Sometimes I make an analogy between the arising of obstacles and put-ting our hand in front of our face. If we put our hand in front of our face, it obscures whatever is behind it. We can't see whatever is there because our hand is in the way. Our hand, in this case, is an obstacle to the experience of the shapes and colors that lie behind it. But if there's nothing behind our hand, no forms of any kind, our hand doesn't obscure anything. Our hand is there but it isn't an obstruction.

Unconditioned awareness has no structure. It doesn't have a shape, color, or any content, so nothing can obstruct it. Nothing can get in between us and the experience of unconditioned awareness. When we look closely in this way, we can see that an obstacle is just an idea. It's a concept, a label we attach to whatever we think gets in the way of freedom and fulfillment. In fact, the idea of "obstacles to unconditioned awareness" is just another obstacle! But, we don't have to worry because, as we have just discussed, this is simply another concept. There are no obstacles to unconditioned awareness. What are we doing here, right now? We are dancing in a paradox of unconditioned awareness.

You might ask, how do we get from there to here—from the idea and experience of obstacles to seeing that there are no obstacles to realizing unconditioned awareness? We get there—which is here—by seeing that there is nowhere to travel. We've already arrived. There's nowhere else to go. There is only and ever the here and now.

CHAPTER THREE EXERCISES

In these exercises, we will explore the obstacles that can disturb our recognition of the unconditioned dimension of our existence. We'll begin with a set of exercises that will give you an opportunity to recognize the ways you become distracted from unconditioned awareness. These exercises will increase your capacity for "doing nothing" and your tolerance for "not knowing." They will reduce your need to suffer when you don't know what is happening and have nothing meaningful to do.

The capacity to observe the obstacles to unconditioned awareness is a necessary preparation for experiencing unconditioned awareness. First we need to recognize our biases or preferences toward:

- Doing or not doing
- Knowing or not knowing
- Listening for meaning or no meaning

When we are clear and empty, we can see these biases as clearly as we can see the hand in front of our face. To the extent that we're blind to them in ourselves, we are blind to them in others. For example, if we are attached to meaning, we won't see in others their need to find meaning, because their need to make things meaningful supports our own bias.

REMINDERS

I recommend that you photocopy the two text boxes below, which identify different ways we block unconditioned awareness. Make two or three copies, and post them where you'll notice them during the day: on your desk, the bathroom mirror, the refrigerator door, the television screen, and your computer monitor.

For the first week, concentrate on observing the first set of biases. During the second week, direct your attention to the second set.

> **TODAY I WILL BE AWARE OF:**
>
> - My attraction to suffering and my difficulty with happiness
> - My need to be doing something
> - My need to know—what is happening, who I am, and where I am
> - My need to create meaning
> - My positive projections about unconditioned awareness

> **TODAY I WILL BE AWARE OF:**
>
> - My need for happiness and my aversion to suffering
> - My need to be doing nothing
> - My need to become spaced-out and disconnected
> - My need to be overwhelmed
> - My negative projections about unconditioned awareness

PROFILING YOUR PATTERNS

In order to further sensitize you to the ways in which you identify with your cultural and personal conditioning, consider the following questions:

- How and when do you suffer in your life? Is this suffering necessary? How do you tell yourself that you *need* to suffer in order to be fulfilled? What do your private and public conversations look like?
- What do you *do* in order to remove or reduce feelings of boredom, anxiety, restlessness, and fear?
- How do you stimulate your thinking? Typical ways that we keep our minds active include reading, conversations, attending lectures, watching television, writing, and surfing the Internet.
- What sources do you rely on for making meaning of your experience? With whom do you have meaningful conversations? What is the structure of those conversations? Do you create meaning out of "meaninglessness"? What is the "absence of meaning"?
- What beliefs do you entertain about unconditioned awareness? For example, do you think it means you won't suffer any more? Does it mean you won't be reborn? Does it mean you won't fear illness and

death? Do you think you will lose interest in people you care about, or that it will jeopardize your career? Will you be more or less capable of fulfilling your daily commitments?

TOMORROW'S SUFFERING!

We have a multitude of reasons, causes, and stimuli for feeling upset, disheartened, frustrated, powerless, and so on. As a function of our conditioning, we are attracted to difficult and problematic experiences. Consciously or unconsciously, we believe we must move through these in order to be fulfilled. While the causes of our suffering often seem to be outside us, the root cause lies within. It must, otherwise it would be impossible for people to become more equanimous in the face of adverse and challenging situations.

In this exercise, I would like you to speculate about how the moment-by-moment quality of your experience is degraded by reactive responses. Use the following pointers to create, from knowledge of your past behaviors, how you will sabotage yourself in the future. Write down your observations and review them over the coming weeks.

- Over the next week, I will get frustrated when/by . . .
- I will be upset by . . .
- I will feel sad when I think about . . .
- I will feel bored when . . .
- I will feel disheartened when . . .
- I will feel vulnerable when . . .
- I will feel overwhelmed when/by . . .
- I will feel victimized when/by . . .

It's possible that you might feel some aversion to this exercise. You might not want to do it, believing that you are negatively conditioning yourself by repeatedly thinking "I am going to suffer." In fact, in this exercise, you are acknowledging your future suffering, not as something that *must* happen, but as something that will, in all likelihood, continue to occur. If it doesn't, wonderful. If it does, you do not need to be surprised. You don't need to resist it, and you don't need to invalidate yourself, or your practice.

Having identified your patterns in this exercise, there's no need to avoid the situations that trigger difficult emotions, or to try to change your reactions. Change will happen. When we recognize our reactive patterns, we open up the possibility of experiencing the world differently. For example, when we identify the behaviors that keep us busy, we create the opportunity to be present to what is, without needing to escape our conditioning and experience.

Contemplative Practice

Because it is devoid of any innate nature, meditation
does not exist. The act of meditation is not meditation.
Because it is neither substance nor nothingness,
meditation cannot be a conceivable reality.
KALACHAKRA TANTRA[1]

Grasp this paradox my sons and daughters! There is not so
much as a mote of dust upon which to meditate, but it is crucial
to sustain unwavering attention with presence of mind.
SHABKAR, TIBETAN MASTER[2]

To realize the inexpressible truth, do not manipulate mind or body
but simply open into transparency with relaxed, natural grace.
TILOPA (10TH CENTURY), *SONG TO NAROPA*[3]

TO PRACTICE OR NOT TO PRACTICE,
THAT IS THE QUESTION

These days, we live in a marketplace of spiritual practices. No matter what we believe, we can probably find a system of practice that supports our way of thinking. Even though there are huge variations in how people conceive the spiritual path, in essence they can be divided into two basic approaches.

The approach we're most familiar with is based on the premise that we need to change in order to achieve real fulfillment. Spiritual systems founded on this assumption claim that something is missing in our life, and then offer various methodologies to rectify this deficiency. These systems offer "ancient" or "innovative," "easy" or "demanding," "gradual" or "rapid" methods for achieving complete fulfillment—wisdom, purity, freedom, bliss, and so forth—after a period of time: after many lives, within this lifetime, through a single course, or even from one meeting with a teacher. Most systems for spiritual and psychological development, both Eastern and Western, belong to this category. While their methods differ widely, these systems are predicated on the need for change. In other words, they're variations on the core belief that "this isn't it" and we need to be somewhere, or someone, different if we're to be truly happy and fulfilled.

Recently, this assumption has been challenged by the nondual systems of spirituality that have entered the United States and other Western countries. At one level, at least, these traditions teach that there is nothing more we need to do because enlightenment is staring us in the face. The main obstacle to realizing that we're already complete and fulfilled is our fixation with constructing and pursuing spiritual goals. This approach invites us to adopt a new perspective on achieving our highest potential.

Some nondual traditions teach that enlightenment is our natural condition, our essential nature. The only problem, which isn't a *real* problem, is that we haven't realized our enlightened condition. In Zen, this is known as the gateless gate—the paradox that we're already enlightened (our fundamental, "gateless" condition, in which no real or substantial barrier separates us from our true nature), but until we realize this fact (enter the "gate," wake up to who we are), we continue to search and suffer. Such traditions teach that our burdensome thoughts and conflicting emotions are the play or manifestation of our wisdom-mind.

Alternative systems say that the search for enlightenment is a distraction because there's no such thing as enlightenment. As Manjushrimitra said, "Since the state of pure and total presence of the Joyful One does not exist, it is a magical apparition of the [state] that appears to those who are deluded." In other words, enlightenment is not what we think it is. Other traditions and teachers claim to go beyond the belief that "this is it," insisting that there is no "it" to get, either in the future or in the here and now. Thinking that "this is it" only shows that we haven't really got it. As the Chinese master Foyan said, "The minute you fixate on the recognition that 'This is it,' you are immediately bound hand and foot and cannot move around anymore." As you can see, there are many different nuances and stories in the nondual approach.

The main characteristics of these two different approaches to the spiritual path can be summarized like this:

SYSTEMS BASED ON THE NEED FOR CHANGE SUGGEST THAT:	SYSTEMS BASED ON IMMEDIATE EXPERIENCE SUGGEST THAT:
This isn't it.	This is it.
We should do more.	We should do less — or do nothing.
We should try harder.	No effort is involved.
We can control our future.	Life is ultimately choiceless.
In order to progress, we need to study, learn, and know more.	Realization is a state of not knowing.
Reality is meaningful.	Reality has no real meaning.

GETTING IT, LOSING IT, AND REGAINING IT

In my own experience and in my work with others, I've found that the way most of us think about our path is a complex mixture of these two different approaches. Sometimes the experience of unconditioned awareness seems to arise as a product of a spiritual or psychological discipline. At other times, it seems to arise when we spontaneously let go of our concerns and preoccupations. Sometimes we think we need help. At other times, we think we don't. Sometimes we think our problems are real; at other times, we think they're just in our mind. Sometimes we think that what we're experiencing is exactly how it should be; at other times, we're convinced it should be otherwise. Sometimes we feel we must try harder; at other times, it seems more sensible just to let go and give up. And some of the time, we're just confused about which of these approaches is the most true or useful in the moment.

Underlying this complex blend of approaches and the confusion that sometimes arises is the undeniable feeling that we've lost something precious — an experience characterized by serenity, bliss, openness, and love — and we need to recreate it somehow. In truth, unconditioned awareness can't be lost, since it isn't an ephemeral experience that comes and goes. However, in the midst of an experience that we identify as unconditioned awareness, we may think, "This isn't the same. Something has changed. I'm no longer where I was, wherever that was. I've lost it!"

Of course, we may have lost what can be lost—a conditioned experience. But unconditioned awareness itself isn't an experience in the same way that thoughts, feelings, and perceptions are experiences. While other experiences come and go, unconditioned awareness neither changes nor stays the same.

Generally, when we sense that we've "lost it," we're referring to the fact that we've become identified with the contents of our experience, rather than with the space in which those contents arise and pass away. And we've judged that we're not where we want to be or should be. Then we feel we've lost our connection with that which can't be deliberately connected to—unconditioned awareness.

The moment we identify with our conditioned experience—our thoughts, feelings, and perceptions, however sublime—we open up the possibility of losing something we value. As soon as our thoughts and feelings cease to conform to our preferences, we determine that "something is missing."

Rather than seeing those contents of our experience for what they are—thoughts and emotions that come and go—we take them to be an accurate depiction of reality instead of a personal representation. Then we start to struggle within this reality created by our mind, while earnestly believing that we shouldn't be experiencing what we're experiencing. In nondual work, we interpret this feeling of loss as the recrystallization of, and identification with, the thought "I should be experiencing something different from what I am." At the level of our conditioned existence, a gap reemerges between where we are and where we would like to be. This feeling of loss produces a desire to do whatever we need to do to recover the experience of completion.

When the belief that "something is missing" starts to resolidify, we look for a discipline or practice that will assist us in recovering the experience of being fully and simply at home with who we are. Usually we begin by doing whatever we've done in the past that's helped to recreate the experience. If this doesn't work, we look for something else—a new practice, a new teaching, a different teacher. If none of these approaches works, we may experiment with doing nothing. The aim, though, is always to arrive at a point where there's nothing more we need to do.

NONDUAL WORK AND CONTEMPLATION

When we feel that "something is missing," many spiritual traditions suggest that we meditate, both as a way of working with uncomfortable feelings as they arise, and as a way of generally reducing the problems and dissatisfaction in our life. In nondual practice, by contrast, the sole purpose of contemplation, or meditation (I use the two words interchangeably), is to create the circumstances and conditions that allow us to enter and deepen the experience that "there's nothing more we *need* to do." In this sense, contemplation isn't confined to sitting quietly for twenty minutes a day. It applies to everything we do. We can be in contemplation with our eyes open or closed, sitting or standing, by ourselves or interacting with others.

In the following chapters, we'll explore contemplation (1) as a state that goes beyond practice, (2) as an awareness of the deeper structure of our conditioning, and (3) as a practice that we can enter and leave. We will also explore how these three understandings are intimately related to each other. In this way, we'll mainly be exploring contemplation as a specific practice, but we'll also see how it relates to unconditioned awareness and the broader context of our life.

One of the paradoxes of nondual work is that, while unconditioned awareness is unrelated to a structured contemplative practice, at least initially it can be more easily entered within the controlled conditions of a contemplative space. Hundreds of thousands of people over at least three millennia have encountered this same paradox. Thus, the popular argument that talking about optimal conditions is inconsistent with a nondual approach to well-being, because the experience itself is unconditioned, is both true and untrue.

At this point in our evolution, our experience of unconditioned awareness is supported by the presence of certain conditions, such as retreats, satsangs, meditations, and teachings. Outside such conducive conditions, we generally find it more difficult to stay immersed in unconditioned awareness. Of course, we can find it difficult to remain in unconditioned awareness even in a supportive environment, but the opportunity is greatly increased when adverse conditions have been filtered out. Certainly, when we're confronted with intense emotions, the pressure of a deadline, or strong physical discomfort, it's difficult to access unconditioned awareness.

BEYOND PRACTICE

When contemplation goes beyond the need for any effort or structure, it becomes what Tibetans call "natural contemplation." Natural contemplation is the experience of *finding* ourselves in a clear and serene state of mind, without needing any discipline or practice. That is why it's also called the meditation that's not meditation—or nonmeditation. We have no need for meditation because we're complete in every sense of the word. In the state of natural contemplation, we touch everything that arises in our experience without any resistance, we no longer reject or grasp at particular thoughts and feelings, and we spontaneously share our serenity and clarity with others in a simple and uncontrived manner. At this point, meditation has become the context for our existence, rather than a particular activity we do at certain times of the day. It's the experience of resting in unconditioned awareness while being present to, and engaged with, the dynamic flux of our conditioned experience.

CONTEMPLATION AS THE AWARENESS OF OUR CONDITIONING

A natural by-product of more nonconceptual forms of meditation is that we begin to *see* how our moment-by-moment experience is conditioned by an intricate set of causes and conditions that extend back into the past. We see how our capacity to rest in unconditioned awareness is influenced by what we did this morning, yesterday, last week, and ten years ago. Similarly, what we do (and don't do) and say (and don't say) today will influence the availability of unconditioned awareness next week, next year, and on our deathbed.

Within this wider context, our practice creates the conditions that support the direct experience of unconditioned awareness. Our aim is to remove all *need* to be thinking about any one thing in particular! Sometimes our practice allows us to enter unconditioned awareness on the spot—for example, when we inquire into the nature of our own existence and can't find anyone! More often, our practice comes to fruition in the future—for example, we experience the results of our practice when we sit down to meditate and find that we have no concerns about the past or future bleeding into our contemplative experience.

Our practice extends beyond a practice such as "just sitting" to include living our life in ways that we optimize the conditions for resting in the unconditioned dimension of existence. We learn how to create a pressure-free way of being whereby we are simply present to what is—without any unnecessary complications or considerations. As we gain familiarity with unconditioned awareness, the conditions that are required in order to rest in this state will become broader and less rigid. While the optimal conditions will be different for everyone, there are also common elements that apply to most people. For example, most of us find it very difficult to be genuinely complete in the moment when there's a high level of disturbance within or around us, such as when we're feeling angry or hearing some loud and unpleasant noise.

Discovering contemplation as the context of our life doesn't mean that we try to be calm, serene, and contemplative in every situation and interaction. Not at all. Many situations at work, with our children, playing sports, driving our car, etc., demand that we engage the world in a dynamic manner. But whatever we're doing, our actions ultimately support our fundamental commitment to deepen our experience of unconditioned awareness. How we are in the world is guided by an ongoing sense of the relationship between the conditioned and the unconditioned. We see, for example, that if we've been rough with our speech, angry, or withholding this morning, it colors the quality of the rest of the day. Such actions draw on our energy and negatively impact our capacity to be complete in the here and now. We'll return to contemplation as an awareness of our conditioning in Chapter Eight, "Completing in the Here and Now."

CONTEMPLATION AS A CONVERSATION

Usually we think of meditation or contemplation as a practice—something we *do* with our body and mind. In this chapter, we're also going to look at the practice of contemplation as a conversation. By the term "conversation" I mean the stories we have about and within contemplation. For many of us, the story has been formed by the teachings, readings, conversations, and practices we've pursued (*or* avoided) over many years.

This suggestion is not an original one. Two thousand years ago, Mahayana Buddhists said that the structure of our conditioned experience is shaped by the concepts we use to cut the universe up into self and the world, and then we fill these in and make meaning out of our existence. According to Buddhist philosophers, the manifest universe exists as a function of linguistic designation. It comes into being through the distinctions we make and share in language. As inhabitants of this universe, we too are part of the complex and ever-evolving text or narrative that constitutes the universe. As part of this process, contemplative experience is also shaped by the way we think and talk about contemplation. Because of this, we can change the way we experience contemplation by changing the way we think and speak about it.

The conversation that is meditation can be complex and variable. In some conversations, meditation occurs when we sit in a fixed position, close our eyes, and concentrate our attention. In another conversation, meditation occurs when our eyes are open (or closed) and our attention *isn't* fixed on any object. For some people, meditation occurs as a conversation in which they are closely or correctly (or even incorrectly) attending to the movement of their breath. Within this conversation, they can assess that a particular meditation session is effective or ineffective, that they are concentrated or distracted, and so on. These assessments interpret the present experience against a model of successful or effective meditation.

You might think that what I'm saying is a distortion of meditation because meditation has nothing to do with the mind. Meditation may have the capacity to take us beyond the mind, but we can only make an assessment that we are or aren't in the mind when we're in the mind — that is, when we are in a conversation about what meditation is! Hence, any engagement with meditation as a particular practice that we can enter and leave, that has a beginning, middle, and end, and is designed to induce a particular experience, is nothing more than a conversation. When meditation takes us beyond the mind, it is non-meditation, or as the Dzogchen yogis say, "natural meditation." (See the "Beyond practice" section earlier in this chapter, p. 59.)

There's another way we can appreciate how the practice of meditation is a conversation: by observing that often in the middle of a meditation session, we suddenly find that we haven't been meditating. We've lost connection with our body and our immediate environment, and forgotten that we're sitting in a zendo or a room at home. We're no longer engaged in the conversation called meditation — we're off in the future or back in the past. One minute we're engaged in the conversation of meditation, following our breath or witnessing our thoughts. The next minute we're having a conversation with our partner or enjoying our next trip to India! What's happened to produce such a dramatic change? Quite simply, the conversation has changed. (Even the thought that we're no longer meditating occurs within the conversation of meditation.)

The conversations we have within our meditation can have a dramatic effect on the quality and durability of our practice. For example, one of the easiest ways to destroy a contemplative practice is to interpret "sitting" as a series of lost opportunities. As we "sit," we contemplate all the valuable experiences we're missing out on because we can't get up and move around! We can't have a stimulating phone conversation, watch an interesting and important program on television, make love, or go to sleep. In a single twenty-minute session of "sitting," we can watch a series of experiences escape our enjoyment. Clearly, we're not going to sustain a meditative practice for any length of time if we spend a good part of our time in a conversation about "lost opportunities."

DIRECTLY EXPERIENCING UNCONDITIONED AWARENESS

The experience of unconditioned awareness is theoretically available and accessible in every moment of conscious experience. In reality, it's more easily accessed when we're calm and free of internal and external pressures. The conditions that are needed to establish and maintain a contemplative practice are thus very similar to those that make us more generally available to unconditioned awareness. "Just sitting" is designed to create such supportive conditions. In this way, it directly supports our cultivation of unconditioned awareness. The aim of sitting is not to sit for its own sake. In nondual practice, it's not meditation, as such, that's relevant. Meditation or sitting is only relevant to the extent that it supports us in experiencing unconditioned awareness.

Later in this book, we'll explore the use of deconstructive questions, such as "Who am I?" "What is this?" "Where do my thoughts come from and where do they go?" "Where is my mind?" "What am I doing?" These types of questions are designed to reveal the nature of unstructured awareness—unconditioned awareness. In a "sitting practice," we can ask these questions with a degree of focus and awareness that supports their intention to take us beyond the mind.

INCREASING OUR CAPACITY TO BE PRESENT TO WHAT IS

In order to be able to rest in unconditioned awareness in difficult environments and during challenging times, we need to expand our capacity to be present to uncomfortable thoughts and feelings. I call this "broadening the river of life." One of the most direct ways to develop this capacity is through contemplative training. Contemplative training is a little like "working out" in a gym: it increases our ability to accept and integrate emotional intensity and boredom—the presence and absence of strong feelings.

Contemplative practice also lets us see the internal source of our problems. Again and again, we get to discover the core truth of the Buddha's teaching—that our suffering arises through our attachment to or rejection of what is happening moment by moment. By slowing us down, the practice of sitting lets us see that many of the things we feel we "must do"—the necessities—are not so necessary.

CONNECTING US WITH OUR CONDITIONING

The practice of meditation connects us with who we are at the conditioned level of existence, where our identity is largely constructed of the stories we tell ourselves about who we are, what we've done, where we've come from, and where we'd like to be. All this happens in our minds—in our thoughts. When we sit, the structure of our thinking becomes much clearer because we aren't distracted by sense phenomena. The strategies we adopt to avoid experiencing ourselves become more obvious. Through sitting, we learn to accept ourselves exactly as we are.

DEEPENING OUR UNDERSTANDING OF THE CONSEQUENCES OF OUR ACTIONS

In order for a sitting practice to be rewarding over the long haul, we need to organize and live our life in ways that let us move into relatively peaceful and expanded spaces when we're sitting. If our experience of sitting is loaded with problems, planning, worries, and regrets, we can easily become disheartened and depressed.

The quality of our sitting correlates directly with how we live the rest of our life. If we make a mess of our life, our sitting will also be messy. If we act skillfully, our sitting will more likely be peaceful and relatively undisturbed. Indeed, sitting is a litmus test of our capacity to live our life skillfully, creating minimal residue in the form of burdensome thoughts and heavy emotions. The upside is that our sitting practice reveals how and where our actions have been incomplete—where, in other words, we've created karma. The skillfulness or crudeness with which we handle routine and challenging events becomes obvious when we sit. If we can create the conditions that allow and encourage us to sit quietly for some time most days, then by definition, we've begun to organize our life in a way that allows us to expand beyond our conditioned reactions.

No particular intention is needed to begin to see the connections between "how we've been" and "what's happening now." It happens automatically. The thoughts and images that bleed into our contemplation are a direct readout of the consequences of our actions.

Contemplation turns our attention inward. Our awareness is like a high-powered microscope directed at our thoughts and feelings. We begin to see the levels, layers, and patterns of our conditioning with a clarity that is difficult to achieve when we're focused on the outside world.

DOING THE WORK

I'm about to describe a practice called "just sitting." It's extremely simple. I'd love to present a practice that is impossible not to do, but I haven't quite found one. While this practice is very simple, it lets you:

- Directly experience unconditioned awareness
- Increase your capacity be present to what is, without attachment or aversion
- Connect with your conditioning
- Better understand the consequences of what you do and don't do

Nondual teachings have attracted people from a wide variety of backgrounds and with varying degrees of experience in meditation or contemplation. Some people have had no exposure to meditation. Others are seasoned practitioners. Some are lapsed meditators. And some are teachers of meditation. The practice I will introduce here is suitable for everyone, whether they are new to meditation or an accomplished practitioner.

If you are new to contemplation, this exercise will give you the opportunity to design a contemplative practice — one that is suited to your lifestyle and commitments. I will outline a minimal practice. You will identify and anticipate the types of interruptions that may arise, and gain support for your practice from your family and friends if this is necessary.

If you're an experienced meditator, this exercise will give you the opportunity to further explore your relationship to contemplation. You will more clearly see the conversation that meditation is for you. You may begin to rethink and redesign your understanding of contemplation so that you can enter unconditioned awareness more easily.

The practice of this contemplative technique will continue throughout the book. As we continue, I'll introduce different dimensions into this practice, but it will remain very simple and won't conflict with other practices. In fact, the practice is contained within your existing practice. It isn't something separate that you need to be doing.

CONFUSING AN AVERSION TO CONTEMPLATION WITH "GOING BEYOND" PRACTICE

At this point, some people who feel an affinity for nondual approaches to fulfillment might question our introduction of a "sitting practice," especially when we acknowledge that such practices can simply recondition us by establishing a new set of habits and preferences. They might think it's inconsistent with nondual work. Why create something that has a beginning, middle, and end, when unconditioned awareness has no boundaries or containment? They might even feel that this is a regressive move because it will take them back to an earlier, less advanced stage on their evolutionary path, where formal practices were all-important.

The rationale for rejecting contemplative practice is a belief that it invariably conditions the experience that "something is missing." The very act of trying to cut through or transcend so-called obstacles to unconditioned awareness makes these obstacles "real." The idea of meditating in order to experience unconditioned awareness also conditions and reinforces a belief that unconditioned awareness can be lost and found. By conditioning us in this way, the argument goes, our practice prolongs the pain and suffering that it's designed to remove.

People who express these concerns have often discovered the nondual approach after years of heavy-duty practice in which they didn't experience what they would consider to be sufficient return on their investment of time and effort. At this point, Dzogchen and Mahamudra can appear like a fresh breeze, because they teach an effortless path and are presented as the most advanced spiritual perspective.

We need to differentiate the experience of "going beyond meditation" from a state in which someone no longer meditates because it's unrewarding. The state of "non-meditation" occurs whenever we rest in unconditioned awareness. In this state, there's no need to meditate because nothing is missing. Yogis who abide continuously in this state go beyond the need for any formal practice. Such yogis may, of course, continue to practice, purely out of habit or routine. But they no longer *need* to practice, because there's nothing better for them to experience.

Some people confuse the practice of no practice with an aversion to, or even fear of, meditation. They may use their fluency in the nondual conversation to create the deception that they've gone beyond meditation. They explain this by saying that they don't need to meditate. They've meditated in the past but have now reached the point where they bring meditation to everything they do. They practice "being present to what is" with every experience; they're mindful throughout the day. If this is so, it is wonderful. But, if we suffer, if things go wrong, if we get upset and frustrated, then we haven't gone beyond the need for practice. Although practice isn't necessary, we still need to do something in order to realize this! This is the function of our practice. We practice in order to deeply realize that we don't need to practice, but without this practice, we don't see that we don't need to practice!

Although we may gain short-term relief from our suffering by engaging with the nondual conversation, our suffering won't be permanently relieved by simply adopting a different conversation. The fact that you're reading this book probably means that you're still searching for a more reliable and stable form of fulfillment.

There's nothing sinister about misreading the nondual traditions. They are very subtle and deep. Even though nonduality isn't a knowledge- or skills-based experience, it's easy to think we can acquire it by letting go of all effort and giving in to what is. We can acquire a new language that allows us to say that there's nothing to get, and no difference between having it and not having it. We can learn to talk the talk, but in and of itself, that doesn't alleviate our basic discomfort and conflict. The idea of "living in the now" can be a way of saying that we've run out of steam.

In the end, the simplest way to see if we're averse to "sitting" is to do some "sitting." Perhaps we'll discover that we can sit in meditation indefinitely, or maybe we'll find that there's still some work for us to do in order to feel more at home in the mindscape of our thoughts and feelings.

"JUST SITTING"

As mentioned before, this basic practice of "just sitting" is suitable for everyone, whether they are new to meditation or an accomplished practitioner. Throughout the rest of this book, you will be using this simple practice as a laboratory for exploring the causes of suffering and fulfillment.

If you're an experienced meditator, this section may not seem relevant to you, but what you get out of it will depend on who you are when you're reading it. For example, if you read it only for what you can get out of it for yourself, you may find it quite unrewarding. But if you read it as someone who is thinking about sharing meditation with others, these paragraphs may contain valuable new observations that empower you to introduce contemplation to someone who'd like to begin to explore meditation or to a group or community with which you feel an affinity.

"Just sitting" consists of:

- Disengaging from high-level external stimulation such as other people, television, books, and computer screens
- Sitting in a relatively still position
- Being silent and awake
- Then doing whatever you are doing
- For around twenty minutes each day

You can sit on a chair, couch, or meditation cushion. You can even lie on your back if you prefer. The only requirement is that you stay in the one place for around twenty minutes. You don't need to be rigid. If you are uncomfortable, you can move, but you don't need to. Just don't get up and move around. You can move your legs, move your hands, scratch and itch, stretch your neck, and so on. If you prefer not to, that is fine, too. Just don't relocate your body. Remain comfortable, quiet, and awake.

Within these parameters, simply do whatever you're doing. Think what you're thinking; feel what you're feeling; experience what you're experiencing. There's no right or wrong way to meditate. If you're following your breath, follow your breath. If you're reciting a mantra, recite your mantra. If you're doing nothing in particular, do nothing in particular. There's no need to follow your thoughts, nothing to concentrate on, nothing you *need* to do. If you're captivated by a particular line of thought, a feeling, or a physical sensation, that's fine. If you observe this process, you do; if you don't, you don't. There's nothing to correct or adjust, no guidelines about what you're supposed to be concentrating on, such as breathing, thoughts, feelings, or sensations.

If your eyes are open, let them be open. If they're closed, let them be closed. If you open and close them—and then open them again and let them wander around—let all of this happen. If you need to distract yourself, then, within the parameters of this practice, distract yourself. It doesn't matter whether you're concentrated or distracted. In fact, because there's no object of meditation and no need to meditate, there are no distractions. You don't need to do anything other than what you're doing. You can't go wrong. If you enjoy a session, you enjoy it; if you don't, you don't. Enjoying your contemplation is no better than enduring it. You don't even need to know *why* you are doing it. All you need to do is to do it!

Because it consists of doing whatever you're doing when you're sitting, this practice incorporates any other meditation practice you may be engaged in. To begin this practice, you don't need to know how it relates to the other material in this book, or even why you're doing it. And you don't need to know anything about the nondual.

THE TIMING OF THIS PRACTICE

To give yourself the opportunity to experience what you're thinking and feel what you're feeling, you need to minimize external stimuli. For this purpose, it's important to choose an optimal time for your practice when there are minimal actual and potential interruptions. For example, if you have children, you may want to choose a time when they're cared for by someone else, involved in their own activities, or asleep. It's also sensible to choose a twenty-minute period in your daily schedule that doesn't fall too close to a time when you need to be somewhere or do something else that you deem important. As much as possible, choose a time when there are minimal demands on your attention, and factor into your practice a little "transition time" on each side of your session. Finally, it can be helpful to allow some flexibility in your schedule in case you need to move the time of your sitting because urgent matters unexpectedly demand your attention.

PREPARING THE PHYSICAL ENVIRONMENT

First you need to choose a private space for your sitting. If you don't have one, you can create a space where you won't be disturbed for the duration of your practice by posting a note on the door or by just telling the people around you that you'll be meditating for the next twenty minutes or so. Most people find that they can quickly establish a special place they can return to each day that signals and supports their inner reflection. There's no need to get too formal: for example, you don't have to set up a shrine unless you find it supports your intention.

And just as you organize your kitchen before cooking a meal—first cleaning it, then gathering the ingredients and utensils—you need to take care of the physical environment before you sit, in order to avoid possible interruptions. For example, if you have an answering machine within hearing range, you can turn down the volume or put it on mute. If you don't have a voice mail or answering machine, you can take the phone off the hook or turn off the ringer.

Wear comfortable clothes, and adjust the temperature, if necessary, to make sure you aren't too cool or too warm. It's also a good idea to have an alarm clock set for the period of your contemplation so that you won't need to think about the time.

SUPPORT FROM FAMILY, PARTNERS, AND FRIENDS

In addition to preparing the physical environment, you may also need to make sure that the people who share your home environment understand and support what you're doing. For example, you can explain that this practice takes twenty minutes, and that it isn't complicated or mysterious. If the practice of just sitting quietly for twenty minutes or so doesn't make immediate sense to your spouse, partner, or children, you can reassure them by telling them just a little about what you're doing. The type and level of explanation will be influenced by their own relationship to meditation, reflection, or prayer. By explaining what you're doing, you'll put their minds at rest, and you won't have to think about what they're thinking about you. You can even invite them to join you or quietly watch what you're doing for five minutes or so.

Be sure to communicate in a loving, gentle, and respectful manner, without putting any demands on them.

The people around you should also know that you shouldn't be interrupted during your practice period—unless, of course, there's an emergency. It's unreasonable, however, to expect them to be totally quiet while you sit. Noise happens! If sounds penetrate your environment, they're simply part of your meditation. Of course, as I said earlier, timing can address most of the interruptions that may occur. For example, there usually isn't much happening in most households after 10 p.m. or before 6:30 a.m.

If you push the message that what you're doing is very important and you don't want to be interrupted or disturbed, you risk creating a rigid boundary or "hard edge" between you and the people around you that ends up provoking anger, resentment, and envy. If you're attempting to control others or impose your will on them, or you're feeling self-righteous or interpreting the people around you as an obstacle to your practice, you're likely to alienate them.

Deciding to go on an extended meditation retreat might also create a hard edge between practice and everyday life. Again, it depends on your attitude and your responsiveness to others. For example, if your family strongly objects to your going on a retreat but you insist, you're creating a hard edge. Or if you run the risk of seriously jeopardizing an important work opportunity, then your retreat clearly undermines your everyday life situation. Optimally, you want to organize your life so that your practice of contemplation, including retreat, is integrated and coordinated with your other activities and commitments.

ADJUSTING YOUR PRACTICE

Generally, sitting practice is neither too comfortable nor too uncomfortable. In fact, too much comfort can make you sleepy, and too much discomfort can make you so edgy that you can't sit quietly for the allotted time. If you find your sitting difficult or impossible, you need to make some changes at an environmental, physical, or mental level that will allow you to sit with some degree of ease. The particular changes are unique to each person's situation. You'll have an opportunity to explore this in the exercises that conclude this chapter. If you feel you're about to give up sitting because you find it too painful or unrewarding, it's best not to continue doing it in the same way. You may want to bring your practice back a notch, for example, by sitting for a shorter time or playing some soothing music while you sit. Or, if the weather is suitable, you can find some pleasant spot outside where you can quietly sit and enjoy nature. Whatever we do in the area of a contemplative practice, it needs to be generally gratifying.

SOME QUESTIONS YOU MIGHT ASK ABOUT THE PRACTICE

Does a mind-body discipline such as yoga or tai chi count as a contemplative practice for this course? Can I incorporate nondual contemplation into my tai chi or yoga practice?

The variations in methods for meditation and spiritual practice mean that there is no simple answer to this question. Some methods are more stringent than others. I recommend a very simple practice in which you're essentially stationary.

I'm involved in another practice that commits me to specific meditations every day. I don't have time to do an extra twenty minutes of "just sitting." What should I do?

I suggest that you integrate the nondual minimal practice with your other practice. Begin with nondual contemplation, being still, doing whatever you are doing, and let your formal practice arise within this. Similarly, at the close of your practice, let it dissolve into the unstructured practice of doing nothing other than what you are doing. This is consistent with the traditional Tibetan Buddhist instruction of creating your visualizations out of space or emptiness and letting them return to this state.

Can I complete my contemplative practice while traveling by car or in a train or aircraft or cab? I've heard about "driving meditation."

I think it will be difficult. There could be the newspaper headlines sitting right in front of you, there will be people getting on and off the train, and within minutes, you will be doing whatever you are usually doing on a train—there won't be any difference. At least initially, this doesn't fulfill the conditions of satisfaction for creating a contemplative practice.

What is the purpose of doing this?

There are many benefits that are often spoken about in relationship to a contemplative or meditative practice. Many studies indicate that important physical and emotional benefits come from regular meditation. I am not going into these types of benefits here because they aren't our concern. If it's possible for you to sit for twenty minutes—just being where you are, without moving or speaking or falling asleep—then anything else is possible. This is the only discipline. It's possible to do this without needing to know what you're doing or why you're doing it. If these questions arise during your practice, just let them be, without feeling any need to answer or solve them in your meditation.

How do I know if I'm doing this practice properly?

As long as you are following the basic guidelines I've provided, there's no further instruction about *how* to do it. How could there be? You are simply being with what is arising. You don't need to have an absence of thoughts; you don't need to have particular types of thoughts; you don't need to be aware; you don't need to be mindful. It is very simple. You will be adequately mindful (present/aware) without trying. However mindful you are, that is absolutely proper and correct. It doesn't need to be anything more.

Do I need to "sit" every day?

Again, we're not getting into a conversation here about whether you need to or don't need to. I suggest that you make a commitment to practice every day, and see how it goes.

What should I do if I miss a session?

If you miss a session, the best thing to do is to give it no more thought, and meditate today!

SHARED SESSIONS

Up to this point, we have described meditation or "just sitting" as a solo activity—something that you practice in your own time and space. In the *Radiant Mind* approach, we are also interested in introducing the nondual, contemplative experience into our relationships.

A very obvious way to begin is by sitting with another person. You can invite your partner to sit with you, or invite someone who might be interested in coming to your home and sitting together.

You can even practice "just sitting" with someone who is not in the same room as you are. In order to do this, you'll need a hands-free phone or a phone with a headset. You will be sitting in silence, but you will be energetically connected with your partner, knowing that she or he is at the other end of the line, doing what you're doing—just sitting and being present to "what is." Many of my students do this and it's very powerful.

When you first make the call, the only conversation that is needed is to acknowledge each other in a natural way: "Hello," or "Good morning." "Are you ready to begin?" Something along these lines is quite sufficient.

Decide how long you want to sit for. One of you will keep track of the time, with a timer or an alarm, and signal the end of the session. Even ten minutes can be a powerful experience of connecting with unconditioned awareness.

You don't need to debrief. It's enough to just coordinate a date and time for the next "shared session," and—if you plan on meditating again with someone who will not be physically present with you—you can establish who will call whom. Meditation isn't about creating a story about the past, even if this is simply the past ten or twenty minutes. It is about being in the present moment.

If you find the "shared sessions" particularly beneficial or supportive, you should feel free to schedule them with more frequency.

Enjoy!

CHAPTER FOUR EXERCISES

The following questions will help reveal your conversation about contemplation or meditation. Simply by considering them, your relationship to contemplation will change because your story or conversation about meditation will change.

What is your conversation about meditation? Why do you meditate? Why don't you meditate? Is it an integral part of your life? Is it a burden? Is meditation something that seems necessary and important, but just doesn't come together for you? Do you like to meditate, or do you find reasons to avoid it? What is the purpose of meditation? Is it purposeful? Have you rationalized that it's something you have gone beyond?

Generally, breakdowns and interruptions in a meditation practice occur when there's a gap between what we think meditation should be—what it *should* feel like, and what it *should* produce in terms of results—and what it actually is for us. What do you expect from meditating? Is there a discrepancy between your expectations and the actual results of your practice? Is this a source of disappointment and discouragement?

If you meditate, does your meditation practice adapt to your other commitments, including being displaced by them from time to time? Or do your other commitments accommodate your contemplative practice?

Do you assess your meditation practice session by session? Are those performance criteria part of the practice as it has been taught to you, or are they something you have added to your practice?

ENHANCING THE CONDITIONS FOR CONTEMPLATION

As already mentioned, there's a close relationship between the quality of a contemplative practice and what goes on in the rest of our life. This exercise gives you an opportunity to speculate about changes or adjustments you can make in the different domains of your life, including your environment, and in your body and mind. Remember that if the changes are too contrived, they might work once or twice, but you won't be able to sustain them in the face of your other routine commitments. Creating a "hard edge" between your practice and the rest of your life may in fact be counterproductive rather than supportive.

ENVIRONMENT

What changes can you make at home that would support your contemplative practice? What changes can you make in your work that would support your contemplative practice? These may be changes in how you do your work, when you work, and so on.

Do any of these changes require having a conversation with anyone, for example, your partner, children, colleagues, or boss? What type of conversation do you need to have? Do you need to make a request or an offer, or provide some explanation?

BODY

What changes can you make in the area of your health that would positively impact your contemplative practice? These may be changes to your energy level and fitness, what you eat and when you eat, changes to your pattern of sleeping, and so on.

Do any of these changes require having a conversation with anyone, for example, your partner, children, or doctor? What type of conversation do you need to have? Do you need to make a request or an offer, or provide some explanation?

MIND

What changes can you make in the area of your moods, feelings, emotions, and thoughts that would support your contemplative practice? For example, are there any changes you can make that would make you less anxious, worried, excitable, guilty, resigned, or fragmented?

Do any of these changes require having a conversation with anyone, for example, your partner, therapist, supervisor, or children? What type of conversation do you need to have? Do you need to make a request or an offer, or provide some explanation?

Noninterference and the Practice of Natural Release

Empty oneself more and more, finally you reach no action.
Where there is no action, nothing is left undone.
TAO TE CHING[1]

In a pellucid ocean, bubbles arise and dissolve again.
Just so, thoughts are no different from ultimate reality,
so don't find fault, remain at ease.
Whatever arises, whatever occurs, don't grasp — release it on the spot.[2]
NIGUMA, 11TH-CENTURY FEMALE MASTER

Conventional psychospiritual paths assume that the release of intense emotions involves work and effort, deep cognitive insight, cathartic release, or some combination of these. Such paths are built on the principles of discipline and transformation: we change our behavior, purify our minds, and transform our perceptions.

The nondual approach opens up the possibility of liberating disturbing thoughts and feelings by doing nothing! The nondual Dzogchen tradition calls this "leaving what is, just as it is." Dzogchen masters dissolve disturbances and enter unconditioned awareness by letting things be as they are. The moment they really do this, their reactive responses evaporate like water on a hot plate — or, as traditional texts say, "like snow falling on the warm water of pure noninterference."

In the nondual approach, we don't judge some experiences to be sublime and others profane. We don't make more out of our experience than what is immediately given. We don't enhance or accentuate our experience, nor do we trivialize or devalue it. Basically, we don't intervene or meddle in our experience in any way at all; we leave what is, just as it is. Our experience is natural, unaffected, unmanipulated, and free from contrivance. When we connect with the source of our being, we're intrinsically free; we feel spacious and liberated, no matter what our external circumstances or internal condition may be.

When we let things be as they are, contracted emotions and compulsive thoughts often dissipate more quickly than if we meddle and interfere. The ability to let things be, without judgment or reflection, is a central component of the nondual approach. We simply create space around a problem, letting it run its course and dissipate of its own accord. As the great Dzogchen yogi, Longchenpa, wrote, "Do not condition your mind by [trying] to suppress your experience, apply an antidote, or mechanically transform it, but let your mind fall naturally into whatever [condition you find it]. This is the incontrovertible essence of what is ultimately meaningful." In the Dzogchen tradition, the spontaneous dissolution of limiting beliefs and feelings is called "natural release" or "self-liberation."

NATURAL RELEASE

The ability to spontaneously liberate constricting emotions and compulsive thoughts depends on neither grasping nor suppressing any arising thought, feeling, or perception. Self-liberation, or the spontaneous release of reactive emotions, occurs as a natural consequence of identifying with awareness as such. When one's awareness ceases to be conditioned by compulsively or intentionally engaging and disengaging with different sensations, then thoughts and feelings float through one's awareness like clouds in the sky. Emotions dissolve like snow falling on the warm water of one's panoramic awareness. The contemporary Dzogchen master Namkhai Norbu Rinpoche explains it this way:

> When we speak of the path of self-liberation, there is neither a concept of renunciation, because if it is always my energy manifesting, then it can manifest in many different ways; nor is there a concept of transformation, because the principle here is that I find myself in a state of pure presence, of contemplation. If I find myself for an instant

in a state of contemplation, then from that point of view, wrath and compassion are one and the same. Good and evil are one and the same. In that condition there is nothing to do; one liberates oneself, because one finds oneself in one's own dimension of energy without escaping and without renouncing anything. This is the principle of self-liberation. [3]

In other chapters in this book, we'll explore dynamic and engaging ways of dissolving fixations. But in this chapter, we'll focus on the approach of noninterference and natural release.

COMPLETE OR INCOMPLETE

In nondual training, we learn how to observe human experience in terms of whether we're complete or incomplete in each moment as it arises. "Being complete" isn't the same as feeling satisfied, happy, or content. When we're complete, there's absolutely nothing more that we need. Nothing of any value or significance can be added to our experience: it can't be further enhanced.

"Being complete" is another way of describing the experience of resting in unconditioned awareness. Relative to the experience of unconditioned awareness, every other experience is incomplete. In unconditioned awareness, nothing is missing; there's no thought, consideration, or concern for being either complete or incomplete. As the Prajnaparamita (Perfect Wisdom) tradition of Buddhism says, the ultimate experience transcends the concept of freedom or liberation.

The difference between a "complete" and an "incomplete" experience is the presence or absence of a need. If we need anything, we're incomplete. If we need an experience to change, we're incomplete. If we need it to continue, we're incomplete. The Buddha used the word *duhkha* to refer to this state of incompletion. Even though "duhkha" is usually translated as "suffering," it refers not only to painful experiences but to any dissatisfaction caused by our attachment to, or our aversion toward, any circumstance or experience. When we're complete, we have no concern about an experience continuing, because we realize there's nothing to be grasped and held. As soon as we try to hold on to the experience of completion, we're immediately incomplete.

LETTING THINGS BE

The baseline position of the nondual approach to being with ourselves—and with other people as well—is that nothing is wrong or missing, and therefore nothing needs to be done. There's no work to do and no solutions to uncover because, ultimately, there are no problems. As much as possible, we experience directly the space in which there's nowhere further to go, nothing to change, nothing to understand, nothing to know. With others, we have no expectations *unless* they have a problem and invite us to engage with them.

In nondual training, an awareness of whether we're complete or incomplete sits in the background, not as something we monitor, but as a natural, effortless attunement to our state of being. We don't necessarily assume that we or others are lacking in any way. Many practices begin with the assumption that we're inevitably lacking something, inherently incomplete or in need of improvement. The nondual approach begins with no assumptions. If we can't determine whether we or others are complete or incomplete, we wait for the experience to clarify itself, and we may find ourselves doing nothing until an obvious direction presents itself.

LETTING THINGS BE WHEN *NOTHING* IS MISSING

If we're complete, we don't need to do anything. Why? Because we're no longer functioning out of needs and preferences. We're beyond needing anything; there's nothing that can be given or received; there's nowhere further to go. We're resting in a state of nondual awareness in the midst of our functional existence. There's nothing we need to think about, analyze, or process. If we encounter this completeness in others, it doesn't mean that we just sit together in mute silence. We may be quiet, or we may begin to dance in the paradoxes of nondual awareness.

When nothing is missing, we're free of all preoccupations about the future. We don't need to maintain the state we're in. In fact, we realize we can't maintain it, because there isn't anything to maintain. That's why the experience of unconditioned awareness is totally effortless. If we feel a need to maintain an experience, then we're incomplete. Even though we're enjoying the experience, something is still missing.

If nothing is missing, we allow ourselves and other people to enjoy this state for as long as it continues. Sometimes we may draw attention to the presence and quality of this state, but only if we can simply acknowledge the state without adding significance or value to it. If we're inclined to embellish the experience in this way, we may choose to not even identify it.

Unlike some approaches, the nondual method doesn't entail digging for problems when none arise. At first, you may be concerned that you're ignoring or denying real problems or not taking them seriously. After all, we've become accustomed to asking "What's wrong?" or "What's the problem?" Our approach here is to work with our anxieties and aspirations in order to come from a space that is as free of desire and aversion as possible. We need to be comfortable being free of problems and not feel obliged to construct that something is missing when we reach our fill of feeling good. In nondual relationships, part of the task is to increase our capacity to be free of problems and then model this space as a possibility for everyone we relate to. The most profound experience we can offer anyone is our own openness and freedom from compulsive behavior and reactivity.

LETTING THINGS BE WHEN *SOMETHING* IS MISSING

Sometimes, even when we know that something's missing, it's still best just to let things be. When we let things be as they are, we offer ourselves and other people a space around problems that's free of all pressure to change or to be the same. This way of being is extremely respectful, because we don't judge where we are or how we *should* be. We give ourselves permission to be exactly as we are.

When we let things be as they are, we neither energize constructions nor take energy away from them. On the one hand, we take care to not compound an experience of lack or inadequacy by supporting or validating it. Any acknowledgement, suggestion, or interpretation may be appropriated and used to fuel the experience that something is missing. On the other hand, we don't take energy away from a problem by dismissing our troubles and concerns or by rejecting our experience by telling ourselves to stop taking things so seriously or to handle things differently. Any attempt to minimize a problem or to reduce our own or other people's suffering may prompt them to become defensive and to create all sorts of reasons to support and maintain their condition.

When we let things be as they are, we don't know when or even whether a problem will dissolve. We're not trying to accelerate or retard the process of healing, and we acknowledge that things may never change. In this space of pure noninterference, constructions do tend to dissolve in their own time and manner, and problems tend to run their course and dissipate of their own accord. But we make no claims either way. At the most, we may acknowledge the fact that our problem has disappeared or reduced in intensity, for we commonly continue to think we're suffering, even when our discomfort has passed and we're experiencing joy.

How does the practice of noninterference work? Behind every experience of suffering lies resistance. We're either resisting what's happening or resisting losing it. When we identify what we're resisting and let go, we're immediately free and complete. As long as we resist, our suffering persists! Emotions and limiting beliefs liberate naturally from within themselves once they're experienced without resistance. When there's nothing to struggle against, there is no struggle. It doesn't matter if we confront a challenging emotion or try to avoid it. Either way, it seems to be real. When we stop trying to confront or avoid what we're experiencing, we release for more creative purposes the tremendous energy we expend trying to control and manipulate our experience.

Most of us don't know how to let go of our resistance or struggle all at once. And even if we did, releasing it in one bold gesture might feel too risky or intimidating. But we can learn to recognize the moments when our resistance naturally dissolves, and practice returning to those moments when situations become stressful. For example, we've all had the experience of being embroiled in a heated argument, and just when our agitation has reached its peak, we receive an important phone call. Somehow we have the capacity to instantaneously transform our energy and carry on a calm, composed conversation with the person at the other end. Then when we hang up, we may or may not pick up the thread of the argument again.

In the same way, we have choice points in the escalation of any resistance or struggle when we can hold back and return to a more harmonious state, as long as we believe it's in our best interest. Often, for example, there's a brief moment when we ask, "Do I really need to be doing this?" It's as if we're being tapped on the shoulder and reminded that we have a choice. We can give others the opportunity to attune to those moments and return to harmony, rather than ignore them and continue to feed their agitation.

Like everything else in nature, thoughts, feelings, and emotions move through natural cycles of development and dissolution. In a nondual approach, we tune in to the points where problems and heavy emotions begin to dissolve by themselves. By recognizing this process, we can naturally return to a point of equilibrium and balance. For example, we may notice when our agitation spontaneously decreases and observe it as it continues to change. In my experience, it's extremely difficult to remain agitated when we're consciously observing our agitation. By focusing our attention on completion, the experience in which we feel clear, balanced, and serene, and inviting ourselves to naturally return to it, we're training ourselves to value serenity and openness over agitation and reactivity. Instead of being buffeted around by the waves and undercurrents of our emotions, we can learn to ride into the calm waters of pure being—that is, into an experience of unconditioned awareness.

By giving ourselves and others permission to be as we are, we're not saying that we're perfect. Rather, we're acknowledging the fullness of who we are at both the relative and absolute levels, with both our individual idiosyncrasies and our essential purity, our sanity and our insanity, our fears and our aspirations. We're not attempting to avoid or suppress who we are, nor are we trying to capitalize on some conditioned identity in self-serving ways. We're natural and comfortable with our existence in its entirety; indeed, this effortless self-acceptance and fullness of being is the fruition of the nondual spiritual path. There's no one else we need to be and nowhere else we need to go.

The journey of conscious evolution begins when we cut through all pretensions and embarrassment, and encounter ourselves exactly as we are. And, paradoxically, this is also where the journey ends. When we *really* begin, there's nothing more we have to do! There's no beginning, middle, or end, just the unobstructed and uncontrived flow of our unique existence.

CHAPTER FIVE EXERCISES

In the last chapter, I introduced the idea that contemplation and meditation can be viewed as conversations, suggested that our experience of contemplation can be deepened by changing our conversation about meditation, and acknowledged that the idea that meditation is a conversation is part of our conversation about meditation!

I would now like you to reflect on where you are with this practice. My aim in doing this is to help reveal the conversation that meditation is for you. I'd like you to begin by looking at the conversations you may have been in over the past two weeks about the "sitting practice" we introduced.

- Did you begin the practice?
- Did you think, "Great, I'll get into this straight away"? Or did you think, "Great, I knew there was a contemplative practice coming up, but I'm pleased I don't have to do anything right now"?
- Do you need a reason to do this practice? What would be a sufficient reason? What would you need to know about it? What result would you need to expect, and within what time frame?
- In the instructions, I recommended that you sit for "around twenty minutes." Did you read it as meaning somewhere between ten and thirty minutes? Or did it mean to you eighteen to twenty-two minutes? Or do you time your sessions in order to make them clear and predictable?

1. DOING NOTHING

Your primary aim in the following exercise is to explore the path of noninterference or "doing nothing." When you encounter challenging situations, begin to experiment with a way of relating to them whereby you neither confront the problem, nor attempt to avoid or escape it. Take in the challenge — the person, conversation, feeling, and so on — but just let it be as it is. Don't try to change or modify your experience. Your experience will change, but for the moment, let whatever arises continue in your field of experience for as long as it's there. The challenge is to surrender all effort to control or manipulate your experience.

2. MOVING WHEN YOU DON'T NEED TO MOVE

In order to complete this exercise, you'll need a window of two hours during which time you have no other pressing commitments. You may complete this exercise in five minutes, but it may also take considerably longer.

THE INSTRUCTION

Go to a café and order a drink. Stay in the café until you don't need to leave, *then* leave. In other words, don't leave if you need to leave. But leave the moment you don't need to leave. This practice is known in Taoism as *wei wu wei,* or acting when there's no need to act. Once you have completed this exercise, go on to answer the following questions.

QUESTIONS

- What happened for you in doing this exercise? Write a brief report.
- How much of what happened really happened? How much of what you've just described is your interpretation? What really did happen?

Observing Fixations

Don't keep searching for the truth, just let go of your opinions.
THE BUDDHA[1]

Biased attitudes are the factor which binds one. The meaning of nonduality occurs when you're free of opinions and transcend clinging to extremes. There is no other way to disclose this. You can't see it by looking for it. Nor can you find it through logical analysis. Calling it "this" doesn't reveal it, so in relationship to the natural state, don't fetter, or liberate it, with a grasping mind.
LONGCHENPA[2]

In Chapter Three, we explored some of the ways by which we block access to the experience of unconditioned awareness. We identified our needs to be active, to know who we are and what's happening around us, and to create meaning as patterns that keep us identified with our conditioned existence. In this chapter, we explore more subtle and individual ways in which we identify with the conditioned level of our existence and keep ourselves distracted from the unconditioned, which exists as the ever-present core of our being.

Buddha taught that we suffer because of our attachment or aversion to what we're experiencing. The nondual approach takes this core insight seriously and applies it in the here and now, with radical results. Here, we observe and release our fixations as they arise moment by moment. Simply observing and acknowledging their presence releases us from their influence. As this awareness grows, an uncalculated correction occurs. Feelings of attraction no longer magnetically grip our bodies, and feelings of aversion no longer repel us.

A fixation is simply a positive or negative reaction. This chapter offers you a simple set of lenses through which to observe your own and others' fixations as they arise in real time. You have an opportunity to explore your attachment to and rejection of different feelings, sensations, thoughts, beliefs, and values, and you get to see how fixations distort your thinking and cloud your perceptions.

FIXATION: THE SOURCE OF SUFFERING

Whereas early Buddhist texts identify the source of suffering as craving or grasping, the Middle Path, or *Madhyamaka*, tradition of Buddhism uses the term "fixation." The actual Sanskrit word is *drshti*, meaning "fixed opinion or belief," but I prefer the term "fixation" because it bridges the psychological, cognitive, and energetic aspects of the phenomenon.

Fixation refers to the way we grasp on to ourselves and the things that make up our world, believing these to be either real or illusory. Fixation occurs whenever we take a rigid and inflexible position about any aspect of our experience. When we're fixated, we invest mental, emotional, and physical energy in focusing on one particular interpretation of reality. We become preoccupied with ideas of who we are, who we should be, who we shouldn't be, what we need, what we don't need, the goal of our existence, and how to get there. We can become fixated about virtually anything: experiences, substances, material circumstances, ideas, ideologies, people, values, feelings, or practices.

The nondual approach reveals our attachment to or rejection of different feelings, sensations, thoughts, beliefs, values, and situations. In this approach, for example, we may recognize that every time we think "I want this to continue," we're attached to what's happening, and every time we think "I wish this were different," we're rejecting what's happening. Gradually we get to see how fixations distort our thinking and cloud our perceptions.

Ultimately, of course, even the notion of fixation is a construction that can itself become an object of fixation, as I discuss later in this chapter. In other words, we can be fixated on our fixations, monitoring them closely and even searching them out. But if we inquire into the nature of fixations, we find that they don't have any substantial existence. That is, fixations are not things; they're just another way of describing the feeling that something is missing from our experience right now. When we can't find any fixations anywhere, our fixations dissolve, and we realize that there is actually no clouding or distortion occurring and nothing to be clouded or distorted. Everything is just as it is.

When we're fixated, we see things through dualistic categories, such as good and bad, right and wrong, self and other, one and many. We're either happy or miserable, free to do what we want or controlled by our circumstances, responsible or not responsible for our behavior. We're progressing toward our goal, or we aren't. People are either enlightened or unenlightened. To the extent that we're fixated, we introduce a bias or distortion into our experience of ourselves and the world. If we believe that we aren't trapped in these extreme categories, we're immediately caught in the dualistic category of being inside or outside them. Rather than seeing things as they are, we view the world through the filter of our opinions and preferences, likes and dislikes, and we're constantly trying to avoid what we don't like and to obtain or prolong what we do.

Our fixations reflect a need to reduce reality to an identifiable, knowable, and predictable thing. By compelling us to constantly defend and reject different interpretations of reality, they reduce our capacity to simply be with what is, in an uncontrived and unaffected manner. By fixating on dualistic beliefs, we place ourselves in a vulnerable position because we distort reality in an effort to manage and control who we think we are. We live our life struggling to consolidate and shore up our existence or wishing we could slip into oblivion. As basic Buddhism says, we crave either existence or nonexistence.

When we're fixated, we invest mental, emotional, and physical energy in defending or rejecting a particular interpretation of who we are and what we need. The fixations disclosed in this work trace back to a core feeling of incompleteness and a core belief that something is missing in our experience, which could be anything from relief from some mild discomfort to full spiritual realization.

Any thought, belief, or preference that results in a sense of incompleteness is a fixation. Here are some examples:

- It's too noisy, quiet, hot, cold, etc.
- Someone hasn't returned my phone call.
- I would get my work done faster if I had some extra help.
- I have to get there on time.
- I have difficulty finding love.
- Someone close to me is seriously ill.
- I'm not meditating properly or often enough.
- I need to reach full spiritual realization.

Accompanying the thought or belief is the feeling that *"this* isn't *it"*—where *it* represents a particular version of how things should be. Something is happening that shouldn't be happening, or something that should be happening isn't. Either view is a fixation that results in emotional confusion and a struggle to gain whatever *it* is. By becoming involved in this struggle, we experience suffering in one of its various forms, from mere stress or tension to intense emotional pain.

Periodically, the feeling that "something is missing" is displaced by the feeling that "this is it." For a time, everything seems to be on track, and circumstances are just as they should be. We might even convince ourselves that we've arrived at a watershed in our spiritual development. However, the belief that we've "got it" is a fixation in itself, setting up the possibility that we can lose it or that we don't have enough of it. At some point, we question whether this really is it and, even if it is, whether we now want it. In this way, the experience that "I have what I want" is inevitably transformed into an experience of lack or deficiency. Regardless of whether we feel happy or sad about what we think *it* is, we're still locked into a self-conditioning cycle of loss and gain. In Buddhism, this cycle of self-perpetuating suffering is called *samsara*.

CORE FIXATIONS

All forms of fixation can be traced back to a core assessment that something is missing in our life. We feel that "this isn't it"—where *it* represents our particular version of how things should be. We're certain that something is happening that shouldn't be happening, or that something that should be happening isn't. Either view is a fixation that throws us into emotional confusion as we struggle to gain whatever *it* is. We fear not getting *it* and, once having got it, we fear losing it. For spiritual people, *it* may be derived from our concept of a state of enlightenment, that is, a state of limitless possibilities and unending happiness.

As mentioned earlier, the baseline assessment that "something is missing" is cyclically displaced by the feeling that "this is it." For a time, we validate that things are turning out as we would wish, and we might even convince ourselves that we've arrived at the long-sought-after goal of our spiritual endeavors. However, the belief that we've *got it* sets up the possibility of losing it, as we reconstruct that we don't have enough of it and could use more of it. Besides, we question whether this *really* is *it* and, even if it is, whether we now want it or if we want it to continue.

The core assessments that "this is it" and "this isn't it" spawn innumerable secondary fixations. In terms of our personal and spiritual development, we spend enormous amounts of time and energy constructing the alternative interpretations that we're making progress or that we're standing still. As these constructions shift and change, we spend yet more time trying to work out whether we're stuck or mobile and oscillating between trying harder and giving up. We may decide that we do or don't need help, or find ourselves unable to decide whether to seek help or to go it alone. Sometimes we're clear and committed; at other times, we're confused and vague, struggling to determine whether our experiences are meaningful or meaningless, real or unreal.

These experiences seem real when we're in the middle of them, because they're supported by complex "stories" that validate our core assessment. For example, if we assess that we aren't making progress in our spiritual pursuits, we listen to a battery of "supporting evidence" that tells us we should be calmer, more aware, or less reliant on foundational methodologies. Drawing on the claims of others who *are* making progress, we may conclude that there's insufficient payoff for our sincere effort. These fixations lock us into habitual, conditioned ways of living life and interpreting the world, and toss us about between the extremes of elation and depression, excitement and resignation.

Every fixation is actually an expression of one of two core fixations:

1 This is it (I like it, approve of it, want more of it, would like it to last or be there whenever I want it, etc.).
2 This isn't it (I don't like it, want it to go away or stop, etc.).

These basic responses, in which we've decided we either like or dislike what we're experiencing, produce a vast array of evaluative thoughts, moods, feelings, and emotions, which, in turn, can lead to strategic actions designed to remove what we don't like and prolong what we do like.

Observing our fixations is as simple as seeing what's in front of us. Once we know how to recognize them, fixations become apparent just as effortlessly as the sights and sounds that present themselves to us in everyday life.

SPIRITUAL FIXATIONS

Once we embark on a spiritual path, we may believe that our fixations will necessarily diminish. But people can become fixated on spiritual matters like doctrine or practice just as easily as they can on more worldly or material beliefs, experiences, or concerns. Nondual spiritual systems do tend to have built-in mechanisms for ensuring that people don't become attached to the system's methods and beliefs. Nevertheless, the mere fact that we believe we're on the "right path" points to a fixation about right and wrong paths. Likewise, we can become consumed by our search for freedom or driven by the need to deliver others from their ignorance and suffering.

When we're following a spiritual path, we can tend to become self-righteous about our own approach and teachers, and critical of what we perceive to be the limitations or deficiencies of other teachers and approaches. At the same time, we may find it difficult to maintain our practice and our motivation unless we feel secure about the path we've chosen and indulge a belief that we're on the right track.

The question of whether we should meditate or not meditate is a popular focus of spiritual fixation. People tend to have a vested interest in either living a life of spiritual discipline and contemplation or living a life free of structures and practices. Many people on a spiritual path defend the view that it's better to be attached to spiritual practice than to reject it. Our relationship with the practice of meditation also brings out any preexisting bias toward having our attention focused on internal or external phenomena. Most forms of meditation direct our attention to the internal landscape of thoughts and feelings, simply because we're instructed to sit quietly in one position and, ordinarily, to close our eyes. People who feel decidedly uncomfortable when they're confronted with their own thoughts and feelings for any length of time, as many people do, tend to reject meditation or internal reflection in favor of external stimulation. By contrast, people who feel nourished by time spent experiencing the content and structure of their own thoughts and feelings tend to find meditation easy, and can feel deprived, unsettled, or incomplete if they can't regularly turn their awareness inward.

FIXATED ABOUT FIXATIONS

Of course, we also need to be sensitive to the possibility that we can become fixated about fixations. Most forms of spiritual development are driven by the belief that there are fundamental obstructions to being free and liberated. Working with our fixations gives us something to do. If we had no fixations, we might find it unsettling because we would have no obvious reason for our psychological or spiritual practice. We would probably have to invent fixations in order to keep ourselves busy. On the other hand, we may find it convenient to ignore our fixations because then we don't have to take responsibility for the problems we create for ourselves and others. We can just go about leaving a trail of disturbances behind us without bothering to clean up our act—or our mess. Often the only reason people deal with their fixations is that their own suffering becomes too intense or the people in their lives draw their attention to their fixations to such an extent that they can no longer ignore them.

FIXATIONS DO NOT REQUIRE "FIXING"

The path that's consistent with the nondual approach neither ignores our fixations nor takes them too seriously, neither gives into our desires nor resists them. In the nondual approach, fixations don't require fixing. It's sufficient to simply observe and acknowledge their presence. We don't even need to consciously change our behavior. The mere recognition of our reactions is often sufficient to release us from their influence. As mentioned earlier, with the growth of this awareness, an uncalculated correction occurs. Feelings of attraction no longer magnetically grip our bodies, and feelings of aversion no longer repel us. We find that we have less energy to direct to our reactions and fixations, and the problem naturally dissolves.

OBSERVING FIXATIONS

In general, there are two ways to stimulate the observation and transcendence of our fixations. One way is to impose a rigorous level of structure and consistency upon one's physical activity. Fixations reveal themselves as the ego attempts to affirm its own uniqueness and independence against a background of sameness and interdependence that's imposed from outside. Zen Buddhism and other traditions based on a monastic model tend to choose this way for stimulating and working with ego fixations.

An alternative way to observe fixations is to remove all structure and meaning. There's no reason for doing or not doing what we're doing, nor any way of determining whether we're on or off track in terms of our spiritual aspirations. Habitual fixations reveal themselves as we search for grounding and reference where there isn't any and consequently create our own systems of meaning in order to have a purpose and to track our performance and progress.

I find the second method to be particularly effective for disclosing and dissolving obvious and subtle forms of spiritual and psychological fixation. As I practice it, the nondual method occurs in a space that is created by the progressive removal of specific and generic structures and assumptions, which, in turn, allows people to see how their experience is constructed. For example, there are no conversations in my workshops or retreats that allow people to conclude that any activity or practice has or hasn't a purpose. Such a space brings people's constructions of meaning, purpose, and outcome into high profile because it doesn't collude with these constructions. As a result, people get to discover what they, and they alone, make out of the space.

In addition, because the space neither validates nor invalidates people's constructions, it isn't skewed toward any particular personality profile. For example, it's biased neither toward encouraging conceptualization and suppressing emotion nor toward encouraging emotion and suppressing conceptualization. This environment allows participants to experience the structure and behavior of their personality without distortion. Consequently, everything that's created within the nondual environment is an accurate reflection of what occurs away from that environment. The belief that "something is missing or wrong" emerges in the same way it does in other situations in life.

As I've already suggested, the initial practice is to observe how our thoughts, feelings, perceptions, and actions reveal our basic responses in terms of liking or not liking what's happening to us. We begin by observing whether we're attracted to or averse to what we're experiencing as our experience changes and evolves. For example, thoughts that signal attraction include "I like this," "I want this to continue," and "I want more of this." Thoughts that signal aversion include "This is unpleasant," "I wish this would stop," and "I wish I was doing something else." In this way, we become attuned to the signals that indicate we're in a reactive position.

RECOGNIZING OUR PERCEPTUAL LENSES

Inevitably we distort our experience by filtering it through one or a series of perceptual lenses based on our tendencies and preferences. To help us identify these habitual fixations, we can observe how we:

- Attempt to prolong or shorten what we're experiencing
- Resist or give in to an experience
- Draw attention to or divert attention away from ourselves
- Expose ourselves to or shield ourselves from fears and perceived threats
- Help or hinder our own and others' process
- Make things easy or difficult for ourselves and others
- Try to please or aggravate other people
- Feel pride or embarrassment concerning our thoughts, appearance, personal history, etc.
- Try to contract or expand our field of influence
- Try to intensify or dilute our experience
- Dramatize or trivialize what we're experiencing
- Validate or invalidate our own and others' beliefs
- Attack or acquiesce in the face of threats and challenges
- Agree or disagree with what others are saying or doing
- Express interest or disinterest in other people's thoughts and conversations

Some of these tendencies may sound healthy and constructive, and it may seem strange to refer to them as biases or distortions. For example, most people believe it's right and appropriate to express interest in what other people are experiencing or to help them whenever possible. However, such a belief is a consensual bias that limits our ability to accept things exactly as they are. In the nondual experience, we don't hold a position for or against helping or not helping, being interested or disinterested, making things easy or difficult. The nondual experience allows whatever is arising to be there, just as it is, beyond such categories and structures as right or wrong, appropriate or inappropriate, perfect or imperfect. The presence of any of these attitudes or judgments signals a distortion from the free-flowing space of natural, effortless, and uncontrived existence. Any attempt to change or prolong the present moment degrades the quality of the state of pure presence.

NOTICING OUR BODILY RESPONSES

Fixations also manifest in our bodies and nervous systems as contractions, tensions, movements, gestures, postures, and other bodily phenomena. In response to the mind's fixations on certain experiences, the body becomes fixated as energy gets concentrated and stuck in certain parts of the body. Such fixations may cause stiffness or limited mobility, discomfort, and even intense pain, and they may determine how and where we move and how we hold our bodies. On the other hand, these physical manifestations of fixations may go unnoticed. In addition, our fixations draw us into some situations and hold us there and repel us from others. By using the nondual approach, we can learn to use our bodies as sensitive instruments for detecting the presence of cognitive, emotional, and behavioral fixations by tuning in to the movement of subtle energies in our bodies.

For example, we can become familiar with the bodily sensations that signal we're operating from a reactive space, and we can learn to feel and read the physical signs of moods and emotions, such as embarrassment, pride, anger, fear, excitement, and boredom. We can also learn to sense the way we're physically drawn into some situations and repelled by others. As this awareness grows, reactivity no longer exerts such a powerful grip on the body.

OBSERVING OUR PATTERNS OF BEHAVIOR

The behavior patterns to which I'm referring are our predispositions to think, perceive, communicate, and act in ways that constrain and limit our experience of reality. Grounded in our fixations, these predispositions impose an impression or structure on our thoughts, perceptions, speech, and actions. As such, they shape and define our way of being in the world.

The ability to recognize just a few of these patterns, such as complaining, blaming, justifying, enduring, commiserating, explaining, and seeking sympathy, can help minimize our identification with the problems in which we habitually get caught. In addition, if we fail to recognize these patterns in ourselves, we will collude with such patterns when they arise in others. We most often fail to see these patterns in others because doing so would disclose the same pattern in ourselves. But when we can observe a pattern—in ourselves or others—we free up the energy that's involved in its deployment.

From an ultimate point of view, patterns are neither positive nor negative. They are simply structures that define who we are as conditioned individuals. However, to the extent that we believe we must alter our thinking and behavior in order to rest in unconditioned awareness, we can observe patterns in terms of how they disconnect us from a more open, spacious, and spontaneous way of being in the world. From this perspective, patterns can contract our capacity to be open and aware.

The patterns we're describing are not raw impulses and drives. They have a design and subtlety to them. The maintenance of these patterns involves a degree of self-deception. Usually we're aware of some of our patterns and unaware of others. And even when we do recognize some of our patterns, we're not always aware of how they're being expressed in our thoughts, feelings, communications, and actions.

Most patterns can be recognized by observing the way we think about ourselves and through the responses we generate in others. We can, for instance, detect many of our patterns through our attempts to justify or rationalize our behavior. Whenever we justify our thoughts and actions to others or rationalize them to ourselves, we are inadvertently expressing a limiting pattern. Or we can recognize these patterns through the internal discourses or conversations that signal their presence.

We don't necessarily want to examine our patterns. In fact, the patterns are constructed with a dual purpose. They are designed to sabotage our life and the lives of others, but in such a way that we don't recognize them. If they were obvious, we might be embarrassed by their presence and want to do something about them. The survival of these patterns requires that they remain concealed from our awareness.

Although some of the mechanisms described may seem innocuous, it would be unwise to underestimate their influence. The cumulative deployment of these patterns can make a vast difference in terms of our "station in life," that is, who and where we are in the world. Each of these patterns is an entire narrative, a theme that consistently and recurrently surfaces in our life.

In the next few pages, I'll briefly describe some common patterns and the type of discourse or self-talk that accompanies them. I will also give the self-justification for using and maintaining each pattern. Your own recurrent conversations will usually be a mixture of these. As you read through these examples, mark the ones you recognize. I'm sure there are many other significant patterns that I haven't identified. If something comes up that I haven't described here, describe it in your notebook or on a sheet of paper. Try to identify the pattern as well as you can in a format similar to the one I've used for the following examples. Then try to reproduce as closely as possible the inner conversation that justifies the pattern by making it seem useful or necessary.

I'm sure there are many more patterns than these. These are just the ones I have observed in myself. We do not have to get down on ourselves as we observe them. And yet we can appreciate the way that they diminish our presence and aliveness. A swami in India was once asked by a student about the phenomenal level of his energy. "You hardly sleep," she said. "Where does this boundless flow of energy come from?" "Just imagine," he replied, "how much energy you would have if you didn't worry, or complain, or judge, or defend, or resist!"

SATURATING EXPERIENCE WITH UNDERSTANDING

This is a predisposition to saturate our experience with understanding and interpretation. We rarely experience people or ourselves with existential purity because we're attached to thinking and analyzing. We create a thought-barrier to being with ourselves and others.

The justification: "I need to understand what's happening. It will help me in the future. And besides, my understanding will help others. I might even be able to make a career out of it!"

SUSPICION

The pattern of suspicion is motivated by a need for safety and security, which may be based on a lack of commitment or used as an excuse for inaction.

The justification: "I have a higher level of discernment than others. I'm circumspect and not easily deceived or shortchanged."

FOCUSING ON THE NEGATIVE

The problem with focusing on the negative is that we can easily delay or interrupt a new initiative, or unnecessarily derail existing plans and commitments.

The justification: "If I'm not aware of how and where things might fail or foul up, I can't guarantee that I'll be able to fulfill my commitments."

NEEDING MORE INFORMATION

With this pattern, we're in a constant state of preparation. We always need to know more, and we continually elicit responses that threaten our security. We're unwilling to jump in and give things a go. We lack resolution. There's an unrealistic need for the false security of "knowing."

The justification: "If you can bear with me and wait just a little longer until I have all the information I need, you can be sure that I'll deliver on whatever I commit to."

PLAYING THE OBSERVER

As an observer, we're always watching what others are doing. It's safe to be an observer because it involves minimal accountability when problems occur. The "observer" is often a theoretician, someone who habitually assumes a secure and impartial position from which to create hypotheses, explanations, and theories.

The justification: "The world needs observers and theorists. There's an important place for those who act as a witness to the doings of humankind and who can, if need be, explain why things are the way they are."

LEARNING THROUGH MISTAKES

The concealed assumption is that useful knowledge is acquired by learning from mistakes. Often, people who learn from mistakes become experts on what they shouldn't do, and give an ongoing commentary about what they've learned in order to cover up the stupidity of having made the mistakes in the first place.

The alternative is to act on the basis of intuition and unconscious competence.

The justification: "If I make mistakes now and learn from them, I will definitely not want to do them again in the future."

CONFUSION

Confusion is a popular strategy, in part because it is a socially acceptable way of debilitating ourselves. Confusion gives the impression that we are "working at or toward a solution." Of course, confusion can be a precursor to clarity, which emerges when we discover a new distinction. The important point is to not indulge in confusion, that is, to not use it as a rationalization or excuse for inaction and a lack of commitment.

The justification: "I can afford to be confused and at times even parade my confusion, since it shows that I am working very hard at gaining clarity and finding a solution."

SELF-DOUBT: I'M NOT SURE I CAN BE TRUSTED

This conversation usually occurs as self-talk but might sometimes be used interpersonally when we feel a need to appear very honest.

The justification: "My peers and superiors will recognize that I have the very important virtue of knowing my own limitations and inadequacies, and for this they will come to trust me."

PERFECTIONISM

The perfectionist pays a disproportionate amount of attention to incidental detail.

The justification: "People will notice the fact that I have attended to every conceivable detail and will generalize this perception and believe that I consistently bring meticulous care to everything I do."

HESITANCY

Like suspicion, this produces a tightness and rigidity about action. When we are hesitant, we miss out on opportunities because we wait until it is too late, then act. We make up our mind to buy the item on sale just after the sale has finished. Or we decide to enroll in a course just after the registration has closed. The closer we are to missing out on opportunities, the less our credibility is damaged. Typically we are so close that we can't be deemed responsible.

The justification: "I'm cautious and prudent."

JUMPING TOO SOON

By this, I mean the tendency to be impatient and act with an unnecessary sense of urgency—the opposite of hesitancy.

The justification: "I'm enthusiastic and committed. People can see how keen I am. I am always first off the blocks (unfortunately, I'm usually off before the race has even begun)."

IMMATURE ENTHUSIASM

This is a brutish, raw excitement that lacks discrimination and sensitivity as well as serenity and perspective. Immature enthusiasm tends to imply that others are at fault when they don't have the same vision and energy.

The justification: "My raw enthusiasm reflects the degree of my commitment and the amount of energy I am willing to give to this task."

EXCESSIVE SELF-DISCLOSURE: THE "OPEN BOOK"

Here, we disclose everything about ourselves without regard for its impact on others. We don't have any secrets and there's no mystery about us. We tend to "let it all out," warts and all.

The justification: "People see how honest I am. They know what they are getting. I have no secrets and this gives them confidence, for they know exactly what they are getting."

EXAGGERATION

Exaggeration takes the form of distorting who we are by magnifying our virtues and amplifying the mistakes of others. As a result, we are bound to trip up at some point, since people bring expectations about us that we cannot meet.

The justification: "If I exaggerate (just a little, of course, so people won't catch me), then my friends and colleagues will think that I am wiser, more wealthy, more astute, more caring, etc., than I really am."

LEVELING

As levelers, we're interested in making progress and getting ahead by fraternizing with the types of people we aspire to be, rather than by gaining expertise and competence through practice and application. We speak as equals to people who aren't our equals because we want to be acknowledged. As a consequence, we do not learn from authorities.

The justification: "By leveling, I can achieve the competence and prestige of those people who are higher, more expert, or more influential than I am. Besides, it helps the people I level with because they really want to feel like one of the common folk."

FLAKINESS

Flakiness is an expression of commitment (supported by an ungrounded enthusiasm) that does not last the distance. We like ideas but not the hard slog necessary to accomplish them, and we have a poor assessment of our own capacities.

The justification: "I need to check out many alternatives. Besides, I tend to be eclectic. I need to express my enthusiasm and commitment now, just in case I decide to really be committed down the line."

THE DRAMATIST

We have a compulsive need to periodically inject action and intensity into our life by precipitating a crisis. Just when things (life, relationships, career) are going smoothly, we create an upset or drama that intrudes into the lives of others. Common dramas include putting things off so they need to be dealt with urgently later, and overcommitting and then being overwhelmed by what we've agreed to do.

The justification: "Dramas keep me alive and on the ball. The emotional intensity I experience keeps me (and others) from becoming complacent and boring."

THE INTERRUPTER

As the interrupter, we cause small but frequent ruffles and interruptions. We might repeatedly burst in and say, "Look, stop doing that. Something else has come up that needs our immediate attention." Or, "How is it going? What have you done since this morning?" We're inclined to invade others' space for our own emotional needs, and we're preoccupied with our own worries and fears. But in reality, we don't know how to give people space.

The justification: "I need to keep people on their toes. I need to know I'm needed."

EXASPERATION

In our interactions with others, this often leaks out as blame, but with a sigh that is meant to convey our patience and paternal maturity. Exasperation satisfies our need for communicating something but fails to get the message across in a way that will make any difference. This type of response often arises out of a sense of enforced responsibility.

The justification: "I'm giving feedback to people in a form they can handle. Some people can't handle direct speaking but rather respond best to the tacit messages I give them when I express mild annoyance, frustration, or exasperation."

PREOCCUPATION-DISTRACTION

In this behavioral pattern, we listen to our own thoughts while giving the appearance of listening to the person who is speaking to us. Essentially it is a way of not being present to what is happening with someone else. We are more inclined to pick up on the tangential details in a conversation that distract us, rather than lock into obviously relevant ideas. If I am at a meeting, I might be thinking, "I must keep in mind that I have a dental appointment this afternoon, otherwise I might forget about it." In a deep and meaningful conversation, such "deaf listening" can be accompanied by an expression of concern with the well-being of others that disguises the smugness and arrogance of the indulging thoughts that tell us how kind and sensitive we are.

The justification: "I can't afford to be distracted by what's happening around me, or what other people think and need, otherwise I'll be sidetracked from my own endeavors."

EXAGGERATED MEANINGFULNESS

In this pattern, we display a preference for deep and meaningful discussions about the personal concerns and worries of others that deflects attention away from our own concerns and worries. We may feel that people will only love us if we express overt concern for their problems and difficulties.

The justification: "I am being caring and useful."

TRIVIALIZATION

In speaking with others, we might say "Is that the real problem?" or "Is that what you really mean?" in a way that devalues them. Privately, we just don't believe that people can be genuinely interested in such trivial matters as sports, entertainment, or science fiction.

The justification: "Life is precious. It's important that I recognize this myself and also bring it to others' awareness."

I'M TRYING THE BEST I CAN

This is essentially a request to not be asked to do anything more. We are saying, "Don't push me, don't ask for any more of me. Can't you see the sweat?"

The justification: "I'm giving my best to this situation."

I'M TOO GOOD FOR THAT

In this pattern, we deem certain tasks too insignificant for our involvement. We don't want to be associated with people or activities we think are common or too ordinary.

The justification: "I should reserve myself for what I'm really best at. If people see me doing some menial task or talking at length with some unimportant person, they won't realize that I have unique capacities."

FORGETTING THE KEY

This pattern leads us to do everything that obviously needs to be done, while omitting a small but essential detail, possibly even leaving the final task undone. The key could be a vital phone call or letter we let slip by, a gift or piece of advice we fail to acknowledge, or a medical check-up, the forgetting of which leads to serious illness down the track.

The justification: "I can't be expected to keep track of everything. I'm not going to be paranoid. It's important to leave some things to chance."

THIS ISN'T IT

This mechanism fuels all the preceding self-defeating patterns. Basically, we just object to being wherever we are and live inside the conversation "This isn't it," "Something is wrong," "This isn't right," "This isn't how it is meant to be." As a result, we live in resistance and denial, and are alienated from our actual existence, failing to appreciate that things cannot be different from the way they are. How can they be?

The justification: "There's something wrong with the way things are. How could they possibly be this way? This is not the way I want it to be."

CONCLUSION

As I said earlier, these patterns are detected indirectly by the presence of the justifying thoughts that accompany them. Of course, the same conversations can be used in empowering and creative ways. For example, learning from our mistakes, seeking out information, finding solutions, exercising circumspection, and noting the negative consequences are all important resources and abilities for being successful in life. But these and other tendencies can be corrupted into self-defeating patterns of thought and behavior.

Certainly, any form of justification should alert us to the possible presence of a self-defeating pattern of behavior. When we find ourselves repeating certain thoughts about looking impressive, needing more certainty, or getting things just right, we can look to see if this represents the active presence of a pattern that keeps us locked into a conditioned identity. If it does, we can recognize the pattern, and immediately its energy will begin to dissipate. Then we can return to our natural condition, in which are totally at home and at ease with who we are, without any need for change or justification.

CHAPTER SIX EXERCISES

1. OBSERVING FIXATIONS

When we rest in unconditioned awareness, our dualistic fixations are completely inactive. There's no attachment or aversion to anything that arises within our field of awareness and hence no attempt to prolong or escape what is happening. Conditioned mind, on the other hand, is characterized by the presence of dualistic fixations—our likes and dislikes.

In these exercises, I invite you to become more aware of your fixations *as they arise.* For example, when you're in a conversation with someone, observe how you agree and disagree with what's being said, and how you move between feelings of interest and disinterest. In other words, listen to the way you listen to what the other person is saying, and notice the subtle and overt ways you communicate your agreement and disagreement.

- If you're listening to a news report or reading the paper, notice how you approve and disapprove of whatever's being expressed.
- When you're with a group of people, notice how you attempt to contract or expand your field of influence. Observe how you'd like to be acknowledged, or how you'd prefer to be ignored.
- When you're in a social setting, notice how you want to stay where you are, or how you'd like to be somewhere else.
- When you're aware of how other people are experiencing you (i.e., listening to you), notice any energy of pride or embarrassment that might arise. How do feelings of pride and embarrassment manifest in your body?

2. SPIRITUAL FIXATIONS

The next time you talk with a friend about spiritual matters, just listen without responding. Listen to your listening, noticing how and when you agree and disagree with what your partner is saying. Then do the exercise again, but this time you can respond to whatever your partner is saying. Notice how you express your agreement and disagreement.

3. JUST SITTING

Within your practice of "just sitting," gently observe your relationship to your experience in terms of whether you'd like it to change or continue. Simply notice the structure of your thoughts, without any judgment. Are you thinking "This is nice," "This is working," "I wish my meditation was always like this"? Or, are you thinking "I'm bored," "I'm tired," "I must only have another few minutes before I finish"?

CHAPTER SEVEN

NONDUAL COMMUNICATION
Pure Listening and Speaking

Once we have an experience of unconditioned awareness, we can learn to bring this quality of open, nonjudgmental awareness to every moment and interaction in our life. In particular, our relationships with others offer an excellent opportunity to notice the ways that our emotional responses and habitual patterns cause us to interfere with or degrade the nondual space by filtering what we see, hear, and say. By bringing awareness to these patterns in our communication, we can return to our natural state, not only when we're on our own, but in the midst of intimate encounters or difficult work situations. If we work as a counselor, psychotherapist, coach, or other helping professional, the ability to communicate purely, without distortion, can be an especially invaluable asset.

PURE LISTENING

There are three different ways through which we can receive what people are communicating to us: positive listening, negative listening, and pure listening. Negative listening occurs when we listen through a filter of boredom, disinterest, invalidation, annoyance, arrogance, anger, frustration, and so on. Positive listening is marked by moods of interest, enthusiasm, excitement, approval, and validation.

Normally, we listen through a filter of reactions and assessments, whether or not they're overtly expressed. We're constantly validating and invalidating what people are saying and doing. This process generally becomes obvious when it's intense. For example, when we think, "Absolutely, I totally agree," we're likely to notice that we're validating someone's interpretations or opinions. Or when we think, "How absurd! That's a complete exaggeration," we may find it easy to acknowledge that we're in powerful disagreement.

But validation and invalidation also have subtler expressions. For example, saying "yes" or "I understand," or merely nodding are ways of signaling agreement. In contrast, spacing out, looking restless, or just thinking, "How much longer are they going to go on?" are forms of invalidation that express some level of intolerance and nonacceptance.

When we listen through a screen of judgments and assessments, we distort the natural flow of people's experience. Positive listening pumps energy into a construction; negative listening takes energy away. Whenever we agree with someone, we tacitly encourage them to continue what they're doing. Our contribution prolongs an emotional or intellectual construction by giving it attention and positive energy. By contrast, when we disagree, we interrupt the flow of people's experience and undermine their constructions.

Pure listening is a quality of being that we can bring to all our interactions. When our listening is pure, we hear without static or interference. We neither add to nor take away from what is being communicated. We "get things" exactly as they are. When we listen with this degree of purity, we "listen from nothing." We're like a clear mirror, receiving exactly what is communicated—nothing more and nothing less.

Pure listening neither encourages nor subverts another person's communication. We don't need the conversation to continue or stop; we don't need to understand it conceptually. We listen without projecting or interpreting, without anticipating what someone is going to say next, without attempting to reconstruct or interpret their experience for them. From our point of view, it makes no difference whether a friend or partner is talking or not talking. If they stop in the middle of a sentence, we're complete. We don't need them to complete what they're saying. We're completely satisfied with the communication exactly as it is. Such listening arises naturally out of unconditioned awareness. We're not being attentive in an expectant and encouraging way that invites the person with whom we're communicating to continue. Nor do we discourage communication by being inattentive or distracted. We're neither engrossed in our own thoughts nor immersed in the story that we're hearing. We're just listening, being purely present to what's there.

In contrast to pure listening, positive and negative listening distort the nature of authentic relationship by disconnecting us either from ourselves or from the people with whom we're in communication. When we listen positively, we get wrapped up in other people's experiences and seduced by their stories, and we lose connection with our own thoughts, feelings, and values. "This is fascinating. I can really relate to what they're saying. This makes total sense." When we listen negatively, we become preoccupied with our own thoughts and feelings, and we trivialize the significance of what we're listening to. "How can I wrap this up? I wish I could change the subject. I've got more important things to do than listen to this."

When we listen from nothing, we hear everything! Because our attention is relaxed, global, and without intention, we're in equal and intimate contact with ourselves and the people with whom we're communicating. The space of pure listening contains all speaking and listening without giving special attention to either ourselves or others. In fact, the separation between self and others dissolves, and communication arises as a spontaneous and synchronized display of nonmanipulative speaking and listening. Because it respects the integrity of both the speaker and the listener, pure listening is the only form of communication that can take us beyond our conditioned identities into an experience of unconditioned awareness.

The practice of pure listening and speaking is developed in two phases. First, you'll need to practice listening in silence, without judging or assessing. As part of this phase, you'll complete a set of exercises designed to refine your listening by filtering out the tendencies to positively and negatively appraise what people are saying or doing. Later on, you'll learn how to introduce speech from your own side, so that you both listen and speak from nothing.

ENTRAINMENT

As we're all no doubt aware, communication takes place not only when we're talking or listening, but also in silence. By sharing our experience of nondual awareness without words or effort, we invite the people with whom we're in relationship to entrain or attune to this experience themselves. As we rest in this thought-free state, the energy of serenity naturally transfers from one person to another like two bells resonating together. In fact, one of the greatest contributions we can make to others is to offer them the experience of our own serenity, especially when they're agitated or distressed. By remaining in equanimity, unperturbed, we share with others the possibility that there's nothing wrong with what's happening. We model the possibility that there's actually no problem, not because we're creating or inventing that position, but because it's true for us.

We can share this possibility by staying intimately connected with others, yet at the same time not allowing the experience of unconditioned awareness to be compromised. By doing so, we may occasion a creative dissonance between ourselves and those with whom we're in communication. Rather than "coming down" to meet them on their own terms, we're inviting them to "step up" to meet us in the space of unconditioned awareness, where there are no problems. But, of course, we need to monitor the dissonance so that people don't experience us as inaccessible or aloof.

THE EMERGENCE OF SILENCE AND SPACE

In nondual communication, our conversations can be punctuated by periods of silence. This silence is a natural outgrowth of the perspective that there's nothing to say or do because we experience others as already complete. Since we don't feel the need to manipulate other people's experience, periods of time spontaneously occur when all involved are simply being present to the moment, without discussion about what is happening.

These periods of silence that arise are useful because they can help to decondition our habits and fixed beliefs. As people entrain to the nondual experience, their state of consciousness naturally becomes less structured, their stories dissolve into the background, and they will have moments in which they "pop through" to an experience of unconditioned awareness. These moments are generally experienced as exceptionally nourishing and healing, which increases the likelihood that they will happen again.

In our culture, we're conditioned to encourage conversation. However, when we're resting in unconditioned awareness, we may find that we don't have the energy or inspiration to get involved in complex conversations. If we remain silent yet stay connected with another person, we give them the opportunity to wonder what's going on for us. They may become curious about our experience, and this may lead to a joint exploration into unconditioned awareness.

TO SPEAK OR NOT TO SPEAK

When people first cultivate a nondual experience, they may confuse pure listening with listening with disinterest or listening as though the construction is unreal. But pure listening is definitely not disinterested listening. When we're disinterested, we switch off; we're not fully present to the person in front of us. Usually we're involved in our own thoughts, and we may be lightly judging the person who's communicating with us. By contrast, when we listen from unconditioned awareness, we're neither attentive nor inattentive, interested nor disinterested. We aren't looking for anything, and we don't do anything with what's being heard. As a result, the person with whom we're communicating may find that they no longer need to communicate something that previously seemed important. In the face of this pure listening, there may simply be nothing to say.

Because we listen without projecting or interpreting, we don't anticipate what the speaker is going to say next, nor do we consciously search for a common reference point by attempting to relate their experience to our own. We don't feel uncomfortable if they say nothing or don't complete what they're saying; it doesn't matter whether they're talking or not talking. We have no needs either way.

Often we tend to think it's important to hear what we're about to hear, and we listen as though it's going to make a significant difference. If our listening is interrupted, we may feel frustrated, which shows that our listening is anything but pure. Pure listening isn't the same as empathy. In empathetic listening, we're interested, attentive, consciously available, and actively contributing our own experience. When we're attentive in this way, even nonverbally, we're inviting and encouraging the other person to continue their construction. In pure listening, we're neither encouraging nor discouraging; we're simply undistracted.

Pure listening changes the structure of what the other person is saying because they're talking into an awareness that isn't conditioned, and they aren't receiving a conditioned response. In fact, they're talking into nothing. When constructions are neither encouraged nor discouraged, they tend to dissolve by themselves.

PURE SPEAKING: SPEAKING FROM "NOTHING"

Essentially, pure speaking is the communication that arises spontaneously from unconditioned awareness. We're speaking without any forethought or strategizing, without knowing how (or even whether) we'll finish, and without anticipating the future consequences of what we're saying.

In ordinary communication, we tend to formulate our ideas as we listen, and our goal is to deliver those ideas through our speech. But in pure speaking, we don't try to convince anyone of anything. Instead, we focus on responding to what's happening in the here and now. In particular, our speaking is continuously accommodated by and adjusted to the listening of the other person. As we attune to their body language, their verbal responses, and other signs of their receptivity or confusion, we calibrate our speech accordingly, not as a strategy, but as a natural response in the ongoing dance of communication. For example, we may sense that the other person has "gotten" what we've said and we don't need to continue. By acknowledging their receptivity, we may deepen the connection between us. Or we may begin to communicate something and realize, by the quality of the atmosphere surrounding the communication, that it isn't necessary or won't be received. By stopping and acknowledging this apparent lack of receptivity, we may create a bridge between ourselves and the other person that invites them to move closer and express their genuine interest in listening.

Since pure speaking arises from unconditioned awareness, which contains nothing, the content of our communication will also be nothing. Ultimately, the point of such communication is not to convey some information, but to reveal the spaciousness and openness of unconditioned awareness. Sometimes, however, those new to the nondual approach may find themselves talking about nothing and begin to feel uncomfortable. Their words don't have the obvious and familiar structure of ordinary communication, and they may doubt themselves and stop talking, out of embarrassment or confusion.

TALKING ABOUT NOTHING

We've been looking at the nature of nondual communication in terms of pure listening and pure speaking. We can go a bit further here, and move into a special type of conversation that looks like other conversations except that there's no subject matter. We can call it "talking *about* nothing." These conversations are used to induce, or share, an experience of unconditioned awareness. This is where the transmission of contentless wisdom happens: in the sharing of no content. Zen speaks about this as the mind-to-mind transmission; Dzogchen, as "direct introduction." In these conversations, we distinguish that which can't be distinguished. We point to the unconditioned awareness by showing that we can't point to it.

As conditioned human beings, we communicate through the mind. We experience ourselves in some kind of relationship—speaking about events, experiences, feelings, perceptions, and thoughts. We use language for the purpose of sharing our conditioned experience. The question here is, "Can we use this medium of communication to share something which is without content, which is nothing?"

Normally we would conclude that, without content, we are forced to remain silent. Why speak if you are speaking about nothing, speaking from nothing? What's the point? The point is that it is possible *and*, if we talk about nothing, it's possible for that to lead us into unconditioned awareness, especially if we take care to ensure that we can't be interpreted as talking about something!

When we speak about nothing, we don't just babble nonsense words. We still generate grammatical sentences that make sense at some level. We remain in communication at the cognitive level, but when we stop and ask ourselves what it is that we are talking about, neither of us can say. What am I talking about? Be careful! Because whatever it is that you "think" I'm talking about, it's not that.

In the beginning, it's like learning a new language. You will fumble and be clumsy. That's all right. It's a perfectly natural part of the process. The way to begin to explore this way of speaking is to stay connected with contentless awareness and allow your speaking to come from nothing.

We can't really figure out how to do this! It's much more about just being willing, and allowing it to happen without knowing how. The main thing to be aware of is our predisposition to be talking about something, or about nothing as if it's actually different from something. This nothing is not a thing, so it can't be separate or different from anything. There's nothing to be different; there's nothing to be the same. If I think it is different or the same, then I have made a form or a concept out of nothing.

The conditioned mind wants to sneak into this whole experience and have a taste of what talking about nothing could be. But even though we are using words and sentences to speak to each other, when we let go into talking about nothing, the mind hasn't got a single thing to tell us about what is going on. We are just here, in this pure awareness that can never be grasped.

Here is an example of how we can lead a conversation into talking about nothing:

Student: How do you talk about nothing?

Peter: Well, we can begin by talking about something that appears to be something, something that seems to have some characteristics.

Student: Like unconditioned awareness.

Peter: Perhaps. What is unconditioned awareness?

Student: Well, you've said it's a state of being completely at home with ourselves, not rejecting anything.

Peter: Yes, I think at times I have. But that sounds like a conditioned state to me. We're at home with ourselves in contrast to being somewhere also. And we're accepting rather than rejecting. It doesn't sound unconditioned.

Student: What doesn't sound unconditioned?

Peter: What you're talking about.

Student: What was I talking about?

Peter: Your understanding of unconditioned awareness.

Student: Yes. Well, I'm not sure what it is.

Peter: What what is?

Student: Unconditioned awareness. Are we still talking about that?

Peter: I'm not sure what you're talking about. Do you know?

Student: I don't know. Do you know? Are we talking about anything?

Peter: I don't know. Do you know?

Student: I don't know.

LOVE, COMPASSION, AND INTIMACY

In this chapter, we're looking at how the nature of radiant mind can help you to see the relationship between nondual awareness and being naturally and harmoniously connected with others. At this point, it's still possible to think that unconditioned awareness in some way excludes our conditioned reality—the way we experience ourselves inhabiting a particular body, living in time and space. But radiant mind includes it all. We experience it as a radiant presence because it's the way that the unconditioned is directly revealed through our body and mind. Radiant mind is where love and wisdom intersect. When we connect with it, we open to an effortless radiance that ripples positively into all of life and supports the natural emergence of compassion and understanding for the human condition.

On the level of our conditioned mind, we experience ourselves as separate and quite distinct from the world. In fact, the boundary between ourselves and others, even those we are intimate and familiar with, may seem quite solid and indisputable.

If you examine this boundary a little more carefully, you'll notice that it is quite hard to find. Of course, there is a boundary between your body and your environment, which is defined by the surface of your skin. But what about *you?* Where do you actually stop? Where is the boundary between your *self* and the world? It can be startling to experience how ephemeral it actually is, when you begin to look at it directly. We move through our days, assuming the existence of this boundary between us and everything else. And yet when we try to find it, it's not really there.

UNCONDITIONED AWARENESS: WE ARE THE WORLD

When we rest in unconditioned awareness, nothing falls out of the picture; nothing disappears. We are totally and fully present. All our faculties are available to us on the level of our humanity. When someone enters our field of experience, their experience becomes ours. This may seem like a radical possibility, but it actually occurs quite naturally when we have "seen through" our sense of separation. When we lose our boundaries, it's as though the universe becomes us. We are experiencing our own selflessness—the absence of our own defined sense of self. We're not there to get in the way of anything. Everything that's happening in the world is happening in us, and yet our personality and our faculties are fully functional. We do not have to evaporate into a golden cloud of nothingness. If we are clear about this, we can make ourselves more available to a genuine experience of love and compassion.

RESPONDING TO OTHER PEOPLE'S DIFFICULTIES

How do we respond to the difficulties of others when we rest in unconditioned awareness? A richness and subtlety enters our communication. We're more functional and much more capable of naturally supporting those around us, because we're no longer preoccupied with our personal agenda. The resources we have for connecting, communicating, listening, appreciating, and empathizing are just there, available, at hand—naturally and effortlessly.

When other people are challenged by physical, environmental, or emotional difficulties, these instantly become our concerns. We naturally recognize and feel their problems. We could not have a more intimate relationship with other people. We deeply connect with their pain and difficulties, because we've experienced that same suffering, those identical restrictions, ourselves. So when we're resting in unconditioned awareness, we don't see other people's problems and challenges as things that shouldn't be happening. We recognize them as natural occurrences—inevitable at this stage of our evolution. We respond to their difficulties in exactly the same way we do when something is arising in us—there's no separation.

If you're being challenged by something, and I'm completely open, your experience, your difficulty, is entering my field, my experience, and this is what's there for me to work with. It's not that I'm creating a label that this is *your* issue that *you* need to deal with. I'm not thinking in those terms at all.

In this space of nonseparation, it's impossible to think of myself as someone who's listening or interacting from a "higher" state. Certainly, I can share my unconditioned experience, knowing how lucky I am to be enjoying this freedom and fulfillment right now. But in the next moment, it could all switch—*I* may be the one struggling or in difficulty; *I* could be the one receiving the love and compassion. So there are no hard and fast roles or boundaries here at all. No one "owns" unconditioned awareness.

When there's no boundary, it's clear that love is an integral aspect of unconditioned awareness. When you open to this experience, you can feel the clarity and simplicity of it. There's nothing to understand or hold on to. Love is totally natural in this state. When you and I interact, it looks like two separate people, but there really is no separation between you and me. You are a part of my existence—you're in my reality. And I'm part of your reality. I've entered your mind, perhaps also your heart. You are certainly in my heart and my mind. And if I look a little deeper, I can't really find myself at all—so in a way, you are everything.

INTIMACY EMBRACES EVERYTHING

Often I prefer to use the word "intimacy" to describe this experience, rather than "love," because it's an experience in which there's no division between myself and others. Unconditioned love isn't a feeling. It's more a sense of embracing everything because I have no choice. I embrace, I include everything that is without judgment or reservation, not because it's a good idea or some kind of moral standpoint, but simply because there's no one here to resist anything.

If I'm not identified with my conditioning, I can receive you totally. You and I experience a sense of real connection—our realities interpenetrate in a space of deep intimacy and openness. I am totally open and available. I can't push anything away; I can't let anything more in. How could I? There's no resistance. It's just total openness—a feeling that you can totally and completely enter into me.

If you are resting in unconditioned awareness, you will naturally allow each person you meet to become a part of your existence. You totally appreciate who they are, and where they are in this moment. What they're thinking, what they're feeling, whoever they are, however they're being—there is no resistance from your side for them to fully enter you. This intimacy has no limits.

We could say that pure listening creates a clearing for the liberation of other people's suffering. From this pure listening, you can authentically question the structure, the texture, and the nature of other people's suffering in a way that begins to dissolve contracted experiences of the present moment. You identify with the suffering and then allow it to dissolve into your own experience of nothingness, of having no fixed identity. If your experience of unconditioned awareness is firm and deep, and people stay connected with you, they have no choice but to experience the evaporation of their problems.

You don't push for change. Through the energy of love, you're drawn into the structure and full intensity of other people's pain and suffering. And with wisdom, you know that this pain is unreal—it isn't what it seems to be. In reality, it doesn't exist anywhere. We know that despite our conditioning, even the most intense pain can't be sustained in the presence of unconditioned awareness.

OUR RESISTANCE TO THIS OPENNESS

This kind of experience might sound terrifying and foolhardy, perhaps even a bit insane. If I open myself up and let someone enter me, what's preventing them from walking all over me? Being so open and so available could be an invitation to be used and abused. It might feel like I'm putting myself in front of a locomotive.

This is why it's important to be authentic to your experience—to your real state of being—and not to be deluded about where you are on the path. You can't pretend that this kind of intimacy works on the level of your conditioned mind. So if you find yourself worrying about this question, then you should probably be careful. If this kind of intimacy does not threaten you, if you are just living your life in an open and natural way, then you probably don't need to think about these contingencies.

NO ONE AND SOMEONE

The main point is that when we're no one—when we're resting in unconditioned awareness—there's no one to be hurt. We're actually invincible, because we're connected with an unconditioned space that can't be hurt, damaged, or harmed, no matter what happens.

If we are "someone"—if we're identified with our conditioned personality (our body, feelings, values, etc.)—all our protective mechanisms kick in the instant we feel threatened. That's the nature of an identity. We're trying to either preserve it, change it, or destroy it. If we feel threatened, our defense mechanisms come into play, and we do whatever we need and can do to protect our identity. When we're no one, there's no one to protect. And when we're someone, we do whatever we need to do to take care of ourselves and our needs.

You might still have doubts about all of this. For example, you might wonder, "Isn't it still possible that when I'm in unconditioned awareness I might just not see that there's something or someone out there who might hurt me? How can I just let all kinds of people enter into my being?"

Of course, anything can happen. There are no guarantees. But it's important to understand that most of the time when you get into trouble, it's because you get lost in your conditioned mind, in constructs and concepts that cloud and cover the natural clarity of your being. When you are in unconditioned awareness, you have direct access to a clear and potent wisdom (in Mahayana Buddhism, they call it *prajna*) that is fully able to face and deal with each situation exactly as it is. So the fears that come up in you about opening in this way are a lot like the initial projections that arise in relation to unconditioned awareness. You can create all sorts of fantasies about what will happen when you let go of your boundaries, but the actual experience is radically different from all your thoughts about it.

RADIANT MIND: THE UNION OF LOVE AND WISDOM

When we are unconditionally present in this way, there's a complete disidentification with the other person's experience, and at the same time, we're totally identified with them. In Buddhist terms, this is the union of love and wisdom.

In this case, wisdom is the experience that no matter how much suffering there is, the essential freedom and wholeness of unconditional awareness is never lost. Nothing obstructs it, not even death.

And love, in this sense, is the experience that as human beings, we all suffer; we all know hunger, thirst, loneliness, grief, rage, heartbreak, and joy. When we can enter into the experience of another, this love has the power to dissolve suffering.

When we rest in unconditioned awareness, wisdom and love are both alive in us. This seems like a great contradiction, a mystery—that I can see you as whole and complete, and at the same time, open my heart to the depths of your pain. I don't wish that you weren't suffering. I *know* that you're suffering, but at the same time, I *know* that there's no suffering. This is love without pity or sympathy. Pity and sympathy take your suffering to be real, and thereby compound the suffering and resistance.

Here we have a living paradox. And radiant mind won't help us to resolve it. Unconditioned awareness is totally different from the conditioned fabric of our thoughts, feelings, and perceptions. On the other hand, unconditioned awareness is nothing, so it's impossible for it to be different from anything else. This is a paradox. It will never be resolved. At the conditioned level, we could struggle for eternity, trying to resolve this paradox, but it's a complete waste of time. Radiant mind does not fixate on the side of wisdom or compassion; it embraces both. If I hold your suffering as unreal, it negates the compassion; if I hold it as real, it negates the wisdom. In order to really experience this union of love and wisdom, I have to let go of the struggle to understand. I don't need to hold any kind of idea about anything. This experience is not mental. Radiant mind is totally clear and lucid when you are in it, and impossible to make sense of, when you are not.

Nisargadatta, the great Indian nondual sage, put it like this: "With wisdom, I see that I am nothing; with love, I see that I am everything. And between these two, my life turns."

CHAPTER SEVEN EXERCISES

LOVE, COMPASSION, AND INTIMACY

1 In this contemplation, you will be exploring the possibility of opening to someone in the way we have been describing.

Take a moment and choose someone to work with—maybe a dear friend or partner, maybe someone with whom you are having difficulty. Just visualize that person in front of you, and imagine that you are engaging them in some kind of intimate conversation.

Instead of listening to them from "your" side, and then presenting your viewpoint or your reality, see yourself just letting go of all that, and opening to their whole being, everything about them, without resistance. Allow yourself to keep opening until you have a sense of them entering right into you, into the whole field of your experience. You can still interact with them, but now it's almost as if you can understand them from the inside.

The things that they say, the habits or viewpoints that may have bothered you before, are now a part of who you are; they are no longer foreign, no longer something you cannot relate to.

Take all the time you need to allow the depth of this state to penetrate you, so that your whole being is included in it. If your mind is chattering about how this isn't real, or how this could never really happen for you, include the chattering in your wide openness, just as you included the other person. Nothing needs to be left out.

2 Here is a very simple visualization you can do anytime you like. Sit gently, and allow your spine to straighten as you breathe fully and freely. You can use an image or a gesture with your hands, as if you are opening and lifting your whole rib cage, to support an opening of the heart. Just breathe and feel the upper body opening and expanding, and the heart softening.

Experience the open nature of unconditioned awareness—like space—and let this permeate your entire being—your body, your breath, your life force. See yourself doing this, lifting the heart, pulling the rib cage open, and walking through life with no resistance, no need to protect or defend yourself at all, just moving in the flow of love and compassion.

PURE LISTENING

This exercise is designed to help you distinguish between the three types of listening that were introduced in this chapter: positive, negative, and pure listening. The next time you have an opportunity for a prolonged conversation with a close friend, divide your listening into three separate phases as outlined below. Be sure to tell this friend that you will be experimenting with three different approaches to listening, some of which may feel uncomfortable to them, and ask them to give you their feedback when the conversation is over.

1   Positive listening: Listening to your friend as though their construction is real

Listen to your friend with interest and validation, as though their construction is real. Allow yourself to be taken in by the story. Here you will confirm, validate, agree with, give energy to the speaker's story (or construction), and encourage elaboration through verbal and nonverbal cues. Notice how your attention fuels the energy of the story. Verbal cues may include saying "I see," "I understand," "Tell me more," and so on. Nonverbal cues may include nodding, leaning forward, and so on. Don't get involved in interpreting your friend's experience. Here, you're primarily exploring how we affirm and validate other people's experience through our listening. Take about three to four minutes for this and each of the subsequent phases.

2   Negative listening: Listening to your friend's construction as though it is unreal

Listen to your friend as though their construction is unreal or trivial. Here, you'll listen as though what your friend is saying isn't really happening, at least not with the meaning and significance that they are imputing to the story.

In this phase, you're giving more attention to your own thoughts than to your friend's communication. You're uninvolved in their story and caught up in your own experience, and you hear your friend's words as an echo. Notice how this sends signals to your friend that you're disconnected, and takes energy away from or even invalidates your friend's story. With this listening, your friend may feel that their problems aren't being taken seriously. They may experience you as distant, detached, even self-absorbed, which may cause them to give up in frustration or make them more determined to be heard.

3   Pure listening: Listening without interest or disinterest

Now listen to your partner in a way that neither validates nor invalidates their experience. Listen without interest or disinterest in what they are presenting. You're neither engaged nor disengaged, neither involved nor uninvolved, but you are totally present and undistracted. You are wide open, taking in everything your partner is saying. You're neither encouraging nor discouraging their sharing. There's no difference whether there is speaking or silence. No one story is preferred over any other.

From the space of pure listening, your partner could continue indefinitely, or stop mid-sentence—it make no difference. You listen because your partner is sharing—you have no agenda of your own. You take everything in, but without judgment or assessment. Here, there is no distinction between self and other. This space of pure listening contains it all—your interpretations, your listening, and the experience of your partner. There is no emphasis on one or the other.

Write a short report on your experience with this exercise and on your friend's feedback.

CONTEMPLATIVE PRACTICE

I hope you're continuing with your contemplative practice. Remember to begin and proceed as you normally do: do what you're doing—nothing more and nothing less.

But just for fun, for the last five minutes of this session, I'd like you to *not* do what you're doing. In other words, don't do what you're doing. If you aren't doing what you're doing, then don't do that! And whatever that is, don't do that!

When you're finished, consider the following questions:

- Were you able to *not* do what you were doing? If yes, how did you do this?
- Was any effort involved in the final five minutes of your contemplation? Did you find it difficult?
- Is it possible to experience effort or struggle if you're doing whatever you're doing?
- What does the presence or absence of effort signify?
- What would you have been doing if you were doing what you were doing, rather than not doing what you were doing?
- Is there any difference between doing and not doing what you're doing?
- No effort is required to do what we're doing. Was there any effort or struggle?

Completing in the Here and Now

[T]he energy that comes out of your primordially
pure nature is more valid than anything else.
SHYALPA RINPOCHE, CONTEMPORARY NYINGMA LAMA [2003]¹

In Chapter Five, "Noninterference and the Practice of Natural Release," I introduced the distinction between being complete and being incomplete. In the exercises that accompanied that practice, we explored a process called "natural release," which is designed to free the emotional charge associated with various beliefs, feelings, expectations, fears, memories, and so on. In order to employ this process, you needed to be in an unhurried state of still contemplation.

In this chapter, we'll explore ways of achieving completion that don't depend on a state of contemplation. You'll be introduced to different ways in which to complete the past. Sometimes all that's needed is a simple, authentic conversation. You'll also learn how to stop creating a future in which you continually need to "go back" and fix up the past.

In order to rest in unconditioned awareness and remain fully open to the ever-changing modulations of the eternal here and now, we need to be free of the burdens of guilt, regret, worry, and anxiety. We need to be complete with the past and fearless about the future. We need to live in a state of ongoing completion, in which the past lives in the past, and not in the present.

How do we know if an action is complete? It's simple. Once it's finished, it no longer requires our attention. We don't need to regret, process, celebrate, or worry or think about what we've done. When an action is complete, we're free to move on and fully encounter the next moment. We don't need to go back and rectify situations where we've left ourselves or others incomplete. In this way, we keep the present moment fresh and alive. At the end of each day, there's nothing to process or mull over. We don't have to think about what we should or shouldn't have done, or feel uncomfortable about how we've been selfish, insensitive, lazy, or overbearing earlier in the day.

COMPLETE IN THE UNCONDITIONED

The only experience that's complete in this sense is the experience of unconditioned awareness, because it's the only experience in which attachment and aversion can no longer function. Why? Because unconditioned awareness isn't anything, and therefore we can't accept or reject it.

Unlike pleasurable experiences (something we'd like to continue), we can't be attached or hold on to unconditioned awareness. Neither is unconditioned awareness a painful experience (something we'd like to change) that we can ignore or push aside. Because it doesn't exist as such, unconditioned awareness can't arise and disappear. When we're present to it, we know we can't lose it. After all, you can't lose nothing! At the same time, we know we'll experience its loss, because in the instant we think that it's something, we lose it. Now it's no longer unconditioned awareness, and it can seemingly be lost or maintained. Paradoxically, when we experience its loss, we know that we've lost nothing, yet the loss seems quite real because we're once again in conditioned mind, where things seem real and unreal.

When we rest in unconditioned awareness, our present experience no longer conditions us. The structure of the present moment may be conditioned by the past, but the present no longer conditions the future. In Buddhist terms, our life continues to unfold as a product of karma, but we're no longer creating new karma. Karma is only created when we're holding on to or rejecting what's happening. When we lose our grounding in the unconditioned and identify with the conditioned, we begin creating karma again. Now our actions are incomplete because we're projecting a time in the future when the results of our actions will come to fruition. Rather than being in the now, we're looking ahead, either for the continuation of an experience we're enjoying or for the end of an experience we find unpleasant. Every moment in which we lose our connection with unconditioned awareness, we're incomplete and creating incompletion.

INCOMPLETE EXPERIENCES

Some experiences are obviously incomplete. If we suddenly find ourselves out of a job, suffering a life-threatening illness, or abandoned by our partner, it's easy to think that things have gone terribly wrong. Our experience is more than incomplete: it's disastrous. What have we done to deserve this? Has God betrayed us? We might feel that we've failed dramatically or even that life isn't worth living.

At an everyday level, we experience feelings of incompletion in numerous ways. Every experience that falls outside the range of our preferences is incomplete, including times when:

- We forget to enter a meeting into our diary and find ourselves in the dilemma of being double-booked
- We oversleep and have to gulp down breakfast and rush around in the morning
- Our children become ill and we suddenly need to reorganize our commitments
- We wait impatiently at the supermarket checkout
- We find ourselves ill-prepared for a presentation
- We forget an anniversary and feel bad about hurting someone's feelings
- A flight is cancelled and we find ourselves at loose ends with nothing to entertain or amuse us

These are routine incompletions—inconvenient occurrences that we would prefer not to happen. They're the situations that throw us into a tailspin or leave us bored, with time on our hands.

Any experience we have to tolerate or accept is incomplete. Why? Because the experience stops us from being in the flow of the here and now. If we're running late for an appointment, we have no cosmic obligation to feel incomplete. The only reason we feel incomplete is that we're thrown into the past or future, wishing that things were different and that we were somewhere else. All these experiences produce stress, anxiety, and frustration. If they continue year after year, their effect accumulates, leaving us resigned, bitter, exhausted, depressed, and physically ill.

How do we know if an experience is incomplete? Because we're compelled to react to it. If we struggle with or rejoice in what we're experiencing, we're incomplete with it. If we endure or enjoy it, we're incomplete. "But where's the excitement?" you may wonder. Without enjoyment or struggle, life would quickly become boring. But buddhas don't get excited, and our aim in working with the nondual is to become a buddha—someone who rests permanently in unconditioned awareness while remaining fully immersed in the functional, interpersonal reality. If this is our aim, then moods such as excitement, enthusiasm, doubt, embarrassment, resignation, and boredom will slowly disappear from our experience. They will be replaced by experiences of serenity, sensitivity, natural patience, vulnerability, invincibility, unconditional forgiveness, openness, bliss, joy, and love.

POSITIVE EXPERIENCES

In the West, we often think that only negative or unpleasant experiences—those we'd prefer *not* to continue—are incomplete. However, from the nondual perspective, positive experiences can also be incomplete *if* we want more of them. No matter how sublime an experience, it's always possible that it could be better. No matter how pleasurable, soothing, sensual, peaceful, exciting, or stimulating an experience, there's always some way in which it could be improved. At the very least, we'd like to be able to control its duration and intensity.

Even experiences that are aligned with our preferences—the way we desire things to be—are incomplete, because they continue to reinforce the value of having desires and preferences. When our preferences are fulfilled, we come to believe that fulfillment is a function of having our needs met. Every time our desires are realized and we feel satisfied, it confirms that fulfillment is a product of fulfilling our desires. In other words, we make a positive association between "having preferences" and "being fulfilled." But this structure for fulfillment is necessarily incomplete because we can't control our reality. We can't control our thoughts and feelings, and we can't control what goes on outside us. As a result, we can't continually have our needs met. In Buddhism, this is called the suffering of conditionality (*samskrta-duhkha*).

Our conditioned mind takes pleasurable experiences and transforms them into incomplete ones. As soon as we say, "This is better than anything

I could imagine," we're already contrasting and comparing. Before long, we imagine some way it could be better. For example, we may start thinking:

- "Imagine if I could hold on to this forever!"
- "This is remarkable, but is this really enlightenment?"
- "This is incredible, but it would be even better if it wasn't quite so intense."
- "This is beautiful. I'd really like to be able to share it with others."
- "This is exquisite, but imagine how pure it would be if I wasn't even judging it!"

At the very least, we can be concerned about whether such experiences will last. Positive experiences come and go—they always have and always will. If we're attached to an experience, we'll always feel loss when it disappears.

Does nondual teaching reject positive experiences of pleasure, serenity, and so on? Certainly not. Some of these experiences are profoundly healing. Experiences of bliss, for example, soothe our minds and repair the damage done to our nervous system by pain and trauma. Nondual practice produces deep experiences of bliss, joy, and tranquility, which arise like clockwork when our thinking slows down and we move into the here and now. Pleasure, contentment, and deep satisfaction happen en route to unconditioned awareness as we progressively let go of our needs and preferences. Even though these experiences are pleasurable and rewarding, they're not the final experience of nondual work. Nor are they the final experience we seek. Ultimately, everyone strives for an experience that fulfills all their needs and can never be taken away from them.

CREATING INCOMPLETIONS

Our worlds are very complex. Each of us lives at the center of an intricate and complicated mandala of conditioned events that includes our concepts, thoughts, values, aspirations, feelings, moods, emotions, bodily structure, living circumstances, the environment, and the thousands of people with whom our life intersects. All of this is constantly changing and at the same time interdependent. Changes in the environment affect our thoughts and feelings, and vice versa. Changes in our moods influence our interactions with people, and these, in turn, shape our thoughts and feelings.

In the midst of this complex and constantly changing world, we naturally create incompletions in the process of taking care of our concerns. In fact, it's inevitable, because a community of people who are driven by their desires and preferences can't possibly coordinate their interactions in such a way that every action benefits everyone. At a fundamental level, we're self-interested. In taking care of our own needs, we damage opportunities for others, in the same way that other people can thwart or obstruct the fulfillment of our needs. We hurt other people's feelings and are hurt by them. We produce feelings of mistrust and fear in others, in the same way that they trigger these reactions in us.

There are two ways in which we create incompletions. Either we don't do what needs to be done, or we do what doesn't need to be done. Often, we only realize some seconds, minutes, hours, days, or years afterward that we've been careless, lazy, or unconscious with our words or deeds. Again, we know we've created an incompletion if we need to go back and fix up a situation to avoid being burdened by feelings of guilt, revenge, and so on.

If we look at the phenomenon of incompletion carefully, we see that all incompletions are created in conversations. This includes conversations we've omitted that would have produced completion. They arise as breakdowns or miscommunications in our conversations with others and with ourselves. An example of the latter would be an internal conversation about "failing to live up to an ideal or a commitment we've made." Toward the end of this chapter, we'll look at how we can design our conversations to minimize incompletions.

Some people who are attracted to nondual forms of spirituality and therapy aren't willing to work with their conditioned minds to clean up the incompletions that invariably accompany actions motivated by desire and aversion. In effect, they're in *denial* of their conditioning. They reject conditioned mind and try to jump straight into unconditioned awareness. They're reluctant to work at the level of their conditioned existence, believing that their environment and personality are unreal and that any actions that affirm the reality of their conditioning only perpetuate their suffering.

In this work, we acknowledge that we're both conditioned *and* unconditioned, and we take care of who we are at the conditioned level. It's like being at home. When we create a mess—on our desk, in the kitchen, in the bedroom—we clean it up because it's the responsible thing to do. We don't deny the consequences and needs of our embodiment. We embrace our existence and come to accept how we're conditioned by our physiology, upbringing, education, and life experience. Perhaps it's possible for unconditioned awareness to arise intermittently when we ignore the demands of our mind and body, but it can only arise as a more constant and stable experience if we take care of ourselves at the everyday level of our relationships, health, and material needs.

SOME WAYS TO ACHIEVE COMPLETION

There are different ways in which we can achieve completion. We can:

- Transcend our conditioning by connecting with unconditioned awareness
- Clean up the past, in the present
- Discover a desireless way of being
- Tune in to the future consequences of our actions as we're doing them, and adjust our actions accordingly
- Shift our negative moods
- Design our conversations so that we remain complete in the present moment

In this chapter, we'll explore the first four ways, and we'll deal with "managing our moods" and "designing conversations" in Chapter Seven.

TRANSCENDING OUR CONDITIONING

The most direct way to be complete is to rest in unconditioned awareness. If this is possible, there's nothing else we need to do. In this state, we're beyond being complete or incomplete. I call this "achieving completion from without." We're complete because we've gone beyond conditioned mind. There's nothing left undone because we've transcended the flux of our conditioned existence. This doesn't mean that incompletions from the past won't arise again. It doesn't mean that we'll no longer resent someone who we feel has betrayed us, or experience guilt about not having been available to our children in the long-distant past.

If we can enter the experience of unconditioned awareness using any of the instructions I've presented in this book, the negative and painful consequences of past behavior can no longer arise. We see that nothing is ever wrong or missing. As long as we're resting in unconditioned awareness, feelings of lack and incompletion can't arise. We're protected from the influences of our conditioned responses.

If we can't springboard into unconditioned awareness, it indicates that we should work within our conditioning. If something from the past that we've done (or not done) occupies our attention and energy, and we can't see through it with the power of our unstructured awareness, we need to "complete from within"—from inside conditioned mind. We need to clean up the mess, the residues, that we invariably acquire through living in an egocentric world. We observe and take care of our moods, our patterns, our communications. We need to manage our existence at the conditioned level in order to stay complete.

LOOKING BACK: CLEANING UP THE PAST

The reason we're unable to rest continuously in unconditioned awareness is that the consequences of our past bleed into the present as limiting patterns and predispositions. The influence of our early childhood experience on the quality of our present life is well understood. Most psychologies acknowledge that we enter our adult life with a set of fears, aspirations, expectations, and defenses that can be traced to our childhood. It's difficult to emerge from our childhood completely unscathed by our upbringing. As infants and children, we are essentially defenseless, and even the most loving parents can never fulfill our every need and requirement. At some level, we were all abandoned, neglected, shamed, and intimidated. As such, most people can benefit from some form of inner-child work, which releases the defensive patterns created in our childhood that trigger fight-or-flight responses to challenging situations throughout our life. There are many high-quality programs around that heal the damage inflicted in growing up. The better-known ones are Colin Tipping's "Radical Forgiveness," Robert Hoffman's "Quadrinity Process," John Bradshaw's programs, "The Work" of Byron Katie, Raphael Cushnir's *Living the Questions*, Stanislav and Christina Grof's "Holotropic Breathwork," and Phyllis Krystal's *Cutting the Ties That Bind*.

As we progress through our adult years, we keep adding to the damage that accrued in our childhood by creating incompletions with our children, partners, lovers, friends, colleagues, and, of course, our parents. We transfer our childhood experience with our parents onto the significant people in our adult life and relate to them accordingly. We create incompletions by doing (or not doing) and saying (or not saying) things that damage other people's opportunities and hurt their feelings. There are innumerable ways in which we create incompletions. We withhold love and affection, become a "people pleaser," speak roughly and abrasively, lie to ourselves and others, promise more than we can deliver, and so on. We also create incompletions when we're hurt by others and allow ourselves to be victimized by the experience. The presence of incompletions in our psyche locks up energy and decreases our capacity for love, intimacy, and spontaneity.

In order to ensure that we're not left feeling victimized, holding a grudge, or needing to retaliate in some way, we first need to recognize that our capacity for warm, open, and free expression has been depleted through an exchange with someone, or with ourselves. Besides the more obvious ways by which we "get back at people," there are many subtle or covert ways that we may not immediately recognize. We get even with people by being self-righteous and a know-it-all; by using sarcasm and humiliation; by withdrawing; by withholding and being unavailable; by being cold-hearted, depressed or overly sensitive in a way that demands the concern of others; or by giving without receiving, thereby making someone indebted to us.

If any of these patterns arise when we're with someone, or even just when we're thinking about them, it means that we're incomplete with that person. Another way to identify how and where we're incomplete is by contemplating the conversations we'd like to have if we knew we were going to die this time next week. If we *knew* that we only had a week to live, we'd prize the opportunity to complete with people. Whom would we like to see, and what would we like to say to them?

Yet, in life, we create all sorts of fearful consequences surrounding the action of completing with people. We fear that in the process of completing, people will negatively judge us. We fear going down in their esteem, or looking mean-spirited, weak, or emotional. Often, it's only when we're close to our death—when we won't have to deal with the negative consequences that we project—that can we afford to become complete with people. The tragedy is that by remaining incomplete, we continue to hurt, and be hurt by, people. Conversely, by becoming and remaining complete, our relationships are continually fresh and inspiring.

Once we've recognized that we *are* incomplete, we need to clear the incompletions that have been created, through a process of healing. Sometimes the most efficient and direct way to heal is to have a conversation with the person or people involved in the event that produced the difficult feelings.

If we created the incompletion, we can ask for forgiveness and promise to be more tolerant, caring, and considerate in the future. If we've been hurt, we can take responsibility for our reaction and apologize for holding this against the person who hurt us. Rather than react by becoming resentful or vindictive, we address the breakdown in communication in a more upfront and responsible way—as we're doing *now* by talking with them. This way of completing is possible in close relationships with our family, friends, partners, and lovers, past and present. Sometimes it isn't easy to have these conversations. We may need to swallow our pride. But generally, if we've worked through blaming ourselves or others and we feel a genuine need to reconcile, the conversations will manage themselves.

To some extent, we can think through what we'll say, but we can't script the conversation in advance because we're communicating from our heart rather than our head. In fact, in order to give the person with whom we're communicating real freedom to express their thoughts and feelings, we need to let the conversation be "out of (our) control."

DECLARING COMPLETION

Sometimes we can't complete by having a conversation with the person with whom we're incomplete. Perhaps they're no longer alive, we may not know where they are, or they may not want to have anything to do with us. Sometimes it's obvious that we're incomplete with someone, but we genuinely have no idea what's "gone wrong" and no way of determining it.

If it's not possible to speak with someone with whom we're incomplete, we can complete internally during our private contemplation by asking for their understanding and forgiveness, and forgiving them for any harm they might have brought to us. We can also "declare completion." We simply declare to ourselves that we're complete and don't need to give any more energy or attention to what happened in the past. If this doesn't work, we can even declare ourselves "complete about being incomplete" for situations that occurred during our childhood: we can be complete at the same time that we're feeling scared and damaged from past experiences.

LOOKING FORWARD:
DISCOVERING A DESIRELESS WAY OF BEING

According to nondual traditions, lasting fulfillment can only be achieved when we're free of desire. Desirelessness is one of the most effective ways to decondition our experience. The beautiful Indian scripture, the *Bhagavad Gita,* speaks about this as "desireless action." It's the essence of what is called "karma yoga." Some people say this is the most important yoga for the modern world in which work and relationships consume so much of our time. The concept of "acting without desire" or "acting without any desire for the goal of our actions" can sound too difficult and a little idealistic. So we prefer to speak about discovering the place in our experience that is free of strong desire, and learning to acknowledge and respect this place as a reliable source for effective action and effective stillness.

When our actions are based on our needs (our desires and attachments), our perceptions are inherently unreliable. Many of us have experienced this in our relationships or careers. We move through a cycle of projecting that happiness lies somewhere other than where we are. We're propelled from one relationship into no relationship or a different relationship, all the while thinking that it's going to be better—it certainly looked "better" back when we were in the pain of our previous relationship—only to find that within days, months, or years, we've reconstructed the prison or our former existence. We're repelled by one situation or idea toward a fantasy—a projection that's energized and distorted by our aversion to where we are. Our vision of the future is contaminated by our feelings of desire and aversion. We don't see what's really there. We think and see through the deluded lens of attraction and repulsion.

At some point, we come to mistrust anything that seems to be attractive or unattractive. When we think, "I want," we know that we're not going to get the happiness we expect. We can never trust that anything we're attracted to can bring substantial, lasting fulfillment. And when we think, "I don't want," we know that we may well be rejecting something that will give us a great deal of pleasure!

The alternative to being driven by "attachment" and "aversion" is to rely on "desirelessness" as the guide for living and relationships. In effect, we say yes to the experience of being relatively free of feelings of attraction and aversion. We trust desirelessness as a more reliable foundation for engagement and fulfillment than being driven in an endless cycle of attraction-disappointment-aversion-fantasy-attraction-and so on. In the Dzogchen tradition, the experience of desirelessness is also called the experience of "one taste," which can sound terribly boring—a little like having muesli for every meal. But the experience of one taste simply means that we're not being thrown around by our reactivity. In fact, the experience of desirelessness opens us to far deeper levels of intimacy, trust, and confidence than can be built on attraction and aversion. The experience of desirelessness produces an equanimity that lets us stay wide open without needing to manipulate and control what comes and goes in our experience. The range of experiences we can accept and process is greatly expanded. We no longer run hither and thither seeking "the experience" that fulfills our momentary needs. Instead, we experience ourselves in a way that's simultaneously more stable and more expanded. We move around in the world with a composure and a serenity that spring from the core of our being.

How does "desirelessness" translate into our daily life, where we're compelled to make offers of, and respond to a continual stream of requests for, our time, money, energy, expertise, attention, or interest? Initially it means that we're guided in the generation of our commitments by the mood and atmosphere that surround the cycles of requests, offers, and promises within which commitments are created.

For example, when someone says, "Would you like to join me on this project," or go to a restaurant or a party, we respond not only to the specifics of the request or offer, but also to the mood with which the invitation or request is made.

If someone comes on strongly, perhaps out of a mood of panic or excitement, saying, "We must do such and such. It's an incredible opportunity. We shouldn't waste any time. It'll be disastrous if we don't do X, Y, or Z," we don't get caught up in their urgency but automatically begin to correct for their agitation. This is not a calculated form of compensation. We sense that some thought needs to go into making this commitment. It's easy to underestimate the time and resources involved in bringing a project to completion.

What we can do is to "commit to commit." We can say, "I hear what you're saying. I'll give you a response. I need to look at my other interests and commitments. I'll get back to you in a week." What we're really requesting is time to just be with the request and feel and see how it sits in the larger context of our life, and to appreciate the moods associated with the activity at the conditioned level: What's actually required of me? Where am I doing it? Who am I doing it with? Then we are taking care of ourselves. We are exercising our preferences and taking care of ourselves at the conditioned level. When we're asked to take on an extra commitment, we take in the mood surrounding the offer or request. Is it intense? Is it generous? Is it in line with the way I want to be living my life?

In the context of nondual study, we particularly consider how the commitments we may generate will support or damage our ability to cultivate unconditioned awareness. How do they commit our time, energy, investment, and so on? Also, who are the people with whom we'll need to interact in order to fulfill the commitment? Are they part of our spiritual community (*sangha*), or will we be working with people who are agitated, racy, addicted to "knowing," or always complaining? Will we be working in a nurturing or a toxic environment? Will the commitment nourish us or stress us out?

TUNING IN TO THE FUTURE CONSEQUENCES OF OUR ACTIONS

When we're more open and less reactive, we're also able to tune in to the present moment with a subtlety and depth that lets us sense the potential of our speech and behavior to condition the future. In fact, this happens naturally when we connect with unconditioned awareness. When our actions come from conditioned mind, they're not optimally responsive to the needs of the moment. We're unable to read and respond to the uniqueness of every situation, because we're operating from a model of what has worked in the past.

On the other hand, if we listen deeply inside at the same time that we're engaged in a dynamic world, we receive meticulous guidance about when to talk and what to say. Our conversations seamlessly and effortlessly calibrate to the unique structure of each and every moment. In order to do this, we also need to be willing to engage with situations as they arise. We can't afford to be controlled by our need to avoid uncomfortable feelings, meetings, or conversations, since this is how we create incompletions.

In the midst of a conversation, we might perceive that the person we're talking with hasn't taken what we've said the way we intended, or that we've unintentionally hurt their feelings. They don't say anything, but we know or sense it. Perhaps they feel that they need to be tough. Rather than let this slide, we address it on the spot, as it arises. If we don't, it may fester, creating distance, mistrust, and resentment. We recognize that our communication is temporarily incomplete. We can feel that we're losing the depth of our connection with the person with whom we're communicating, and that we can't move on with full engagement if we don't acknowledge and address the feelings that are arising.

When I say that we "tune in to the future consequences of our actions," I don't mean that we're kidding ourselves that we're clairvoyant and can know precisely how things are going to pan out as a consequence of what we're doing. Rather, we know that if we don't take some action to recover our connection, there'll be a loss in intimacy and connection. We ongoingly sense how and when our communication becomes incomplete, and we make the necessary micro-adjustments to how we're listening, what we're saying, and how we're saying it, in order to stay connected with the energy, vitality, and immediacy of the present moment.

In order to stay complete, we have to be willing to engage in conversations we're not particularly familiar with. We need to become skilled in creating different types of conversations. We develop ways to recover from a breakdown in communication without placing a load on the person with whom we're communicating. One way to do this is by saying what we want to say, while providing a degree of latitude for how the person we're communicating with will take it. The message we're wanting to communicate is that what we're saying is important, but there's no need to make a big deal about it. In this way, the disconnection that's emerging can be handled easily and effortlessly, and perhaps even transparently.

The following examples give you some ideas about how to share in ways that keep a conversation ongoingly complete. The earlier we intervene in a conversation that's producing some incompletion, the easier it is to remedy. Some of the examples are quite routine, and I'm sure you use them already.

Others are probably different from how you usually communicate, though I'm sure you can imagine situations in which you're saying something similar.

- "It's very difficult for me to listen to what you're saying at the moment. It's bringing up a lot of strong feelings. I know it's important for me to hear what you're saying. But can you go slowly with this?"
- "I need to share with you that my mind's started to wander. Actually, to be really honest, I'm starting to feel a bit bored. I'm sharing this because I want to stay connected with you. So something needs to change. Either I need to change how I'm listening to you, or you need to change what you're saying. Can we work on this together?"
- "I don't understand what you're saying. I'm a little confused. Can you say it again slightly differently?"
- "You seem a little preoccupied. Would you like me to stop what I'm saying? Perhaps you'd like to share what's happening for you. We can come back to what I was saying later."
- "I spaced out a few sentences ago. I'm sorry. Can you please repeat what you were saying?"
- "I'm concerned at the moment that something I've said is disturbing you, maybe even making you feel a bit agitated. Are you feeling uncomfortable with what I'm saying?"
- "Look, I'd like you to stop what you're saying. I think you could go on complaining for a long time, but I don't know where it's taking you. I believe I've got the essence of what you're saying. So, let's just stop a minute. I'd like you to tell me in one sentence what you want me to hear right now."

OBSERVING HOW WE CONDITION THE FUTURE

In the process of tuning in to the future consequences of our actions, we also recognize that how we think in the present conditions how we will think about and interpret our life in the future. This is the very nature of conditioning. Every time we generalize from the present moment, we condition the future by limiting the way we'll experience it. For example, if we think that relationships are difficult, we look for problems and condition a future in which significant relationships will be experienced as problematic or burdensome.

Conversely, if we believe that significant relationships are easy, we create the conditions for disappointment when relationships encounter their periodic difficulties. This conditioning is compounded if we find external support for our thinking.

We have a responsibility here for others as well as for ourselves. If we collude with people's beliefs that change is always difficult, we impede their enthusiasm for growth and development. But if we suggest that change is easy, we set people up to become disillusioned and despondent when the going gets hard.

It's important that we learn to recognize how we contribute to or hinder people's evolution by supporting limiting beliefs. The ways in which beliefs can be energized can be very subtle. The very way we listen to people contributes to their conditioning. We influence their future simply by listening to them through the filter that they should or shouldn't be experiencing what they're experiencing.

CHAPTER EIGHT EXERCISES

NEITHER GIVING IN TO NOR RESISTING YOUR DESIRES

This exercise moves through three phases. You can complete one phase each day for three consecutive days.

Day One: Today you will "give in to your desires." As much as possible, do whatever you'd like to do. Within the parameters of "keeping out of trouble" and "not creating a mess," do what you're inspired or motivated to do. Remember, in this chapter, we're exploring "being complete in the here and now."

Of course, if you'd *like* to resist a desire, then do so. If you *want* to feel that you can control or curb a desire, then do that! Whatever desires come up, act them out, including the *need* to restrain yourself. If this becomes confusing, then just "give in to your desires" in whatever way makes sense for you.

Day Two: Today you will "resist your desires." As much as possible, don't do what you'd like to do. Whatever you feel like doing, don't do it. If you don't feel like doing this phase of the exercise, this needn't stop you from doing it. If you're enthusiastic about exploring how you "resist your desires," then "resist your resistance." If you're keen to do this exercise properly, you don't need to get it right. If you don't *want* to resist a desire, then don't resist your resistance. If you're rejecting your resistance, do whatever you're resisting. If this becomes confusing, then just "resist your desires" in whatever way makes sense for you.

Day Three: Today, neither "give in to nor resist your desires." Explore how your day unfolds when you neither fight against your desires nor act them out.

Write a short report on your experience with this exercise. How differentiated were the days in terms of their pace, mood, activities, and your overall level of happiness and well-being? Did the fact that you were doing this exercise contribute to the flavor of each day? How much of what seemed to happen actually happened? How much of your conversation was about what was happening?

DISCOVERING DESIRELESSNESS

Ultimately, the only time we're free of desire and aversion is when we're resting in unconditioned awareness, because then there's nothing to long for or reject. Through the following exercises, I'd like you to explore the space of desirelessness. This is actually an extension of your exploration on Day Three of the previous exercise. In these exercises, you'll be exploring how you move, where you go, what you do, who you see (and for how long), and what you think and feel when you're neither giving in to nor resisting your desires.

In the coming days, if there's something that's very appealing or attractive, you don't need to rush into it. Of course, you might be worried that if you don't capitalize on an opportunity when it's available, it might disappear. So in this exercise, you'll be working with the possibility of missing out on something that seems attractive.

If something comes up that you'd prefer not to deal with, you don't need to drag your heels. You might think it's a little crazy to consciously step into a potentially unpleasant experience, so in this exercise, you'll also be working with your beliefs about how best to take care of yourself.

COMPLETING WITH THE PAST

Imagine that you have one week to live. Whom do you want to speak with before you die? What do you want to say to them, or ask of them? I invite you to have two or three conversations over the next two weeks, in which you restore a relationship that is incomplete. You can acknowledge a grudge you hold toward someone, expressing regret for sitting on your resentment, and tell them you value the relationship and would like to repair it. You can simply acknowledge to someone that you have been less than skillful in your communication with them, and ask for their forgiveness. Or you can express your deep love and appreciation for someone who doesn't really know how you feel about them. If you're concerned that some of these conversations may become convoluted or not accomplish their objective of achieving completion, find some support for this process. Ask a friend, counselor, teacher, or coach for guidance.

DECONSTRUCTING DESIRE AND AVERSION

Consider the following questions: Does the thought "I'm resisting a desire" mean that you're resisting a desire? Is it possible to think that you're resisting a desire and *not* be resisting a desire? What makes the difference? If you say, "Well, if I'm resisting a desire, then I'm stopping myself from doing something that I'd like to do," is it possible to think that thought *without* resisting a desire? Is it possible to resist a desire without thinking that you are? How would you know you were if you didn't think you were? How do you actually give in to a desire? And similarly, how do you actually resist a desire?

Deconstructing Fixations

I n this chapter, we'll be focusing on a very different set of conversations. These are the conversations that can decondition our thinking and let us enter and rest in unconditioned awareness. Some of these conversations occur in our interactions with others. Other conversations take place in silence, though, of course, they too have a profound influence on how we interact with other people.

The work in this chapter will add to your appreciation of other nondual practices and teachings and deepen your experience of the direct introduction to awareness (*rigpa*) in Dzogchen, insight in the Vipassana tradition, self-knowledge (*atma-vidya*) in Advaita Vedanta, and *sesshin* and *dokusan* in Zen.

DECONSTRUCTIVE CONVERSATIONS

A unique feature of nondual practice is the use of conversations that directly reveal unconditioned awareness. These conversations dismantle the structures of our conditioning and introduce us to the experience of contentless awareness. They are the lifeblood of the nondual traditions of spirituality, and penetrate the seeming reality of our reactive feelings and emotions in a way that dissolves their existence. They are rarely encountered in daily discourse, where our constructive conversations generally interpret what's happening in the moment, produce histories to explain what has happened in the past, and project into the future, anticipating what will happen. One thought follows the next as we elaborate, modify, develop, rework, add detail, change direction, validate, invalidate, approve, disapprove, and so on.

Deconstructive conversations move in the opposite direction and reverse the process of elaboration and complexification. They locate the "core distinctions" upon which a conversation rests, and then show that these distinctions don't refer to anything. This might sound mysterious at the moment, but it will become clear soon.

The most powerful technology for deconstructing fixations was developed in the second century AD by Nagarjuna, Buddhism's greatest philosopher and the founder of the Madhyamaka system. This system offers a comprehensive set of deconstructive tools that are used by yogi-philosophers in their private meditation and transformational debates with fellow philosophers. The Madhyamaka method for dissolving limiting constructions is called deconstructive (*prasanga-vichara*) or unfindability analysis. This type of inquiry lies at the heart of Mahayana insight meditation (*vipashyana*) and is designed to break apart interpretations of experience to allow a person to experience reality directly.

The nondual form of Hinduism called Advaita uses a similar form of inquiry in the practice of wisdom, or *jnana* yoga. Jnana yoga leads to a disidentification with the conversations that structure our personal identity and experience of the world. These traditional methods are forms of cognitive surgery that presuppose a level of concentration and thought control that exceeds the capacity of most people. This makes them relatively inaccessible to most of us.

In nondual practice, suffering and limitation are deconstructed in conversations, rather than through meditative or debating routines. The final experience — that our problems can't be found — is the same, but it's delivered with an informality that's consistent with the repartee of normal conversations. The conversations may seem casual, but they're highly precise. They can unfold gently or as a dynamic and fast-paced exchange of questions and responses that deconstruct a nest of ever more subtle assumptions and fixations. Generally, these conversations take place in group or individual interactions with an accomplished teacher or counselor; but they can also occur spontaneously, both on an inner level and as we interact with the people in our world.

The interpersonal conversations I describe in this section are those I use in my work with groups and individuals. The conversations aren't original; the same or similar ones are used by other teachers and practitioners, and can be found in the spiritual texts of Buddhism and Hinduism. As you read this section, you might imagine how similar conversations might occur in your interactions with friends, family, and co-practitioners.

A CONVERSATION ABOUT THE TERM "CONVERSATION"

Some people may feel that speaking about nondual teaching and practice as a specialized conversation undermines a primary function of this approach—to take us beyond any identification with our stories. People may think that because unconditioned awareness has no structure, speech and concepts can play no role in revealing this dimension of being. But I can't imagine introducing another person to unconditioned awareness if I couldn't speak. Indeed, I find language to be a powerful tool for transforming *and* transcending our minds.

I use the term "conversation" to refer to both the audible interactions we have with other people and the silent conversations we have with ourselves. In this sense, we're nearly always in conversation. In silent conversations, we're both the speaker and the listener, as we listen to the stream of what our own thoughts are speaking. We're in silent conversations with ourselves about what is happening, what has happened, what we could do, should do, etc.

I also use the concept of a conversation to include the silent conversations we have with others. In fact, I'm in a silent conversation with you at this moment. Neither of us is talking! Even before you read this book, you were in some kind of silent conversation with me regarding your thoughts, feelings, beliefs, images, and expectations about radiant mind. Even now, as you're reading this, we are having a kind of silent conversation even though I don't know that you're reading this. Nevertheless, we're conversing with each other, on a level beyond what we normally define as conversational. These kinds of silent conversations are going on all the time, but the scope of our conditioned awareness is far too narrow most of the time to recognize their existence.

TYPES OF DECONSTRUCTIVE CONVERSATIONS

In nondual practice, there's no agenda beyond our constant openness to the possibility of introducing the experience of unconditioned awareness, stabilizing the experience, and allowing our painful thoughts and feelings to dissolve in the fresh experience of unconditioned awareness. Our task is to facilitate this movement and not interfere with it. The main thing required of us here is to be aware of the opportunity to drop into this space of effortless being. Then there is nothing more to do, and we come home to the state of complete fulfillment.

When I'm working with people, I don't predict what will happen next. I don't know in advance how a session will unfold. I don't know if it will be punctuated by periods of deep, meditative silence, or consist of a dynamic exchange of questions and answers. The skills I present throughout this book, including the different types of deconstructive conversations, rest in the background as an ever-present set of possibilities, any one of which may come into the foreground and guide the interaction. In this chapter, we'll explore koans and silent conversations.

DECONSTRUCTIVE CONVERSATIONS WITH YOURSELF: NATURAL KOANS

Koan practice is usually associated with Zen Buddhism. Koans are questions or puzzles that cannot be solved—at least not conceptually. In Zen, koan practice was formalized and institutionalized. The entire koan system of Rinzai Zen is a form of contemplative inquiry that deconstructs the conceptual mind in order to reveal unstructured awareness—an experience that in Zen is called "no mind." But koans are actually timeless. Koans arise naturally in our minds when our experience of conditioned mind expands to include unconditioned awareness .

As the familiar parameters and boundaries of our conditioned experience begin to dissolve, we find ourselves in a place where our "knowing mind" is no longer functioning in the same way. Things we were certain about no longer seem to exist. The ground we have been standing on starts to fall away, and in this dissolution, questions about the nature of reality, and who we are, naturally arise.

The silence that occurs in nondual work is often filled with these natural koans. As we move into a less familiar way of being, we begin to wonder what's happening and what we should be doing. As our familiar points of reference dissolve, questions arise, such as "What is this?" "Where am I?" "Is there something I should be doing?" "Am I moving forward or backward?" "Am I moving at all?" "Is there something special I should be doing?" "Who am I?"

These questions are natural koans. They're arising naturally. We're not inserting them into our mind. They arise because our conditioned mind—the mind that can know—is still trying to work out what's happening as we move into a more unstructured state.

Each of these koans is a key that can unlock the conceptual mind and take us into the unknown. If we let our thoughts ride on these questions, they can take us directly into the infinite expanse of unconditioned awareness. When we ask "What is this?" there is no "this"—there's nothing. There's only buddha-mind—or unconditioned awareness. Even though it appears that there might be answers to these questions, in reality, each one of them is like the famous koan, "What is the sound of one hand clapping?"

In nondual practice, we use naturally arising koans as tools for deconstructing our habitual ways of thinking. The silences that punctuate nondual work, whether in counseling, group situations, or on our own, often give birth to a gentle cascade of natural koans. By letting our thoughts ride on these koan-type questions, fixed ideas about who we are dissolve into the infinite expanse of nondual awareness. We surf the koans through the deepest layers of our consciousness into unstructured mind.

A common feature in all these naturally arising koans is that they refer to "this"—the experience that's happening—or "I"—the person who is meditating, working, or thinking. Often we don't go on to ask the next question—"What is this?" or "Who am I?" We assume that we already know the answers to these questions. But these two questions—"What is this?" and "Who am I?"—are at the heart of many forms of deconstructive inquiry.

"WHO AM I?"

The Hindu form of nondual inquiry is based on the question "Who am I?" This question aims at connecting people with "witness consciousness." I find that it can be more effective to ask a question such as "Who is experiencing this (problem, feeling, etc.) right now?" This question is more immediate and keeps us in the experience we're having in the present moment. What we're asking is, "Is there an experiencer separate from the experience?" Or, to put it somewhat differently, "It's clear this experience is happening, but *who* is actually experiencing it?"

"WHAT IS THIS?"

In Korean Zen, the main koan is the question "What is this?" The first record of this koan occurred in an exchange between the Sixth Zen Patriarch Hui-neng and a young monk named Huaijang, in which Hui-neng asked

Huaijang, "What is this and where did it come from?" Huaijang couldn't answer. But he took the question away and used it as his sole form of inquiry for several years, until he realized what it was pointing to. He then returned to see Hui-neng, who again asked him, "What is this?" Huaijang replied, "To say it is something misses the point. But still it can be cultivated."

In Korean Zen, one sits in meditation and asks over and over, "What is this?" This can lead to the questions "What is what?" and "What is the 'this' that I'm trying to work out?" In nondual practice, we ask ourselves this question in an authentic way. At some point, we realize that "this" isn't anything. The "this" that we are now experiencing—indeed, always experiencing—does not exist. It is and yet it isn't.

Personally I prefer the question "What is this?" to the question "Who am I?" "Who am I?" tends to point us inward and may disconnect us from our problems rather than deconstruct them. The question "What is this?" doesn't point in any direction because "this" includes everything, both inside and outside us. We don't know where to look—and this is what the question is designed to do.

WHEN AND HOW TO ASK THESE QUESTIONS

If used inappropriately, these questions, which can release us from our thinking, can also embed us further in our thoughts. Generally, we need to be in a fairly refined, unstructured state of mind before we contemplate these koans. If we ask them prematurely, they only invite elaboration and interpretation, lock us into our belief systems, and lead us to constructive rather than deconstructive responses. In other words, they produce more thinking rather than disidentification with thoughts. By contrast, if the questions are well-timed, they lead you directly into an experience of the present moment, beyond the discursive intellect. The point is to not think about the questions—they aren't designed to be answered.

COMMUNICATING IN DEEP SILENCE

Nondual work leads us naturally into the experience of being present in the moment, without any concern or discussion about what "this" is. The space is one of effortless, uncontrived being, in which there's nothing to communicate. In the nondual experience, people may spend many minutes in deep aesthetic appreciation, as their thoughts dissolve into unconditioned awareness. Silence is as potent as dialogue in its capacity to enhance or diminish the experience of unconditioned awareness.

The experience of deep, natural silence can decondition our habits and fixed beliefs by de-energizing our constructions. These periods of silence can test the depth of our nondual experience, because they challenge our need for structure. When we rest in unconditioned awareness, it's sometimes impossible to generate the types of conversations that are expected of us. We find that we don't need to respond, and yet in the absence of a verbal reply, everything is communicated and taken care of. We don't contrive to produce an experience of resting in silence. It arises naturally in this work.

But not all experiences of silence decondition our minds. Silence can do the opposite: it can exacerbate and amplify our fixations. If we feel uncomfortable, silence can intensify the feelings, especially if we feel that the opportunities for communicating are being curtailed or suppressed, as in group settings where silence spontaneously occurs. In such instances, the silence can become oppressive rather than liberating, and can send people into an even stronger identification with their discomfort.

WORKING CREATIVELY WITH SILENCE, BOTH WITHIN OURSELVES AND WITH OTHERS

Because the experience of silence can move us toward or away from unconditioned awareness, nondual practice requires that we "know how to be with silence," and this, in turn, requires that we understand silence. This kind of understanding allows us to open more and more to the totally natural and unstructured nature of silence. When we understand silence, we're able to take ourselves and others into deeper states of natural contemplation. When we don't understand silence, or if we're at all uncomfortable with the silence that emerges in this work, the periods of silence can devolve into something analogous to a meditative practice. In a meditative practice, we are creating a silence that comes from controlling the mind. Although it may seem quite peaceful at the time, this kind of contrived and structured silence is a conditioned state that feels quite dense and narrow.

Sometimes "nothing" happens in the periods of silence that occur. At other times, the silences are rich with communication. Both are wonderful!

But silence has depth and naturalness only to the degree that we're aware of the silent conversations that may be occurring, both within ourselves and with others. To work creatively with silence, we need to be sensitive to the different types, or flavors, of silence. For example, there's the silence of confusion, in which we don't talk because we don't know what to say. There's an impulse to communicate, but we aren't sure what we want or need to say. By contrast, there's the silence that results when we're withholding, either through fear of the consequences of communicating or through embarrassment. The sweetest silence is the one that emanates from nondual awareness—when there's nothing to do and nothing to say, and we're resting in "what is" because there's no need to communicate anything.

As we develop the ability to rest in unconditioned awareness, we find that more and more silence creeps into our interactions with others. Our capacity to relate silently is limited by our attachment to talking *and* not talking. It's obvious that if we're attached to speaking—our own or someone else's—we predispose ourselves to interrupt the experience of silence, either by saying something ourselves or by encouraging others to speak. But our attachment to *not* talking, to not sharing or communicating, also disturbs the experience of deep silence. If we're attached to the experience of meditative or interior stillness, we're still exercising a preference. If, in any moment, we'd prefer the experience of silence to continue or stop, this acts to condition the next moment and flatten the potency of the silence to accommodate everything: more silence or renewed speaking. If we're bored of waiting for someone to speak, or hoping that no one will interrupt the silence, we're conditioning the space. Attempting to control the occurrence or duration of these periods of silence—to "do silence," as it were—is counterproductive. The nondual experience neither discourages nor encourages speech or silence.

ADJUSTING TO SILENCE

Many of us simply don't have the experience of being in quiet communion with others. We're conditioned to "break the silence" when we sense the slightest discomfort in the person with whom we're communicating. A friend who spent years living in a community of mystics in Java once told me how these simple, rural people have a practice of sitting quietly together for an hour or so after eating their communal meal in the early evening. They aren't meditating; they just silently enjoy their own and each other's company, smiling, looking at each other, or gazing into space, in innocent appreciation of the present moment. We don't have any models for how to be at ease with, let alone empowered by, the experience of "shared silence."

EXAMPLES OF SILENT CONVERSATIONS

There are two types of silent conversations: conversations we have with ourselves, and conversations we have with others, in which we speculate about, or anticipate, how they might respond to what we could say or do. The power of silent conversations rests in the fact that we can play through, in detail, what might happen *if* we say something, without saying a word. Of course, these are not the same conversations that *would* play out if they were spoken. If we have some experience of deconstructive inquiry, we can deconstruct our beliefs in the imaginary conversations that happen in our mind.

Of course, silent conversations rarely happen in ordinary discourse, but as we become more involved in nondual practice, we may connect with others who are also experimenting with allowing natural silences to occur in their interactions. When we aren't given the same level of content or feedback that we normally receive in a conversation, we may begin to wonder what to speak about, or if there's anything to speak about at all. We become engaged in silent conversations with ourselves that can take us all the way through to unconditioned awareness. For example, we may think, "I'm feeling nervous at the moment. I wonder if I should share that. What would I say? I could just say that the silence makes me a little nervous. How does it make me feel nervous? How can silence do that? Maybe I'm just feeling nervous. Actually, I'm not feeling nervous any more. I'm very comfortable. Really, the silence is lovely. I'd be comfortable for this to continue forever."

The value in letting conversations unfold silently is that they allow us to dance in a set of open-ended possibilities without prematurely conditioning the space by asking a question or making an observation that's simply a reflection of our own insecurity. At the same time, this needs to be balanced with an awareness of the fact that we can also protect ourselves from other people's judgments and perceptions by keeping our mouth closed. In nondual practice, we're often dancing at the confluence of the conditioned and the unconditioned, sensing the influence of our energy field in activating and releasing fixations.

CHAPTER NINE EXERCISES

WHO AM I?

Begin by sitting quietly and resting in unconditioned awareness as much as you can. Then, in a mood of inquiry, gently ask yourself the question "Who am I?" When thoughts, feelings, or experiences arise, inquire, "Who thinks, feels, or experiences that?" If problems arise, you might ask, "Who has that problem? Who is suffering?" Ask each question without expecting an answer. The question isn't designed to elicit any content. Rather, it points to the uncreated creator of all constructions, unconditioned awareness. When asking these questions, do not create any pressure — there are no answers!

WHO ARE YOU?

This exercise is completed in pairs. There are two roles: a questioner and a responder. Work in one direction for about fifteen minutes, then change roles. If you arrive at a space of shared silence, enjoy it together. This can be done face-to-face or over the phone.

Instructions for the questioner:

- Ask your partner, "Who are you?" Do this in a mood of inquiry.
- However your partner responds, invite them to discover "Who thinks that?" "Who feels that?" "Who experiences that?" and so on.
- You need to adapt the question to your partner's response. Some of your questions will be:
  Who feels that?
  Who thinks that?
  Who created that?
  Who thought that thought?
  Who thinks they thought that thought?
  Who has that problem?
  Who is suffering?
- Your questions need to follow the structure of your partner's response. In other words, you need to use the same language as your partner. It isn't as simple as repeatedly asking "Who are you?" If you try to rely

on this one question, you'll disconnect from your partner. And you'll start to sound like a robot.

- Ask the question without expecting an answer. The question isn't designed to elicit any content. Rather, it points to unconditioned awareness.

THE "WHAT IS THIS?—WHERE IS THAT?" EXERCISE

This exercise is completed in pairs. One partner is the questioner; the other, the responder. The questioner and responder sit together for a few minutes in silent shared contemplation. The questioner then asks, "What is this?" This question refers to the whole field of experience, both conditioned and unconditioned, all the objects of experience, and also the one who is experiencing it all. There is no specific focus for this question.

Whenever the responder replies, the questioner asks, "Where is that?" (i.e., "Where is that to which you are referring?" or "Can you find the place where this experience is located?").

The questioner only asks these two questions. The first question is asked only once, to begin the exchange. All questions should be asked from a state of unconditioned awareness, or no-mind. Do not ask the second question as though you believe there is an actual location to the experience.

The exercise continues until the responder cannot locate the experience. Once you have completed it in one direction, change roles.

TRANSCENDING YOUR PERSONAL STORY

In this exercise, I'd like you to have a conversation with someone for a minimum of about fifteen minutes, but you're welcome to go on for as long as you'd like. This can be done face-to-face or by phone.

The aim of this exercise is to communicate outside of your personal history and beliefs. You might begin the conversation with the question "What can we talk about that's not personal?"

You can filter out your personality in two stages. Begin by not referring to your past experience, and then let go of your beliefs and opinions.

If you think your partner's conversation has devolved into a personal history or personal beliefs and opinions, you can offer them gentle and non-judgmental feedback.

SILENT COMMUNICATION

Over the next two weeks, I'd like you to explore silent communication in an informal way. There will be dozens of opportunities. For example, when you're asked for your opinion about something, look inside yourself a little longer than usual and see if you may not be as certain as your first thoughts suggest. Then try to communicate from that "relative space of not knowing."

Other opportunities for exploring silent communication will arise when you're expected to talk, for example, in telephone calls, over a meal, or even in meetings. If you have nothing to say in the moment, you can respect your inner silence by remaining true to that fact, even though it changes the energy and dynamic of the situation.

Try to push the envelope a little, but not too much! If the silence becomes heavy, you're probably heading in the wrong direction. On the other hand, if the silence is punctuated by a gentle smile or a mutual recognition that transcends the present moment, then let it evolve in that direction.

CHAPTER TEN

Broadening the River of Life

If you expect your life to be up and down,
your mind will be much more peaceful.
LAMA THUBTEN YESHE[1]

When we truly hate what's happening, our instinct is
to flee from it like a house on fire. But if we can learn
to turn around and enter that fire, to let it burn all our
resistance away, then we find ourselves arising from
the ashes with a new sense of power and freedom.
RAPHAEL CUSHNIR[2]

After all, what is so scary about things just as they are?
If we see things as they are, at least we know the truth.
What should frighten us is denying things as they are.
SHYALPA RINPOCHE, A CONTEMPORARY NYINGMA LAMA[3]

I n nondual traditions, the nature of the spiritual path changes from cultivating positive states and avoiding negative states to expanding our capacity to
be present to everything that human life can produce—open to the full force
and richness of our conditioned existence. The more time we spend resting in
unconditioned awareness, the less we're able to structure our life around pursuing pleasure and avoiding suffering. In fact, the nondual approach requires an
increasing disidentification from the pleasure-pain cycle, and a growing interest
in the peace and bliss that characterize the experience of the unconditioned.

As we rest in unconditioned awareness, we progressively increase our capacity to receive all experiences without fear or addiction. When we rest in unconditioned awareness, there's nothing to resist or avoid because there's no desire for anything to be different from how it is. Rather, everything that arises is effortlessly accepted and released. In Buddhist terms, we're broadening our spiritual horizon to include the bliss of nirvana and the full range of samsaric experiences. This breadth and inclusiveness differentiates nondual liberation from the goal of dualistic spiritual paths. The dualist says there is some state (like nirvana or salvation) that is preferable, whereas the nondualist opens up entirely, without rejecting anything.

Nondual practice naturally increases our capacity to accommodate a wider range of experiences—in both intensity and variety—because we're no longer dominated by our reactive emotions. We don't automatically try to avoid difficult situations and seek out agreeable ones. We become more tolerant and accepting, and we discover how to face life with more balance and equanimity.

DENYING OUR CONDITIONED EXISTENCE

We live most of our life in constant reaction to the ever-changing realities of our conditioned existence. We speak about our problems as though they shouldn't be happening, and about our suffering as though we shouldn't be experiencing it. "What's wrong?" we wonder. "Why is this happening to me?"

For example, how often do we think, "I'm not meant to be doing this," with respect to our work and family obligations? I know an Indian doctor who works day and night, seven days a week, at a tiny clinic treating impoverished villagers for routine complaints and more serious conditions such as malnutrition and hepatitis. Yet he's always joyful, passionate, and appreciative. Why? One of the major reasons is that he isn't thinking that it isn't fair, or that he *should* be doing something else. Unlike me, he fully accepts and owns his circumstances, and he doesn't seem to be indulging thoughts or conversations such as "This isn't the right line of work for me. I'm meant to be doing something easier and less demanding. I should move on to a different calling."

We habitually resist, object, and deny the reality of our experience. It can be difficult to take a trip across town, read the newspaper, or spend a day in our office or an evening at home without someone or something disturbing our peace and serenity. We reject the volume of music in a restaurant, the actions of our politicians, our own and other people's appearance, the quality of the produce in our supermarket, the way people speak to us, the time we have to wait in line. At some level, we attempt to avoid everything that's unpleasant and painful.

This constant denial saps our energy and demoralizes us, because we're engaged in a losing battle with a reality that simply isn't interested in our existence. As the Tibetan lama Shyalpa Rinpoche says, "When we ignore the present moment . . . there are consequences: we create karma, we create suffering. If we live this moment only fifty percent, the fifty percent we failed to live will surely cause us difficulties later." [2003]4

If we explore our resistance carefully, we'll see that we're in denial every moment we've lost our connection with unconditioned awareness. In fact, if we aren't resting in unconditioned awareness, we're either resisting or holding on to "whatever's happening for us." This might sound extreme, but if we're identified with our conditioned existence, we live in the construction that there's a right or a better place to be. By doing so, we're denying what is—the reality of our conditioned experience. At the same time, we're denying the reality of unconditioned awareness itself. Essentially, everyone participates in this denial. No one has ever won the battle against "what is." And no one ever will. Yet we spend a good part of our life denying our conditioned existence.

At this point, you might feel that I'm being excessive in my description of our daily, conditioned existence. You might also feel that I've betrayed the nondual focus because elsewhere in this book I've said that "in reality, it's impossible to reject or be attached to anything. The phenomenon of avoidance is an interpretation. It doesn't actually exist." This is true. From the viewpoint of unconditioned awareness, there's nothing to reject or grasp. And if we try to find the process of attachment and aversion, we'll see that they simply can't occur.

"But," you might ask, "doesn't 'nondual' experience imply that we can't avoid reality in any case? After all, if all experience is truly nondual, then it includes everything without exception." This is true by definition, but on a relative level, we do attempt to avoid our conditioned experience, the reality that's composed of our perceptions, feelings, and thoughts. We can't avoid the reality of unconditioned awareness because there's nothing to avoid. Avoidance and denial are always avoidance and denial of something. The reaction of denial always has an object. The only thing we can avoid or attach to is a conditioned construct, an image or projection that we take to be unconditioned awareness, whereas the space itself has no structure and thus can't be grasped or resisted.

RESISTING SUFFERING

In the affluent West, we take pleasure and satisfaction to be our birthright, and live with a profound denial and rejection of pain and discomfort. In fact, we seem to share the belief that we shouldn't suffer at all. In nondual practice, suffering isn't represented as something wrong, something that shouldn't happen to us. We all suffer and will probably continue to do so until we die. Problems and difficulties are a natural part of life. There is no doubt that most of us will be forced to negotiate periods of deep suffering at various points in our life. Problems inevitably arise as an aspect of our conditioned existence. Only a fully enlightened individual ceases to create problems.

Much of the time, we're trying to protect ourselves from our experience because we believe it would somehow overwhelm or destroy us. In fact, the only thing in danger of being overwhelmed or destroyed is our carefully constructed and maintained ego identity, our comfort and our illusion of being in control of life. In an attempt to perpetuate the illusion of control and separation, we distort, fantasize, project, and otherwise avoid the reality of our experience—including feelings, ideas, people, places, and situations. We reject what's happening because our survival seems to depend on avoiding experiences that threaten our preferences. We fear that if we don't resist thoughts, feelings, and situations that we'd prefer not to experience, they will continue to plague and disturb us—and possibly even overpower and consume us.

When we fixate on the belief that problems should be absent from our experience, we merely compound our problems. When a problem arises, we struggle to get rid of it. When a negative thought arises—for example, "I'm bored"—we try to remove or reject it. By pushing the problem away in an attempt to access or maintain an experience of nondual awareness, we actually undermine the experience of nondual awareness, which, after all, includes everything and rejects nothing. Similarly, thinking that we *shouldn't* create problems creates the idea that something is missing—that is, the absence of problems—and this blocks the experience of full awareness.

Even though unpleasant experiences continue to manifest independently of our refusal to accept them, we operate, year after year, as though our rejection will de-energize a negative experience. If this was how things worked, surely we would be able to remove unpleasant experiences expeditiously and with ease. Yet we try to avoid our pain, and year after year our suffering continues. The energy of denial or resistance is always wasted. Not one ounce of this kind of energy makes a productive contribution to changing our experience. The source of our suffering lies not in the circumstances of our life but in our resistance.

AVOIDANCE TACTICS

Our methods for avoiding reality are numerous and complex. We try to deny our experience by thinking that something has gone wrong, or that what's happening shouldn't be happening. We fantasize about alternative circumstances and outcomes, including self-improvement or some imagined enlightenment. We distract ourselves or numb our feelings through drugs, media, and superficial conversations. We judge and blame ourselves and others in various ways, for example, "I could have avoided this by listening more carefully" or "This clearly means I'm an inadequate person" or "It's his fault. He should have behaved differently."

We analyze and interpret what's happening rather than experience the raw energy and texture of our feelings and sensations. We categorize, contrast, and compare. We try to work out who's responsible for our pain and then seek a solution, or at least some form of compensation. We try to dilute what we're feeling by blaming ourselves, our karma, other people, our spiritual teachers, or God for putting us into the predicaments we find ourselves in. "What produced this?" "What did I do?" "What does it mean?" "How will this impact my future?" We try to think our way out of our pain and discomfort by creating comforting and tranquilizing explanations. We disconnect from our bodies and feelings by getting tied up in our thoughts and confusing ourselves. In all these ways, we attempt to avoid what's happening.

Another way we try to avoid the full force of painful feelings is to negotiate our way out of our pain by making commitments that are designed to compensate for our failures and weaknesses. "If I survive this illness, I'll take better care of my health." Or we bargain and plead. "I can't stand this." "I'm not strong enough." "Give me a break." "It wasn't my fault." "If this stops, I'm happy to accept the consequences!" Or we look for a payoff. We might think, "There is something in this experience for me. This is a lesson. At the very least, it's expanding my capacity to be present to 'what is' without freaking out or complaining."

We can also spend our life waiting for a better future or missing out on the pleasures of the moment. We wait for painful experiences to disappear, and we degrade the moments of enjoyment by anticipating their inevitable destruction or fantasizing more of the same. We hold ourselves back or drive ourselves forward, rarely finding a pace and rhythm that accords with the conditions of our body and environment.

When we resist reality, we tighten up. Our bodies become tense; we feel paralyzed or agitated. Try to remember some of the times you'd resisted what was happening to you, and see if you can recall how resistance shows up in your body. Don't try to interpret those experiences; just scan your body for how denial manifests in your chest, belly, groin, shoulders, arms, hands, neck, throat, face, mouth, brow, and scalp. Where are the feelings located in your body? Is the energy stable or moving? Is it solid, like a constriction, or more like an absence or a gaping hole?

BROADENING THE RIVER OF LIFE

The conscious cultivation of a more expanded and inclusive relationship to life has a vital place in nondual practice. The experience of unconditioned awareness arises as a function of our capacity to let go of preferences, including the need to be happy and content. If we're fixated on our happiness, we can't enter desirelessness. In the nondual approach, we can expand our capacity to enjoy pleasure and endure pain, while also discovering a space that transcends pain and pleasure. We acknowledge our conditioned existence and learn to live gracefully with our habits and weaknesses. We accept our tendency to create problems, without being seduced by the illusion that we can leapfrog our karmic conditioning.

I call this "broadening the river of life." We have ups and downs, great times when life flows smoothly, and difficult times when things get heavy and intense and don't necessarily work out well. That's life. If we act as though life shouldn't be like this, we deny a fundamental aspect of our existence.

By acknowledging that we do suffer, however, we aren't necessarily committing ourselves to suffering. We accept our circumstances without becoming resigned to our lot in life. Instead, we may think, "At this point in my evolution, I suffer from time to time because I'm still controlled by judgments and preferences. Even so, I don't feel resigned. I'm definitely not committed to the inevitability of this situation. I'm working with my reactive emotions so that, over time, the situation will definitely change. I can even accept the fact that I become resigned to my situation from time to time."

By broadening the river of life, we increase our capacity to be present to the whole range of human experience. We welcome what is, and this welcoming becomes a gateway into the nondual state. When we welcome what is, our suffering dissipates. We let what is happening happen and don't object to it. There may still be pain, but it no longer causes suffering.

GETTING REAL

Ultimately, the only way to break our obsession with resistance, denial, and suffering is by getting real and accepting the nature of our conditioned life. In nondual practice, we acknowledge and accept that suffering still happens for us at this point on our path. We cut through the fantasy that something is wrong when we suffer, and we stop making a problem out of having problems! We accept the basic structure and patterning of our experience and our life circumstances, not in a defeatist way, but with dignity and grace, because we know that "welcoming what is" is the gateway to unconditioned awareness.

First of all, we accept the truth of suffering, which is, of course, the first of the Buddha's Four Noble Truths. Yes, our conditioned existence is characterized by different forms of suffering, and we don't have to make that into a problem. Instead, we can say, "Yes, I've got a problem, and I'll work with it in the most mature and responsible way I can." In fact, it's immature and irresponsible to say that it shouldn't be happening. A more responsible response would be, "Yes, I have a problem, now what can I do about it?" Or we could ask ourselves, "Do I *need* to do anything about it?"

As we accept the fact that we have problems, we find ourselves relaxing and lightening up, because we're not making our problems into a problem. Rather, we realize that we're simply having a common human experience—loss, illness, physical pain, financial difficulties, and so on. We can also notice the tendency to escape from our problems into wishful thinking, which is essentially a constructive conversation in which we imagine a more desirable outcome. At this point, we can ask ourselves whether the fantasized future is actually likely, and gently bring our attention back to the present moment. "What's it like for me right now?" Gradually we may begin to recognize that it's possible to be whole and complete without achieving the particular circumstance we predicated as necessary for our happiness. We can feel complete in the moment and in touch with reality without the fulfillment of certain conditions, and we can go beyond any need to adjust our circumstances, by connecting with the presence of unconditioned awareness.

LIVING WITHOUT RESISTANCE

When we rest in unconditioned awareness, there's nothing to resist; everything that arises is effortlessly accepted and released. There's no need to avoid anything because there's no desire for anything to be different from the way it is. We don't hold ourselves back for fear of being confronted by something that's unpleasant, uncomfortable, or overwhelming. Rather than close down and try to protect ourselves, or drive ourselves forward through fear of missing out on some valued experience or opportunity, we face everything that arises in our experience and avoid nothing, without resisting it or believing it shouldn't be happening.

However, it takes courage to accept "what is" when our emotional reactions have been triggered, because this runs counter to what we've done in the past, and to what we've learned. It also requires confidence that our deeper unconditioned nature is a source of bliss and contentment. Our fear is that if we let go of our resistance, the feeling we're fighting to avoid will gain power and influence, and perhaps completely consume us. So when we open up, we also accept our fear that things might get more intense and even much worse. We need to take full responsibility for our existence, including our potential and our deepest fears, and accept that we can't know or control the future.

Opening up in this way—accepting what is without any resistance—is heroic because we risk losing everything we're attached to. In order to open up to what's happening, we let go of our sense of self-control. "True fearlessness comes from the knowledge that we will never lie to ourselves, that we will never evade a single moment of our lives," says Shyalpa Rinpoche. "We will be fully present for every moment and every consequence." Rinpoche speaks of this "willingness to see things as they are, without having any motive or intention whatsoever to them." (*Shambhala Sun*, May 2003)[5] He calls this "real honesty" because we no longer deceive ourselves and others about what we know and don't know.

One way to begin to accept our experience is to simply say yes to it when we realize that we are saying no to it. When we hear ourselves objecting to what's happening, we can think, "Okay, I will be present to this experience. The nature of conditioned reality is such that when something is, it is. And when it isn't, it isn't. So when something is, I will experience it; I won't try to push it away. And when something isn't, I will accept this. I won't chase after it, or pine for it, or fantasize about it. And when I realize that I am attempting to push something away or chase after it, I will accept that as well."

Much of our pain is caused by our denial of the physicality and factual nature of our embodied existence, and the nondual perspective can add to our confusion. For example, the nondual perspective teaches that when the unconditioned is, it isn't, and when it isn't, it is. But in the domain of forms, feelings, and thoughts, the opposite is true: when something is present, it's present, and when it's absent, it's absent. This is what it means to have a physical body and live in the material world. The world of matter functions in very specific and precise ways. Relative to thoughts and feelings, our physical bodies are highly conditioned. If someone dies or leaves a relationship, they will no longer be around for us to enjoy their physical presence and company. If we lose our investments, we won't be able to go on the vacations we've dreamt about or give our children the education we've planned. In accepting our conditioned existence, we accept what it really means to be living in a body that's conditioned by the past and present and by other people and our physical environment.

OPENING UP

It's easy to think that in order to let go of our resistance, we need to change and become a different type of person. But when we let go of our resistance, nothing needs to change. In fact, that's exactly what we're doing in letting go of our resistance. We're letting go of the need for anything to be different. We accept that things may change, and they may not. We allow our circumstances and our responses (our thoughts and feelings) to be exactly as they are. We let go of what we think is happening, and we let go of what should be happening, in order to allow ourselves to be present to what is actually happening. We stop waiting for anything more to be happening than what is.

In unconditioned awareness, there's nothing to wait for, because nothing *is* happening. The only way to enter unconditioned awareness is to stop waiting. When we stop waiting for our circumstances to change or continue, there is only the here and now. We can't wait for the future, because the future never comes — it never arrives; it never has and it never will. All there ever is, is the moment that is saturated with a level of conditioning that spans infinity and yet, at the same time, is totally ephemeral.

BLISS

The moment we accept what's happening to us without any resistance, pain transforms into bliss. Bliss is available to us simply by letting things be as they are. This is why Tantric Buddhism talks about the indivisible union of bliss and emptiness (*sukha-shunyata*). In other words, the experience of emptiness, which is the same as the experience of unconditioned awareness, is always and naturally experienced as a state of supernal bliss. This bliss goes beyond both the experience of pain and pleasure. It cannot be characterized as the removal of pain or even as an experience of somatic pleasure or emotional ecstasy. It's the bliss that arises when we stop seeking and relinquish all demands for things to be different than they are. It's the bliss we experience when we rest in the certain knowledge that what we're experiencing cannot be enhanced or degraded, and cannot be taken away from us by any change in our conditioned circumstances.

The word "bliss" may not be the best term to translate the Sanskrit word that's used in Tantric Buddhism. In fact, Indian nondual spirituality has many words for bliss. The two most common are *sukha* (which is mainly used by Buddhists) and *ananda* (which is mainly used in Hinduism). Just as Eskimos have many words for snow because they distinguish subtly different types of snow, cultures that practice yoga and meditation have many words for bliss because they experience various kinds of bliss. You might have noticed that most Indian swamis have the word "bliss" (ananda) in their names: Yogananda, Satchitananda, Jnanananda, and so on. The reason why some yogis and contemplatives live in a state of nearly constant bliss is because they have minimal needs and make minimal demands on the world and their bodies. Consequently, they're easily, and normally, complete and satisfied.

In English, the word "bliss" has several associations that can block resting in unconditioned awareness. For a start, the concept of "spiritual bliss" has been degraded in the world of commerce and advertising, which speaks about the bliss of driving the latest model car or eating a particular candy bar. In our own conversations, we talk about how the chocolate mousse was pure bliss, that our vacation in Bali was pure bliss, that we are ecstatic about getting a promotion, or that it was sheer bliss not having to go to work in the morning. At the very least, these usages show that bliss is important to us.

But many of our associations are negative in some way. In particular, we're reluctant to acknowledge that our life is driven by the search for unending bliss and contentment. Spiritual seekers can be embarrassed to acknowledge that they seek a state of permanent and transcendent bliss. We judge ourselves, or fear being judged by others, as being selfish, narcissistic, or hedonistic. We place limits on the amount of pleasure we feel safe to enjoy. If we have too little, we feel starved and cheated. If we have too much, we worry that we'll become addicted to pleasure and lose perspective on the rest of our life.

THE HEALING POWER OF SENSATE BLISS

The experience of unconditioned bliss is different from the experiences of sensate bliss that arise as a function of changes in our thoughts, feelings, and body chemistry. Unconditioned bliss is sourceless. We can't say where is comes from; it doesn't come from inside our body, or from an external source. It's the nature of awareness. Nondual work produces experiences of both sensate and unconditioned bliss.

Experiences of sensate bliss arise in the slipstream of unconditioned awareness. They occur like clockwork when our thinking slows down and we move into more subtle states of consciousness. In the context of nondual practice, these experiences can be profoundly healing, especially for people who deprive themselves of pleasure. They are medicine for the mind and the soul. They soothe our minds and repair the damage done to our nervous system by pain and trauma. We recognize their healing power and let people rest in these experiences for as long as they arise.

Energy and consciousness disciplines such as tai chi, yoga, and meditation produce experiences of sensate bliss—the bliss that can be felt as ecstatic joy, or as the somatic bliss that arises when our nervous system is perfectly integrated with our mind. The most powerful practices are those that are based on knowledge of the energy movements (*prana*) in our subtle physiology of energy pathways (*nadi*). Experiences of bliss, rapture, deep contentment, serenity, and imperturbable peace arise like clockwork when people practice deep contemplation.

However, like all conditioned experiences, sensate bliss comes and goes. Though it can be healing to rest in sensate bliss, nondualists know that there is still further to go: to the place where there's nowhere to go. So if we find ourselves in an experience of sensate bliss, we let these experiences do their work, and then gently move forward into the ultimate experience of unconditioned awareness.

DEATH AND UNCONDITIONED AWARENESS

Of course, in broadening the river of life, we are compelled to include death—the deaths of everyone we love and care about, and definitely our own death, whenever and wherever it occurs. Working with death invariably brings us back to unconditioned awareness, because unconditioned awareness will be the ultimate resource when we're dying, just as it's the ultimate resource for living.

THE ULTIMATE DECONSTRUCTION

Death is a great opportunity for the practice of letting go and deconstruction, because everything is being torn away from us in every moment anyway. Death is the ultimate deconstruction—the final disintegration. Even though there's no possibility of control at this point, the more familiar we are with the process of letting go of our points of reference, the easier it will be to let go when everything disintegrates around us and within us. The more familiar we are with the inner, dynamic processes that let us connect and reconnect with pure, nondual awareness, the better chance we have of negotiating this transition without being terrified or freaking-out. Anything we can do that increases the possibility of staying with unconditioned awareness when we die is worth doing.

We know from our experience of unconditioned awareness that there *is* a state in which we need nothing: we know firsthand that there are moments when we don't need the "things" we think are necessary for our existence and well-being. When we're in unconditioned awareness, it's clear that we don't need anything. We don't need our possessions, our friends, our smart ideas, our emotional fortitude, our moral integrity, our ingenuity, or our money. We're super-complete—so complete we're beyond even feeling complete. We're complete with nothing!

If we know this experience, then when everything is taken from us—at death—instead of freaking out about everything we're losing, it's possible to look straight ahead, instead of behind us. It's possible to look forward to the precious opportunity of having nothing: no possessions and no identity, no one to take care of, and nothing to defend or protect. No loss, because there's nothing we can lose.

RELEASE AND LETTING GO

A primary message we need to hear when we are dying is, "Let go, let go completely, and keep letting go, again and again." We need to realize, and fully take on board, the fact that we'll never return to our existence as we know it. "I" will cease to exist. There will be no "me" as I know myself. This moment could come at any time. I might not even finish writing this page. You might not finish reading it. We need to be ready for that time, when we know that we're done for. That this is it.

We're saying goodbye, once and for all, to *everything* that we know. If we are deeply rooted in unconditioned awareness, there's nothing to be attached to, and no one—no "I"—to be attached to anyone or anything. Of course, the best preparation for death is to become more and more familiar with unconditioned awareness when we're alive. But we can also prepare ourselves in a more focused manner.

CHAPTER TEN EXERCISES

These exercises are designed to give you opportunities to:

- Expand your capacity to experience and integrate painful experiences
- Become more sensitive to the conversations that signal that you're resisting an experience
- Observe the time you spend "waiting"
- Help you identify and taste the simple and innocent pleasures in life
- Dismantle the experience of resisting an experience

SAYING YES INSTEAD OF NO

Over the next two weeks, when you recognize that you're saying no to what you're experiencing, experiment with saying yes. If this is difficult for you, say to yourself, "Okay. This is what's happening. It's difficult, but I'll be with it. I'll experience it." If it feels unbearable, then do this for just a minute to two at a time. Think, "This is unbearable. Can I stand it for another minute? Yes, I can. I won't try to distract myself. For the next minute, I'll be fully present to this feeling."

EMBRACING YOURSELF AT A LEVEL BEYOND
COMFORT AND CONVENTION

Another way to move beyond your normal comfort zone is to have a significant communication with one or two people (or types of people) with whom you normally wouldn't interact. For example, these might be people who you feel aren't worthy of your attention, people you're averse to, people whose time you wouldn't want to waste, people who are arrogant, people who live on the street, people who are timid and shy, people whose lives and values you totally disagree with. After interacting with them, take on their values, beliefs, and behavioral characteristics for a short while. See if you can do this in spite of the resistance you might be feeling. Feel what life might be like for them.

INNOCENT PLEASURES

Over the next two weeks, expand your opportunities for bringing simple pleasures into your life. Do something that you wouldn't normally do. This could be going dancing, having a massage, having a manicure, nursing a newborn baby, listening to Mozart, or giving a gift to a child in need.

Continue to explore the koans in your daily life. Whenever you think "I like this," "I don't like this," "I'm busy," and so on, ask a second question: "Who likes this?" "Who is busy?" When you think "I don't like this," "This is boring," or, "This is great," ask a second question: "What is this?"

DEATH SCRIPT

Sometime in the next two weeks, I invite you to prepare a script in which you're guiding yourself through your own death. Imagine that you're on your deathbed, listening to your own voice through headphones. You're guiding yourself through the final hours before you'll be clinically dead.

What do you want to hear, now, and even beyond the time of your clinical death? What can you say that will help you to stay connected with unconditioned awareness? What would be the most helpful thing to hear at that point? Just open yourself up and see what comes to you.

Sketch it out on paper, or record it on a recorder. What would you like to be hearing when you're dying?

For example, I might say something like this to myself: "Hey, Peter. Your death is approaching. You can feel that. You know it. It might be tomorrow, it might be today, it might be happening right now. But you know it's coming. *This* is the time to let go. Try to stay conscious, Peter. This is the time to remember unconditioned awareness. You know, the space where 'nothing' is happening. Nothing is happening right now, Peter. Nothing is happening. Tune into this, Peter. You know it. Nothing is happening. Forget about your body. It doesn't matter what your mind is doing. Just tune in. You know this, Peter. Just listen. Just listen to the silence. [Silence] . . . . Peter, if you can, look at this. *Who's* dying? Where are *you*? Peter, there's no one to die. There's no death. There's only now.

Serenity and "Seeing Through"

In its essential form, nondual practice is the unimpeded and uncontrived expression of a contentless wisdom that instantaneously and effortlessly reveals the free and open nature of all structures of existence. As the Buddha says in the Mahayana teachings:

> *When the universal panorama is clearly seen to manifest without any objective or subjective supports, viewless knowledge awakens spontaneously. Simply by not reviewing any appearing structures, one establishes the true view of what is. This viewless view is what constitutes the Buddha nature and acts dynamically as the mother of wisdom, revealing whatever is simply as what it is—empty of substantial self-existence, unchartable and uncharacterizable, calmly quiet and already blissfully awakened. (Hixon 1993)[1]*

The Buddha is quite clear: The wisdom that awakens us to the true nature of reality has no structure whatsoever. That is why it's also called "the wisdom of no-wisdom" or the "experience of nothingness." It has nothing to do with gaining cognitive insight or seeing things from a different perspective. It is radically uninterpretable—we can't even think about it—which makes it a unique occurrence in the mind-stream of any person.

In Buddhism, the experience of contentless wisdom, or unconditioned awareness, is cultivated through the twofold practice of serenity (*shamatha*) and clear seeing (*vipashyana*). Shamatha means peace, tranquility, or serenity. Vipashyana means penetrating insight, clear seeing, or "seeing through." Just as we can see through a window without becoming preoccupied with the specks of dirt on the glass, we can see through the obstacles to the unconditioned without having to obliterate them. In orthodox Buddhism, serenity is cultivated prior to, and in parallel with, "seeing through." The two practices support each other and ultimately merge in the union of shamatha and vipashyana.

The practices of serenity and insight suggest that we must create the sense of settlement or resting peacefully in our experience before inquiring into what it is that we're experiencing. Without shamatha, we can't have vipashyana, because our thoughts are racing and inquiry would only result in what Eastern traditions call "conceptual proliferation." Once we have rested, then we can invite ourselves to inquire—and, of course, this inquiry then leads to more resting because it opens up more space in which to rest. As I mentioned earlier, the two practices complement and ultimately merge with each other.

Nondual work traces the same path as orthodox Buddhism, except that we don't need to segment our practice into two different methods. As with every dimension of the nondual approach to fulfillment, dualistic structures of practice and interpretation tend to be integrated from the outset. During this course, for example, we've consistently worked in a way that bridges the divide between:

- Speech and silence
- Concepts and experience
- Conditioned and unconditioned
- Path and goal
- Action and meditation
- Love and wisdom

Nondual practice similarly integrates serenity and "seeing through" into the one fundamental practice of "having nothing to think about" or, to put it slightly differently, "thinking about nothing."

SERENITY: THINNING OUT OUR THOUGHTS

Many psychospiritual systems—Buddhist and non-Buddhist—offer practices for calming the mind and producing inner serenity. Some approaches are based on bringing coherence and stability to our thinking by concentrating on a single object, for example, a sound, visual object, or mental image. Other systems focus our attention on raw bodily sensations such as the cycle of our breathing. Though the techniques differ, they're all designed to reduce the density and turbulence of our thoughts.

Pushing the practice of serenity to the extreme, some systems of meditation reason that if our confusion and inner disturbance can be reduced by thinking less, then it's best to stop thinking altogether. Some spiritual teachers talk about the need to find the gap between our thoughts. Others exhort meditators to try to bring about a complete cessation of all thought. Such thought-stopping might be possible, but it takes a tremendous amount of discipline and effort. To be successful at it, one needs to be a "career yogi." Besides, from the nondual point of view, thought-stopping is completely unnecessary because the experience of "seeing through" allows thoughts and feelings to be present without disturbing our experience of the unconditioned. When we're resting in unconditioned awareness, our thoughts, no matter how light or dense, are incapable of giving rise to negative emotions.

In practice, however, "seeing through" our fixations can be difficult if our energy is tied up in struggling to escape from the burden of boring or uncomfortable thoughts. For this reason, the time-honored wisdom of Asia's contemplative traditions teaches that initial access to unconditioned awareness can be greatly enhanced by slowing down our thinking so that we feel peaceful and serene. In nondual work, if our thoughts are racing or disturbed, a crucial step is to slow down and discover a place where there is more composure and less urgency. We don't need to eliminate thoughts completely; we just need to arrive at the point where thoughts can float through awareness without producing any disturbance.

The reason we feel burdened by repetitive, negative thoughts and believe we need to stop our thinking in order to be free is that we identify with the structure and content of our thoughts. In other words, we forget that thoughts are just thoughts, and believe instead that they're an accurate representation of reality that we need to pay attention to. When the same heavy thoughts begin to recycle, we crave for a break from our obsessive mind. Sleep becomes a better alternative than being awake.

The essence of serenity practice is to slow down our thinking and reduce the density of our thoughts. "Thinning out our thoughts" is the term I use to describe the process of slowing down the thinking process so conceptualization occurs less frequently and becomes less important. Thinning out our thoughts produces an experience of inner peace, within which unconditioned awareness can more easily be recognized. Traditional teachings use the metaphor of clouds and the sun: The clouds don't have to disappear in order for us to see the sun, but they do need to thin out a little.

NOTHING TO THINK ABOUT

In nondual work, thinning out our thoughts generally occurs in two stages. First, thoughts can be thinned out by not feeding the interpretative process, not digging for problems, not offering ourselves anything additional to think about. We remain present to our experience while gradually reducing the ideas, concepts, and judgments we layer on top of our experience. We may find it challenging to stay awake and aware when we have little or no cognitive stimulation to entertain us. But just as fasting can be easier if we gradually eat less and less over a period of time, thinning out our thoughts by reducing conceptual input can gradually prepare our minds for thinking about nothing. There is no need to eliminate thoughts completely and no need to understand what is happening in the present moment. We reduce the burden of thought by learning how to be complete in the here and now, and also by increasing our capacity to work, relate, and live our life effectively, without needing to process everything as much as we do.

"SEEING THROUGH": THINKING ABOUT NOTHING

In stage two, when our thoughts have slowed down somewhat, we can move our thinking into an inquiry into the nature of unconditioned awareness. When we try to think about nothing—not an idea we have about nothing but absolute nothing itself—we can quickly enter into the experience of the unconditioned. When we think about nothing, we have fewer and fewer thoughts, because our thoughts have no content to attach to and so our capacity for conceptual elaboration is seriously undermined. This is the point where the cultivation of serenity transforms into the practice of "seeing through." The practice of not giving ourselves (or someone else) anything to think about reduces the topics we can use to stimulate our minds. The practice of "thinking about nothing" becomes untenable—in fact, impossible—because it doesn't provide a basis for our conceptualization. We have nothing to think about. Of course, we can think about nothing as a concept. People have written books about "nothing." But that's not what we mean. When we think about nothing, we aren't thinking about anything.

The practice of serenity—which may take the form of contemplation in which there is no object of reflection or contemplation, and no theme or issue in our life that we need to explore—begins by giving us less to think about. As this practice evolves, we have less and less that we *need* to think about, until finally there is nothing to think about. At this point, the practice converts into an inquiry into nothing. We might ask, "What is *this* state that has no structure? Is it a state at all?"

At a certain point, "having nothing to think about" is the same as "thinking about nothing," which is the practice of seeing through all presenting structures (vipashyana). In turn, "thinking about nothing" becomes untenable because there's no foundation for our thoughts, and this naturally slows our thinking down even further. This, in turn, gives us less thought material with which to identify, which deepens our ability to see through conceptual structures. In this way, serenity and seeing through empower each other.

There are many ways in which we can invite another person to think about nothing. If they're relatively open and spacious, we might ask, "What would you say is happening right now?" They may recognize that there isn't much structure or content to hang on to; they can't identify or conceptualize what's occurring. Then, at some point, they will begin to relate directly to nothing, the experience that has no content, which reveals unconditioned awareness. The following dialogue will give you some idea about how this might unfold:

Peter: I'm wondering what this is?
Beth: Well, we're sitting quietly, talking.
Peter: Yes, but I'm wondering what "this" is?
Beth: What?
Peter: This. What's happening now.
Beth: I don't know what you're talking about.
Peter: I'm not sure I can describe it. I'm talking about this.
Beth: You mean this moment?

Peter:	Perhaps. I'm not sure I can even say if it's this moment, because . . . well, it's not this moment in contrast to another one.
Beth:	It's this . . . right?
Peter:	Yes.
Beth:	This—right now?
Peter:	Are we talking about the same thing or not?
Beth:	I don't know. What are you talking about?
Peter:	This. I can't say anything more than that.
Beth:	It's not anything, is it?
Peter:	It's certainly not a thing—not a thought or sensation.
Beth:	I know what you're talking about.
Peter:	You do, do you?
Beth:	Yes, it's this. I've got it. There's nothing more to say, is there?

EXPERIENCING "NOTHING"

By simply being for an extended period of time with nothing to think about or know, we automatically invite ourselves to rest in unconditioned awareness. The lack of stimuli or positive and negative feedback sets up a creative ambiguity designed to free up fixed ways of thinking. Ambiguity naturally gives rise to questions that tend to deconstruct or dissolve fixations.

En route to experiencing contentlessness, we may find ourselves thinking, "This is strange. I don't know what's going on. I'm not sure what I'm saying or thinking or what I know or believe any more." As we move from the known to the unknown, our experience can be quite ill-defined. We aren't sure how to interpret what's happening around us, and our experience of ourselves keeps changing—to the point where we may not know who we are. The habitual story we have about ourselves doesn't seem to apply.

In fact, the experience of not knowing who we really are can become routine. Through this work, we become familiar with experiencing ourselves as someone whose existence is being continuously and freshly revealed as aspects of our conditioning, and as the primordial and constant dimension of unconditioned awareness. The unconditioned provides a clear and open space within which we can evolve in an unimpeded way. In this process, we continually encounter ourselves as a stranger—as someone we've never met before. When we're experiencing nondual awareness, our belief system no longer limits the boundaries of our identity. Even during the intervals between our experiences of unconditioned awareness, our belief system becomes more relaxed.

Rather than pushing the panic button when we fail to understand why something is happening or how we can control it, we can just see it for what it is, without needing to know. Contentlessness is revealed to be a completely valid experience in which we remain fully functional and effective, and our thoughts and behavior are clear, coherent, and precise.

In this state, there is no need to know, and also no object of knowing. When we ask "What is this?" there is no "this"—there isn't anything—which is why it is sometimes termed "no thing" or "nothing." We can't know because there's nothing to know. That is, what there is to know is nothing, and what we know is nothing.

Of course, this doesn't mean that we suddenly forget everything we do know in a bout of temporary amnesia. Knowing nothing in no way interferes with the things we need to know in order to function in the world—our name, our social security number, the knowledge required for doing our work or relating to our family and friends. We're simultaneously present to everything we know and present to the fact that there's nothing that can be really known. Knowing and not knowing are not inconsistent. It is the simultaneous arising of form and no form.

MOVING TO A METAPOSITION

Clear seeing, or "seeing through," can happen in stages. One of the simplest ways to see through a problem is to disidentify from it. This approach doesn't completely deconstruct the problem, but it does release us from the grip of our reactions by creating distance and detachment. Although we don't move completely through the structure of our stories and interpretations, we do move to a metaposition where we stand outside them and see them for what they are, rather than being caught up inside them. In other words, we shift our perspective and see what we're doing from a more spacious and detached point of view. Some people call this "going meta."

One way to produce the shift to a metaperspective is to ask the question "What am I doing right now?" There's nothing particularly spectacular about this technique. We catch ourselves doing it all the time in ordinary life.

Perhaps we've been caught up in some painful story, defending our position or worrying about what might happen or what someone might be thinking about us, and suddenly we see that it doesn't really matter. In that moment, we move to a metaposition. When we move to a metaposition, we *see* what we're doing, in contrast to just *doing* it, which produces immediate detachment and peace.

Being able to apply just a handful of different labels helps us to create some distance from our problems. By simply recognizing that we're complaining, blaming, justifying, enduring, commiserating, explaining, seeking sympathy, and so on, we can de-energize and begin to disidentify from our reactive constructions.

From the viewpoint of nondual practice, what's most significant about a problem is its presence, rather than the particular details. We're always generating problems, which we construct from a never-ending set of circumstances, memories, and interactions. What's significant is not the content of the particular problems, but the simple fact that we keep using our minds, our emotions, and the energy available to us to construct problems at all. By constructing problems, I mean that we construe that something is happening that shouldn't be, or that something should be happening that isn't.

CHAPTER ELEVEN EXERCISES

BALANCING SERENITY AND "SEEING THROUGH"

In order to move toward resting in unconditioned awareness, we need to balance the experiences of serenity and "seeing through." If there's too much serenity and insufficient penetrating insight, or "seeing through," we may sink into feelings of comfort and tranquility that leave us with little motivation to move through to unconditioned awareness. In other words, we may confuse relative feelings of peace with unconditioned awareness, which goes beyond relative stillness or movement.

If there's too much critical insight and insufficient serenity, we may become overly concerned with the acuity of our perceptions, and attached to the releases that happen when we see things from a metaperspective or cut through a fixation with our deconstructive skills. In these situations, we can become overly excited about what we're seeing in ourselves and others.

I invite you to consider your own tendencies and assess your particular ratio of serenity to critical insight. You can do this when you're "just sitting" or when you're involved in a nondual teaching. If you're heavy on the insight, you can work to slow down your thinking so that you're less prone to identify with your thoughts. If you're heavy on tranquility, you can work with inquiry to directly enter a space that transcends any attachment to feelings and sensations.

SHIFTING TO A METAPOSITION BY OBSERVING PATTERNS

In this chapter, I spoke about shifting to a metaposition by seeing what we're doing as we're doing it. Recognizing just a few patterns, such as complaining, blaming, justifying, enduring, commiserating, explaining, and seeking sympathy, can help create distance and less identification with the problems that preoccupy us. When we observe a pattern, we free up the energy that's involved in its deployment. All we have to do is pause in the moment that we sense the presence of one of these patterns, and ask ourselves, "What am I doing?"

These patterns are predispositions to think, perceive, communicate, and act in ways that constrain and limit our experience of reality. By imposing an impression or structure on our thoughts, perceptions, and behavior, they shape and define our way of being in the world.

From an ultimate point of view, patterns are neither positive nor negative. They are simply the structures that define who we are as conditioned individuals. However, to the extent that we believe we must alter our thinking and behavior in order to rest in unconditioned awareness, we can observe patterns in terms of how they disconnect us from a more spacious and spontaneous way of being in the world. From this perspective, patterns can contract our capacity to be open and aware.

SHIFTING TO A METAPOSITION

In this paired exercise, you take turns being the speaker and the listener. Invite your partner to begin speaking about a current challenge or concern. As you listen to your partner speak, stop them every once in a while, and ask them, "What are you doing right now?" You can refer to the section that identifies common patterns and fixations, or just have a simple list on hand like this:

blaming, complaining, justifying, explaining, denying, resisting, avoiding, rationalizing, judging, defending

See if you can help your partner to disidentify with the pattern they are involved in, by inviting them to observe it without judgment, as though they were an external observer.

CHAPTER TWELVE

Deconstructive Conversations

Reality is not as it seems. Nor is it different.
LANKAVATARA SUTRA[1]

Nothing happens and we report it.
THE DOT (BUDDHIST MAGAZINE)[2]

The Buddha asked, "Manjushri, what should one rely upon for right practice?" "He who practices rightly relies upon nothing." The Buddha asked, "Does he not practice according to the path?" "If he practices in accordance with anything, his practice will be conditioned. A conditioned practice is not one of equality. Why? Because it is not exempt from arising, abiding, and perishing."
DEMONSTRATION OF BUDDHAHOOD SUTRA[3]

I n this chapter, I will introduce you to a comprehensive range of deconstructive techniques drawn from the major nondual traditions. Generally, these conversations are used by nondual teachers and therapists to introduce students and clients to unconditioned awareness. But you don't have to be a teacher or therapist to benefit from them; they can also be adapted for individual use or applied in relationships with spiritual friends.

In nondual practice, different deconstructive conversations can merge and blend into each other. If we don't gain traction with one conversation, we can seamlessly convert to another approach. Of course, the range of conversations can seem daunting, but don't worry. At this point, it's sufficient just to know that there are many types of conversations that can fully dismantle our own and other people's fixations. If three or four of them strike a chord with you, you may wish to practice and refine them. If you're a therapist, you can use them with some of your clients. If you're a member of a nondual spiritual community, you may find opportunities to explore them in group discussions or casual conversations. And if opportunities don't yet exist, perhaps you can create some.

In Chapter Nine, we showed you how to recognize and use natural koans, and how to use silence in the service of deconstructing fixations. In Chapter Eleven, we described thinking and talking about nothing, and introduced the idea of partially dissolving our fixations by moving to a metaposition.

In this chapter, we'll complete our presentation by briefly describing how to:

- Make impossible requests
- Ask for demonstrations of phenomena that don't exist or can't occur
- Inquire into the unreality of interpretations
- Use checking questions to determine the depth of someone's experience of unconditioned awareness
- Dance in the paradoxes of nondual experience

IMPOSSIBLE REQUESTS

One important way to ease someone's mind from being exclusively identified with the conditioned dimension of experience is to ask them to fulfill an impossible request. Masters in nondual traditions such as Zen, Dzogchen, Mahamudra, and Advaita have asked their students to respond to impossible requests for millennia. For example, Zen teachers sometimes say to their students, "Show me your mind." A standard method in the Mahamudra form of "seeing through" or vipashyana practice is to ask, "Does your mind have a color or a form? Is your mind inside or outside your body? Where is it?"

On careful inspection, such requests can't be fulfilled; questions about the location and structure of the mind can't be answered. For example, when someone says they're disconnected from the here and now, a teacher may say, "Show me how you can be somewhere other than in this moment." When someone says they're attached to what's happening, the therapist can ask them to show how they hold on to this experience. If someone is forever planning what they're going to do tomorrow, next month, or next year, their teacher can ask them to show how they can change the future. "How do you actually do that? How do you get hold of the future and change it?"

ASKING FOR A DEMONSTRATION

"Asking for a demonstration" is closely related to "making an impossible request." In fact, the two often amount to the same thing. In requesting a demonstration, we ask someone to show us, in the present moment, what it is they say is happening. For example, if someone says they are living in the past, we can ask them to show us how they can actually be in the past (or the future). If someone says, "I'm attached to my thoughts," we can respond by saying, "Can you show me *how* that's happening? Can you give me a demonstration? Can you become attached to and then detach from a thought so we can see the difference?" We can also ask ourselves the very same questions.

When we look with clarity and penetration, we find that something we thought was happening isn't happening at all. "How can we be attached to an experience? What does that mean, exactly? How can we be attached to this moment? How can that happen? Where is this thing called attachment?" The more we try to grasp the phenomena we're describing, the more they slip through our fingers. In the end, we discover that there is *no one* attached to *any thing*. What we call attachment or fixation is simply repetitive thinking. If we're recycling the same thought, we say that we're attached to it, but there's no such thing as attachment per se: it is merely the same thought process being repeated. The feeling that we're attached occurs because we can't prevent some thoughts or images from appearing again and again. Attachment and fixation are conceptual overlays to describe the experience of repetitive thinking.

In the space of nondual awareness, attachment and fixation don't exist. We observe our thoughts coming and going, changing or staying the same. But it doesn't make any difference, since nothing needs to be different.

INQUIRING INTO THE UNREALITY OF AN INTERPRETATION: UNFINDABILITY CONVERSATIONS

Normally, when we listen to people talking, we assume that there's some truth or reality to what they're saying — or at least that what they're saying could be true or false. In ordinary conversation, there's a strong consensual pressure to listen in this way. When we don't understand what people are saying, we still assume it's meaningful, and we typically try to work out what they mean by inviting them to say more.

When we listen to a story, whether our own or someone else's, with unconditioned awareness, we don't take what's being described as true. What seems to be happening may *not* be happening. For example, we no longer assume that people's problems and difficulties are real or fictitious. This innocence and freshness opens up the possibility of engaging with our own and other people's constructions from the viewpoint of "beginner's mind."

From the nondual viewpoint, meaning is not intrinsic; it's a human construction. We may join people in their constructions, agreeing or disagreeing, but we're not compelled to do so. We can listen in such a way that we understand that what they're saying is meaningful to them, but we don't find any meaning there. This is pure listening. Out of this pure listening, or listening from no reference point, comes pure speaking.

How does the experience of unconditioned awareness guide the deconstruction of our constructions? Let's look at the statement "I think I'll be happy when I find someone who loves me."

Usually when someone says something like this, we assume that it's meaningful, even if we disagree with it. We think we know what thinking and love are and what it is to be happy. However, when we listen to this statement from unconditioned awareness, we find that we don't take the meaning for granted. At one level, we can identify with the person's longing and aspiration by considering our own histories and memories. At another level, we can't find any reference to the terms they're using; they have no intrinsic meaning for us.

The way to inquire into the reality of an emotional construct is to first identify the core concepts upon which it is built. Then we can inquire into the reality behind the concepts and dissolve the painful feelings associated with fixed ways of thinking. Suffering dissolves when it's examined by the mind that rests in the unconditioned. In this way, we can discover the truth taught by the *Heart Sutra*—that there is no suffering, never has been and never will be.

If we hear ourselves or someone else say, "I think I'll be happy when I find someone who loves me," this statement replays like an echo in our mind, and we gently scan the statement for any intrinsic meaning we can unlock. We hear what has been said, but the statement deconstructs because we fail to find anything that our thoughts can lock into. The process works something like this:

STATEMENT	DECONSTRUCTION
"I"	"You? Who are you? I don't know who *you* are. Who am I?"
"think"	"What is thinking?" "Where does that thinking happen?"
"happy"	"What does happiness mean?" "Where is that?"
"find"	"How do you find someone?" "I can't find someone by looking for them because this presupposes I haven't found them. For as long as I'm looking I haven't yet found them. And I can find someone without looking. So how do I find someone?"
"love"	"What is love?"

With this going on in our minds, we might say (or think, if we're working with ourselves), "I hear that you're saying that you'd be happy if someone loved you, and I'm sure that the word 'love' has many associations for you. But what does it refer to? What actually is love?" We can say this in a way that invites them not to elaborate their story, but to join us in an inquiry into the possibility that neither of us knows what love is. Or we may simply say, "I do not know what you're talking about." We communicate this in a way that doesn't imply any deficiency in the person with whom we're talking. We ask these questions because *we* genuinely don't understand what's being said. The other person may think that we should know. However, if their words are deconstructing in our mind, then we actually don't know what they're talking about, even though we understand the language they're using. This inquiry opens us to the possibility of dropping our constructions and resting in the natural silence and serenity of unconditioned awareness.

Like natural koans, deconstructive inquiry should only be used when we sense that the timing is right. We're inviting ourselves and other people to enter the space of wonderment and uncertainty, and experience what it feels like to not take things for granted. For this to occur, there must be a certain readiness and a level of trust in the relationship.

Any interpretation can be deconstructed in this way. The primary limitation is the extent to which we identify with the interpretation in question.

Stories that may be deconstructed include:

- Personal beliefs (for example, "I'm a serious person.")
- Spiritual beliefs (for example, "When X happens, Y happens.")
- Constructions about suffering (for example, that it is bad, that it shouldn't be happening, and that it is happening)
- Constructions about fixations (for example, that we shouldn't have them, and that we're not enlightened until we remove them)
- Stories about enlightenment
- Stories about the deconstructive process

THE ULTIMATE PURIFICATION

Even though it can seem imprudent or even arrogant to question our own or other people's inner experience, especially when they say that they're suffering or in pain, if we're genuinely resting in unconditioned awareness, suffering (our own and others') doesn't exist. Prompted by love and compassion, we may then inquire into the reality of the suffering. For example, we might ask "Where exactly is your suffering?" in a way that allows people to go beyond their assumptions and look into their suffering directly, rather than just tell their story about it. "Is your suffering in the nature of your thoughts? If so, is it the structure of a particular thought, or the way a number of thoughts are put together? Where exactly is the suffering? Is it in the way you're feeling? If so, where is it? Is it in your body? What is that feeling? Is it always associated with suffering? If it isn't, there must be some other factor that's present. What is that other factor?" If we pursue this line of thinking and questioning with rigor and determination, we'll invariably discover that we can't find what we're looking for. If our attachment to our suffering doesn't outweigh the sincerity and rigor of our inquiry, the experience of suffering will invariably dissolve.

Not only does our experience of our suffering in the present dissolve, but we also see that past and future suffering don't really exist either. This experience represents the ultimate form of purification. In Buddhism, it's called the "healing salve of emptiness." When we're resting in unconditioned awareness, we can pass thoughts and memories that are associated with painful (even highly traumatic) experiences through our mind without triggering any contraction or reactivity. This doesn't happen because we've desensitized ourselves or suppressed our feelings or memories. We're fully open, rejecting nothing, available to whatever arises. Yet we see clearly that there's no suffering or absence of suffering, even though the experience we previously called suffering does not go away.

CHECKING QUESTIONS

In nondual practice, it's important to be able to determine the quality and purity of our unconditioned experience. We do this by asking ourselves "checking questions." The experience of natural presence or having no point of reference can be transmitted and realized with varying degrees of purity. The challenge is to transmit the purest experience of nothing, free of conceptual overlays and interpretations, while also recognizing that there is no such thing as a pure experience of nothing, since, as the nondual traditions say, unconditioned awareness is neither pure nor impure.

Checking questions can be directed to ourselves or to others, and are designed to detect any conceptual structures through which the unconditioned is being interpreted and experienced. Even when we have a clean experience of "nothing," if it lacks depth and stability, it's easy for us to begin to create some significance around the experience. One checking question that reveals whether we're resting in a structured or unstructured state is, "Can we enhance *this* experience (the one that's happening right now)?" The answer yes shows that we're in a structured experience—that is, we believe we're experiencing something that can be enhanced and diminished. Once we've discovered this, we can choose to go one step further, into the fully unconditioned state, by seeing that our "metaphysical interpretations of the absolute" are completely unrelated to unconditioned awareness. Or we may be content with a minimal level of conceptual activity and decide to enjoy the feeling of peace and serenity that arises when most of our concepts have dissolved.

Another way to check the purity of an unstructured state is by asking, "Is there anything we need to be doing at this moment?" This will give us direct feedback on where we are in relationship to nondual awareness. If we say yes, then we are still inside the construction that something is missing. If we don't say anything, or say no, then there isn't anything to do, and we can just rest in silence.

If we respond that the experience couldn't be better, we may or may not be holding on to a structure. We could then ask "Can we hold on to this?" If

no response is forthcoming because there is no energy or need to communicate—nothing to say—then we may be resting in unstructured awareness.

Other checking questions include:

- Is anything missing right now?
- Is there anything that we need to be doing at the moment?
- Is there something that we need to be thinking about?
- What would you say I'm doing right now?
- Can this be enhanced?
- What is this that I'm trying to enhance?
- Can we do more of this?
- Could we lose it?
- Is this pleasurable?
- Where are you now?
- Are we making progress?
- Are we going anywhere?
- Is there anywhere to go?

These are the types of questions that naturally arise in the journey from the
conditioned to the unconditioned and can be used to gauge the presence of
conceptual residues.

In asking these checking questions, we need to take care that they do not
provide a trigger for a conceptual construction. Normally, we only ask these
questions when we're in a fairly open and spacious state of being—when we
sense that we've reached a space that transcends loss and gain. If the questions
prompt us to elaborate the space conceptually or increase our uncertainty
about whether we're in an unstructured space, then they have missed their intention. Checking questions often become natural koans because they direct
us back to the experience of unconditioned awareness.

DANCING IN THE PARADOXES OF
NONDUAL EXPERIENCE

In the West, we are in the habit of being quite serious about our psychological and spiritual endeavors, and we feel compelled to communicate without
any hint of inconsistency or inner contradiction. If we say one thing in one

sentence and contradict ourselves in the next, we fear that people will judge us negatively and think we're confused, superficial, irrational, or even a little crazy. We are uncomfortable with paradox. Think about how Zen is often parodied in popular culture. If we say something abstruse or contradictory, people may respond, "Oh, how Zen." Unfortunately, this way of thinking is extremely limited.

In Eastern cultures, sages move fluidly and confidently in the paradoxical domain without any trace of self-consciousness or distress. They know from experience that paradox and contradiction are inevitable when we enter the space of unconditioned awareness, and they welcome paradox because it points to the reality that cannot be captured by our thoughts.

In nondual practice, paradoxes arise within our thought-stream in two ways. First, when we try to describe unconditioned awareness with accuracy and precision, we are often led to use statements that contain internal contradictions. The more rigor and clarity we bring to our descriptions, the more we are compelled to use paradoxical formulations.

Second, when we speak from *within* an experience of unconditioned awareness *about* unconditioned awareness, paradoxes can flow forth as joyful and exuberant expressions of mental energy that is usually trapped by the need to appear sane and sensible. An engagement with these paradoxes and absurdities can produce an explosion of hilarity and laughter that shatters the seriousness with which we usually take ourselves and our practices. They also let us experience unconditioned awareness as a highly discerning and dynamic state of consciousness. If we let go of our need for conceptual consistency, these paradoxical thought-forms can act as a springboard to unconditioned awareness, especially for people who are familiar with the unconditioned.

What are some of the paradoxes that emerge when our thoughts encounter the unstructured expanse of pure awareness? One of the most obvious is that unconditioned awareness is simultaneously something and nothing. It *is* because it *isn't*. And it's the *only* thing that is because it isn't. Everything else is because it is. When we try to think about it, we think it is something, but we can't say what it is. It is something and it is nothing. If you are confused by this, don't worry. It doesn't "make sense." If we think it does, we haven't understood it! At this moment, we're playing in two paradoxes of unconditioned awareness—that it is presenced by its absence and known through being unknown.

Another exquisite paradox is that at the completion of the nondual path, we realize that we haven't traveled any distance — no path has been traversed and we haven't attained "anything." But we also realize that if we hadn't believed that there was a path and made the effort, we wouldn't have arrived at the point where we are right now. Even though we now know that our struggle and commitment are both pointless, in the absence of this effort, we would still be drifting in the illusion that there is actually somewhere to go and something to achieve. Without doing what we didn't need to do, we wouldn't realize that we didn't need to do it.

Some people label this play as a mind game when they become frustrated with their inability to make sense of what's being said. However, if we label this activity as a "mind game," we lose an opportunity to keep the experience of unconditioned awareness alive and vital. As long as we don't overdo this play, it can be a delightful way of experiencing unconditioned awareness manifesting as a dynamic display of thought and interaction.

ARTICULATE CONTRADICTIONS

Dancing and communicating in paradoxes is one of the most difficult aspects of nondual work. Somehow we need to make a leap of faith and be willing to articulately contradict ourselves in an upfront and confident way. If someone says to us that we've just contradicted ourselves, we need to be able to say, "Yes, that's right. I have. Because that is how it is. There's no other way to accurately describe this state."

At a certain point, we betray the experience of the unconditioned if we aren't willing to say that unconditioned awareness is because it isn't; that it's totally unrelated to our conditioned existence but indistinguishable from it; that it can't be lost or gained, yet it repeatedly arises and disappears. India's most celebrated and "rational" philosopher, Nagarjuna, had no problem speaking paradoxically. In a verse of praise at the beginning of his famous text, *The Fundamental Verses of the Middle Way*, he says of the ultimate teaching and the ultimate state:

> *It is unceasing yet unborn, unannihilated yet not permanent, neither coming into or going out [of existence], without distinction, without identity, relatively arisen and free of conceptual constructions.* [4]

When our thoughts are born at the point where the conceptual touches the nonconceptual, we are compelled to use paradox, negation, and absurdity.

DECONSTRUCTIVE CONVERSATION IN ACTION

The following dialogue from one of my workshops integrates a number of the conversations we've been talking about in this and earlier chapters, and shows how we can invite others into an experience of unconditioned awareness. It shows you different ways in which the radiant-mind style of contemplative dialogue opens up into the space of unconditioned awareness or natural meditation.

Anne: I'm a little bored with what's happening right now. I want to get into my fixations and release them. I want to see how I'm fixating, and how to avoid this.

Peter: Can you see that you are fixating right now? You are creating that this isn't it. Actually, you can see from your mood and the way you are holding your body that you are stuck. Given the general mood you are in, whatever you say, it will be an expression of the feeling that this just isn't it.

Anne: Yes. I can see that. I know that I'd like things to be different, but just wanting it to be different isn't changing anything. And you're right. I do feel stuck with this.
[Pause]

Peter: You seem to be wanting me to do something. It also feels as though you want some attention directed specifically toward you, in the hope that something will then shift.

Anne: Well, yes. I do.

Claude: I'd like to ask if . . .

Peter: Please excuse me for interrupting. We will come back to your query. But I'm just wanting to observe, Anne, that you are already poised to interpret whatever Claude is about to say as a "more boring description." At this moment, you are predisposed to interpret whatever you hear as less than relevant. In other words, you are predisposed to create that "this isn't it."

Anne: Hmm, yes. Well, I prefer what you are saying now. This is more like what I've been wanting to hear. I'm finding this useful.

Peter: Perhaps. But now you are starting to move in the opposite direc-
            tion. You're interpreting that this is it, or at least that this is closer
            to how things should be. Your experience is suddenly lighter. You
            don't feel particularly stuck at this point. In fact, in the absence of
            any obstruction, this could evolve into an experience of . . .

Anne: I've got it. I just got it. I've got what this whole process is for.
            [Silence]

Henri: What happened? What did you do?

Anne: Nothing.

Henri: But you must have done something. You seem so certain and
            clear.
            [Silence]

Henri: So what is it?

Anne: I don't know. I can't say what it is. I can't describe it, but I've got it.
            [Silence]

Henri: But if you can't say what it is, how do you know you've got it?

Anne: But I have got it. I know. There's no need to know what it is. I've
            just got it. There isn't anything to know.

Henri: But what about the Zen saying Peter sometimes quotes, "The
            moment you think you've got it, you've lost it."

Anne: You can't take this away from me because, in fact, there isn't any
            it. There's nothing to lose.

Henri: I can see that.

Anne: I'm just thinking, "I could lose this." I'm wondering if there is a
            different experience that is completely invincible.

Peter: Be careful! [Laughing] You can't afford to think like that.

Maurice: My understanding is that enlightenment is permanent.

Peter: You have to be very careful who you listen to right now.

Anne: What do you mean?

Peter: If you take Maurice's suggestion seriously and begin to partici-
            pate in his construction, your present experience will quickly
            dissipate.

Anne: So what should I do? Who should I listen to?

Peter: I'm just pointing out the consequences of the different interpreta-
            tions you could take on board.

Anne: I already feel that something has been taken from me.

Peter: But you say that as though you have no role in it. If we hang on
           to something for long enough, it is bound to shift at some point.
           In fact, the moment we judge that it is valuable, we have already
           distorted the original experience which lay beyond any judgment
           of good or bad, desirable or undesirable. However, it is also very
           easy to become fixated on the idea of observing our fixations. We
           can think there is some intrinsic value in doing this. In fact, if
           we think there is some value in doing it, then we will condition
           ourselves to observe our fixations, even when this is quite un-
           necessary. If we become attached to the notion of observing our
           fixations, or any other type of spiritual process for that matter, we
           condition ourselves to becoming perpetual seekers. This is just to
           say that balance is required when observing our fixations, so we
           don't become self-aware in a neurotic or obsessive way.

Michèle: But it still seems to me that you are saying that this is it, because
           you like it. Before, when you were feeling frustrated and bored,
           you said that that wasn't it, and now you are obviously feeling
           great, so you think, "This is it."

Anne: This has got nothing to do with what I want. In fact, I don't want
           this. It just is.

           [Long silence]

Tanya: It seems to me that what you are offering is a form of mindful-
           ness meditation, but extending that into our interaction with
           other people and the world.

Peter: Perhaps. What do you mean by mindfulness meditation?

Tanya: Staying aware of what we are doing in the moment. Being aware
           of what I'm doing, no matter what it is. If I'm washing my dog,
           being fully aware that I'm washing the dog and not drifting off
           into my thoughts about the past or future.

Peter: What's wrong with that? What's the problem in washing your
           dog and thinking about tomorrow?

Tanya: Well, I'm not being present to what is there. I might get soap in
           my dog's eyes, or more to the point, if I'm driving, I might ram up
           the back side of the car in front.

Peter: Sure, in some situations, like driving, our attention should be on
           the road, which it generally is. But we still don't need to block all
           other thoughts. If this was a condition for safe driving, no one
           would have a license. In fact, if we didn't think about the future,
           there would never be a reason to brake or accelerate.

Tanya: I don't know about that. But I still feel that if I'm washing my
           dog, I should have basically all my attention on what's happening.

Peter: But what if other thoughts are part of what is? Are those thoughts
           about tomorrow or yesterday there in the present when you are
           washing the dog, or are they happening at some other time?

Tanya: Yes, they are there, but they are a distraction from being present
           to what is.

Peter: How is that possible if that's what is there?

Tanya: I see what you are saying. They are there in the present even
           though they might be about the past or future. Still, if I'm think-
           ing about tomorrow, it means that I'm not fully appreciating what
           is immediately present to me.

Peter: That's right. Perhaps you're not attending to the smell of soap
           and fur as you wash your dog. Instead, you're attending to some
           internal imagery and thoughts about a meeting you are having
           tomorrow. You're present to some thoughts about something else
           because those are the thoughts that are there. Specific thoughts
           are there to be thought, so you are thinking them, in the same
           way that there are visual sensations of your hands and dog which
           you are perceiving. Still, I do appreciate what you are saying. It's
           just that we can give ourselves a lot of suffering by struggling to
           do something different from what we are doing. This isn't to say
           that we *should* be doing whatever we are doing in some moralistic
           or fatalistic sense. Rather, it is simply recognizing that presence
           includes being present to thoughts, feelings, etc., that we would
           prefer not to be there. Yet, interestingly, if we are also open and
           honest about the fact that we have preferences, the same thoughts
           and feelings can be there in a totally transparent and uneventful
           way. Often we disguise our preferences by clothing them in righ-
           teous beliefs about what we should be experiencing.

[Silence]

Peter: Are you being mindful right now?

Tanya: Yes.

Peter: Show me how you could become unaware, or, let's say, just *less* mindful.

Tanya: Well, I could start to free associate. I could just let my thoughts drift off somewhere else. I could think about dinner in a few hours.

Peter: Can I see you do that?

[Silence]

Tanya: I can't do that right now.

Peter: Why?

Tanya: Because you're talking to me. It's just not happening.

Peter: Well, I'll stop talking a bit, and let you do that.

[Silence]

Peter: You don't seem to be drifting off to me. You seem to be very much here in the workshop setting and in relationship with me.

Tanya: I'm not sure. I am thinking about what we have been talking about.

Peter: So what do you think? Should you be thinking about what we have been talking about, or should you be thinking about something else?

Tanya: I don't know. I guess it's okay to be thinking about what we are doing.

Peter: Is there something else that it would be better to be thinking about?

Tanya: I don't know. I don't think so.

Peter: Is it fine to be thinking that thought?

Tanya: Yes.

Peter: Do you think you should be sitting here?

Tanya: I suppose so. Sure.

Peter: Do you think you should be somewhere else?

Tanya: Well, I can think I should be somewhere else.

Peter: Yes. And is it okay to think that thought?

Tanya: Sure.

Peter: Would you say you are drifting off now, on some unrelated stream of thoughts?

Tanya: No.

Peter: Are you trying to control what you are thinking?

Tanya:	No.
Peter:	Is this mindfulness?
Tanya:	No. At least not as I was describing it before.
Peter:	Is this being mindless—unaware of what is happening?
Tanya:	No. Certainly not.
Sue:	Where is this taking us?
Peter:	Wherever we go.
Charles:	It's taking us to where we are.
Peter:	Where are we?
Charles:	Here.
Peter:	Where were you before you were here?
Charles:	Here, but we might not have known we were here.
Peter:	If you didn't *know* you were here, how do you say you were here?
Charles:	I don't know.
	[Silence]
James:	This seems somewhat nihilistic to me.
Peter:	Is something happening?
James:	Of course. This is happening.
Peter:	So how is this nihilistic? Is anything disappearing out of your experience?
James:	You seem to be suggesting that we should be just doing whatever we are doing. What about choice?
Peter:	Is this in any way stopping or suppressing anything happening? Is anything stopping you from getting up and stretching your legs or having a drink?
James:	Well, only that we are in a conversation.
Peter:	The way to check out if this space is restricting your freedom is to see what's happening now. For example, is there anything stopping us from taking a break right now?
James:	No, there isn't.
Peter:	Would you like to take a break?
James:	Sure.
Peter:	How about others? Would you like to take a break now?
Others:	Yes.
Peter:	Well, let's do that.

CHAPTER TWELVE EXERCISES

IS THAT HAPPENING NOW?

This exercise is designed to help you work in the here and now. It is performed in pairs. There are two roles: a speaker and responder. Explore both roles.

INSTRUCTION

The speaker is invited to present a problem of the type that one might present to a friend, partner, or therapist. The role of the responder is to help the speaker distinguish between the problem that's occurring as a story about the past or future, and the problem as it manifests in the here and now.

RESPONDER'S ROLE

The responder listens to the problem and then asks their partner, "Is that happening now?"

If the speaker answers "No," then ask, "Then what is happening now?"

If the speaker answers "Yes," then ask, "Tell me what is happening in this moment," or "How are you experiencing the problem right now?"

Keep asking and listening until the speaker's sense of the problem dissolves.

SHOW ME NOTHING?

Here is a final exercise to play with, either in your imagination or with a friend. Zen students in the Rinzai tradition are often given the koan "Mu" as their first insight puzzle. "Mu" means "nothing." The challenge for the student is to show the master "nothing." How would you show someone nothing, without giving them the idea that nothing means that something is absent or missing?

CHAPTER THIRTEEN

Some Final Lift-Off Points

Without developing the consummate contemplative art of the
bodhisattva — skillful nonchalance and ceaseless concern —
no aspirant can remain authentically and passionately
dedicated to the boundless task of universal awakening. The
perfection of wisdom alone can keep selflessness and love pure
and steady under all conditions. Such is the realization of
perfect wisdom through the entire body, speech, and mind
of the bodhisattva, who is free from controlling, battling,
repressing, or extinguishing any form of manifestation.

BUDDHA [1]

We've covered a lot of territory in this book — from basic but important communication skills, to subtle and sophisticated methods for entering and sustaining the experience of radiant mind. I hope this book serves you as a resource that you can turn to again and again.

I'm sure you've connected or reconnected many times with the core state of unconditioned awareness in reading this book, and certainly while doing the exercises. I'm sure you know firsthand what it's like to be resting in the state where absolutely nothing is missing.

I sense that you can easily enter this state at the moment, especially as we come to the end of this book! You know, it's interesting. I've been running workshops and retreats for a long time and noticing that as an event progresses, people loosen up and find it easier to complete. At the beginning of an event, we think there's something to do. During the event, we feel that we're on the path, increasing our knowledge and refining our practice. And then toward the end, it comes to fruition.

You might think, well, yes, of course people feel more spacious and complete at the end. That's because of the work they've done during the workshop or retreat: getting mellow, seeing through the experiencer, and so on. But it still surprises me, because I know it's possible to begin at the end. It's foolish to think that this isn't even possible, because this just adds to our work and prolongs our path. Often, I think it's just a question of permission. We don't let ourselves enter the ultimate state until we've done a certain amount of work. We forget that we enter it by doing nothing—yes, the special nothing that's *not* nothing!

That's why I often begin my courses by saying, "Let's just start at the end. Let's just go straight there. If we can, it's great. If we can short-circuit the path and "be complete," that's wonderful. Then we get to spend more time together dancing and sharing in unconditioned awareness. If we can't, it's not a problem. We'll make up some stuff and fill in the time until we are ready to let go into "pure being." More and more, people can do this. People can drop the reasons that have brought them to participate in a course or retreat, and begin to rest in unconditioned awareness within minutes of the start of a retreat.

Anyway, that's why I'm confident. If you've come this far with me, it's easy, at this point, to breathe, to let go, to say, "Wow, yes, I get it. I really do. It's so simple. I'm there, or here, or nowhere—wherever it is. This—that thing, this experience, whatever it is—that's happening right now. I don't know where it is. I don't know what it is. I don't know who's experiencing it. But it's great." Or, as the Tibetans say, "Emaho!"

Why am I saying this? Because there might be a lesson in this. Right now we can see that there's nothing we need to do to rest in unconditioned awareness. Resting in this state has nothing to do with what we've done. This is why it's sometimes described as being acausal—without a cause—or unproduced. It's nothing, so it can't be a product of anything. Unconditioned awareness is completely unrelated to this book. This book is a collection of words on paper, written in English. It's a completely conditioned thing that will disintegrate in a few decades. So it has nothing to do with timeless, ahistorical, transplanetary buddha-mind.

Yet, it's also possible that your experience of unconditioned awareness has been supported by this book. It's paradoxical and there's no way or need to resolve the paradox. It's quite possible that if your weren't reading what you're reading right now, you'd be in a different state of awareness. You might be watching TV, catching up on some email, on the phone with your children or parents, or just dozing.

I wrote this book to keep you connected with the possibility that you don't have to do anything to be complete, to show you that you are complete — beyond complete. You're so complete it doesn't mean anything to say you're complete. This book is a paradox. It was an excuse — a reason — for you to give attention to the unconditioned and explore the connection between radiant mind and your life. I'm sure you also know that it has nothing to do with unconditioned awareness.

Right now we're talking about your state of consciousness — the unconditioned dimension of your being, not what you're reading on this page. But it is a paradox. Your state of consciousness at the unconditioned level has nothing to do with what you're reading now, yet it's supported in some way by what I'm writing. Whatever you need to understand in terms of understanding the words and sentences, it's happening, effortlessly. This is also effortless because there's nothing to understand. There are no secrets; there's no hidden or deeper meaning. There's nothing more, and nothing less, than what's happening in this moment. That's wonderful, because then there's nothing to strive for.

Even though you're reading and taking this in, you're complete. You don't *need* to be reading this. We're not going anywhere. There's nowhere to go, there's just this moment, and even this moment doesn't exist. We can't hold on to it and we can't push it away.

Our natural state — buddha-mind, unconditioned awareness — is with us right now: the experience of being exactly who we are and no one at the same time; the co-emergence of the thoughts, feelings, and perceptions; and the simultaneous presence of the infinite stream of timeless, content-less awareness.

Right now I also know that you know that we can't lose the experience of unconditioned awareness, because there's nothing to lose. The environment will change as we move around, our bodies will get older, and our feelings and thoughts will constantly transform, but unconditioned awareness neither comes nor goes. Unconditioned awareness has never started, it will never stop, and it actually never remains, because it's not that type of thing. You know that when we're in this state, we can't lose it, because there's nothing to lose and no one to lose it.

BUT WHAT CAN I DO WHEN I LOSE IT?

The best thing to do, of course, is to not think about losing this. We will lose it—that's nearly certain—but it's best to not think about it, because a common way of losing our connection with the unconditioned is to get caught in a stream of "concerned conceptualization." I see this happen frequently. We think, "But it's not going to last." And that's often the beginning of a cycle of thinking in which we ponder why we lose it and what we'll do when that happens. But we don't need to lose the experience when this happens. You can practice this now. Think, "This won't last. This won't last." See, right now it doesn't make any difference. It's just a thought, and we can't lose unconditioned mind, because it has no location, it can't go anywhere, and it can't get lost. How do you hide "nothing"?

So, it's a little bit tricky for me at this point. Half of me knows that the *only* thing to do is to be here, neither adding to, nor taking anything away from, this moment. We can't conclude this. There's no conclusion. This doesn't stop and it doesn't continue. That's it. The other half of me leans into the future, anticipating that you'll lose this. I know *I* do. Actually, I'm split three ways because one third of me would like to stay with you forever, reminding us both that "there's nothing to gain and nothing to lose."

Well, it looks like I'm continuing in the second direction, so you need to know that what I'm about to do could be regressive. Whether it is or not depends partially on you. I'm about to buy into the idea that we can lose our connection with radiant mind. It's quite possible you might want to stop at this point, not out of fear of losing anything, but simply because there's no need to continue. Of course, there's no need to stop either. If you're resting in radiant mind, nothing can take this from you, because you're not resting in anything, so, whew, we're still on safe ground!

The reality is that, unless you're extremely unique, at some point quite soon, you're going to feel that you've lost the experience of unconditioned awareness. It doesn't take much. You'll finish this book, put it down, sit for a few moments, stand up, go to your computer, pick up the telephone, walk into your children's room . . . and buddha-mind is history!

You won't even know this has happened. Then, perhaps after a couple of hours, or later in the night when it's quiet and the day has settled down, you might think, "Oh wow, unconditioned awareness. That was good. Where is it? How do I get back there? What can I do when I've lost my connection with buddha-mind?"

Time and again, we seem to fall out of it, back into our regular way of being in which we like and don't like what's happening to us. Even though we know how to drink from the river of nonduality, we somehow become reidentified with our conditioned experience as though this is all that's happening.

I'd like to conclude this book by giving you a few final lift-off points for reentering unconditioned awareness when it seems to have gone missing. I want to trace, in just a few pages, the most important trajectories for reengaging radiant mind. I want to show you how to work with real-life situations in ways that can create an opening into radiant mind.

THERE'S NOTHING TO RECOVER

Not surprisingly, we begin at the end! We begin right here at the level of no-practice because this is the easiest point to reenter unconditioned awareness. If we can reenter the state, when we think we've lost it, by realizing that we can't get it or lose it, that's wonderful. If we realize that there's nothing to lose, it puts us straight back into the state where there's nothing to get and nothing to lose. If this insight doesn't come by itself, it's possible that picking up a book like this one and reading a few lines that are written from the "result level" can be enough to help you reenter the state you never lost.

I find the writings of Dzogchen masters such as Longchenpa to be very helpful. Reading the Asian nondual masters is also humbling, because it reveals how my own experience of unconditioned awareness is extremely limited compared with theirs. My own capacity to work with unconditioned awareness is very dependent on ambient conditions: my material and emotional needs and preferences need to be fulfilled.

From their writings and biographies, it's clear that Longchenpa and thousands of other Tibetan masters lived their lives in a supersaturated state of dynamic bliss-consciousness, with none of the artifacts and comforts that we take for granted on our spiritual paths: conditions such as heating in winter, air-conditioning in summer, good food, and even orthopedically designed zufus.

If you're using this book as a resource, and you're only lightly identified with your conditioned experience, I'd revisit the sections in Chapters Five and Six that present some of the keys for entering radiant mind. You might ask yourself, "Who is it that thinks they've lost something?" or "What is it that I think I've lost?" Often these keys are sufficient to unlock the door that wasn't even closed.

But sometimes these keys just don't work. We get taken over by the dramas of our life and forget these simple keys. This is normal. And even if we do remember them, we can't use them. We put them in the lock—we think the thought "Who is suffering?" or "What is this?"—but nothing happens! The keys don't work. They don't dig in deep enough.

So what can we do when this happens? We go backward until we find something to do—or not do—that gives us some traction.

WHEN THINGS ARE VERY INTENSE

If we find ourselves in the middle of an intense emotional experience, or a crisis, it's difficult, often impossible, to find the bliss of radiant mind. So what to do? We can begin by opening up. We can open our heart and broaden our mind to accommodate our disturbance and distress. Even when we're in a really hostile situation, or feeling very frightened about losing something that's precious to us, we can open up. You can even lie on your back and open your heart to your pain. You might even imagine you're pulling your chest open and exposing your heart to your experience.

You can think, "I don't know what's going on here. I don't understand why this is happening. This is excruciating. But I will let this happen to me, through me. I don't know if I can survive this, but this is my work at the moment. Just to be with what's happening. This is my path. I don't understand the 'work' that's happening within me, but experiencing this anxiety, this fear, this profound disappointment, this loss or grief, is part of my transformation. I'm in the middle of some profound work that's necessary for my maturation and evolution. I'm in training. I don't exactly know how this works but this is working deep inside me. At the very least, this is helping me release my attachment and aversion. Even if I can't stop resisting this transformation, still this is important work I'm doing."

Spiritual surgery can be intense. And unlike physical surgery, it can never be numbed with painkillers. In order to do its work, spiritual surgery has to be experienced, even if it feels like having an open-heart operation without an anesthetic.

THE SUPPORT OF SPIRITUAL FRIENDS

Spiritual friends can be a precious resource when we're struggling to cope. Giving and receiving support from *dharma* sisters and brothers is what a spiritual community, a sangha, is about. It's beautiful if we feel free enough to ask for support in a very simple way. All that's needed is a simple email or telephone call: "I'm really struggling. You don't need to do anything. You don't need to say anything. Just be here with me for a while."

All we're asking for is someone to be with us, in our pain, with an open heart and without judgment. Some people call this "bearing witness." I see it as "pure listening." In a sangha, everyone supports each other: we learn how to ask for support and how to make ourselves available to others. We're willing and able to offer our love (our ability to connect without judgment) while staying connected with a space that's more open and less personal.

In its purest expression, we enter totally into another's experience, and let the pain instantly and continually self-liberate us in our nondual awareness. This doesn't necessarily mean that our friend's or partner's or relative's pain liberates. It means that we're there in total support of our companion in a way that we allow each moment to liberate into the next.

It's not exactly the same as the wonderful Tibetan *tonglen* practice of "taking over and giving." In that practice, we lift the pain of another and take it into our own body-mind and liberate it within us. When we are "purely present" for someone else, we also connect with boundarilessness—the state in which there is no you and me; there is only pure awareness within which we are connected to the totality of our experience, which can include an experience of intense pain. In this sense, our companion contributes their suffering and we contribute our nondual presence, and together we liberate the pain in the infinite expanse of unconditioned awareness.

The results of this type of sharing can be quite miraculous. It's possible to journey through an emotionally intense episode in just a few minutes and to transform emotional and even physical agony into an experience of intense bliss. The fact that we can do this, even just once, shows us that it's possible. And once we've experienced this firsthand, we know we can do it again.

When we open to an experience, it doesn't mean that we roll over like a dead dog. It's not the same as "giving in." Sometimes we can be with our pain in privacy. At other times, it means that we will continue to act, see people, and take care of our concerns, at the same time that we're terrified and screaming out to God, our guru, or the universe for help!

Sometimes we can see the source of our suffering. "I know I'm holding on to something (my reputation, my money) or someone (my lover, my children, my mother, myself). I can't let go, I just can't, but still I can see this is helping me, this is forcing me to let go, which is good."

Other times, we can't identify the source of our suffering. We don't know what's behind it. We might be experiencing "temporary insanity": the experience of going crazy, of losing all our reference points and fearing that we'll never get back to safe territory. Or we might be feeling really frightened or anxious but not know what's behind the feeling. Here, too, we can open up. We open up into "not knowing."

"Just sitting" can be a tremendous resource when our emotions are intense and agonizing. If we don't need to act, we can "just sit." And if it helps to pray, say mantras, breathe in white light, we can do that. We do whatever we need to do; we use our resources to help us accept and integrate our pain and distress. If we're working with anger, we let it well up inside us. We stay with the feeling that we could lash out and hurt someone; we acknowledge our rage and destructive capacity, and accept that we really don't know ourselves and our limits.

When we open up to "not knowing," sometimes something very remarkable can happen. We open into "not knowing" at the relative level, not knowing if we're really going to die from cancer, not knowing if we can control our anger, and this transforms into "not knowing" at the unconditioned or ultimate level. We're in the middle of a crisis and suddenly we're complete. "Not knowing" at the relative level becomes so thorough and comprehensive that it becomes the pure not-knowing, or the knowing of nothing, the state of unconditioned awareness. Suddenly (or gradually) nothing is wrong. Instead of feeling panic, terror, or agony, we feel wide open, spacious, and serene.

Even if things don't open up in this way, we know that at some point, our experience will change. It always has and always will. We will come through this in the same way we've come through *everything* our life has thrown at us up to this point. Even if we feel completely overwhelmed in this moment, it will become a memory that's barely worth recalling. When the intensity begins to subside, a whole range of possibilities will become available to us.

SPIRITUAL TRANSFORMATION IS DIFFERENT FROM SPIRITUAL KNOWLEDGE

Something that's also important to appreciate is that spiritual transformation isn't necessarily accompanied by understanding. This is especially true when our spiritual evolution is following a nondual path. If we try to work out what's happening to us when we're in a process of accelerated change and rapid integration, this can just make us more confused and disoriented. Often we don't have the time or capacity to understand what is happening, or has happened, to us. We have to move on, not knowing where our fears have come from or if we've prepared ourselves to handle similar experiences in the future. Sometimes we can extract some meaning and significance when we come out the other end. But sometimes we never know, and never will know, why we needed to experience whatever was happening for us. The process of transformation doesn't need us to know. All it needs is for us to show up, to be there, in order for the work to happen.

I'M TOO BUSY

Probably the most common reason we give for losing our connection with unconditioned awareness is that we just get caught up in our day-to-day activities. We simply don't have time to stop and listen to the eternal stillness of imperturbable buddha-mind.

People often say to me, "I'd like to spend more time in unconditioned awareness, but I just don't have the time to do this. I'm too busy. What can I do?" First I agree: "Yes, it seems you are very busy." But I also say that it's best to not say, "I'd *like* to spend more time in unconditioned awareness," because it's not entirely accurate. We spend as much time in unconditioned awareness as we can, given our conditioning, our values, and our priorities. If we could spend more time in unconditioned awareness, and if it's what we really wanted, then we'd do it. So, first, it is important to be honest and realistic about your present relationship to unconditioned awareness.

Second, there's no point in complaining, no point in even wishing that we didn't have to do as much as we seem to need to do. No one has ever entered buddha-mind by thinking that they've got too much to do! If we can't stop what we're doing, we have to continue with our work, fulfilling our commitments. We do our work, we fulfill our obligations, without telling ourselves that we'd like to be somewhere else. The *Bhagavad Gita* talks about this as the practice of desireless action (*nishkama-karma*).

To some extent, we can forget about unconditioned awareness, but not entirely. We remember that we're doing whatever we need to be doing in order to do nothing. Unconditioned awareness sits in the background throughout the day as an ever-present possibility that can shine through at any moment in our busy days.

We go to our office, do the shopping, prepare dinner, phone our parents, *in order to* open up some space, to give ourselves some time each day or each week to do nothing, and perhaps some time each year for a retreat as well. When time and space opens up, we recognize it, and take advantage of it. We sense that there's nothing we need to do—and so we do exactly that. We do some deep abiding in unconditioned awareness.

THE BEST PREPARATION FOR THE FUTURE IS ALWAYS TO REST IN RADIANT MIND

If we look at it, our busyness is often related to preparing for the future. That's what keeps us rushing around and lying awake at night. We're making money to pay next month's mortgage, re-skilling ourselves for a career change, seeing if we need to update our software, thinking about our retirement, squeezing in a massage, wondering if we should hire a new manager, and checking out our calendar to see when the next holiday falls. This is fine. But we often trade the possibility of resting in unconditioned awareness for a hoped-for "better" future. We rationalize that we need to prepare for the future instead of resting in our natural state. We think, "Yes, unconditioned awareness is important, it is the ultimate medicine, but it doesn't take care of my life, so I'd better learn how to communicate more effectively, develop more patience, work out how to improve the return on my investments, increase my store of spiritual merit, or do some good works."

Whatever we're doing, we're conditioning our mind to do more of it, or we're in an internal battle, struggling to be different. Either way, we're conditioning our mind. If we're angry—especially if we let ourselves be angry—we're conditioning our mind to do more of this. If we're kind and loving, we condition these feelings and intentions within us. If we develop the practice of "just sitting" so that we feel at home with this experience, we're establishing the conditions to continue it.

Similarly, the more familiar we are with unconditioned awareness, the more easily, comfortably, and naturally we move back into this state, even when we think we've lost it. In a way, it's very simple. So if we have a chance to rest and act from radiant mind, we should do it.

If it's possible to rest in radiant mind, this is *always* the best thing to do, because this is the way we move toward full awakening. This is how we develop and deepen buddha-nature. It's never worth it to forsake the opportunity to drink the ultimate medicine for a lesser reward such as feeling more secure.

In order to make this easier, we can train our mind to automatically return to unconditioned awareness when the winds change and the conditions become favorable again. It's simply a matter of repetition. Rather than conditioning our body-mind to acquire more and more tools and strategies, we can learn to produce a shift into a state of consciousness in which it's no longer possible to suffer. The path to full awakening consists of becoming more and more familiar with less and less suffering.

One of the lovely things that begins to happen as we become more familiar with radiant mind is that we can access this experience even in the midst of intense difficulties and challenges. We might be dealing with a domestic problem or worrying about our health. One second, we're in the heat of an emotional conflict, and the next second, it's totally unnecessary. Our reactivity evaporates without leaving any residual animosity or self-recrimination. We can move from being totally wrapped up in our identity, consumed by our needs and preferences, in one minute, to being open and spacious in the next.

I'm not talking about losing our cool and then moving on without regard for cleaning up the fallout from an emotional outburst that we may have given or received. I'm not talking about moving on by cutting our losses, swallowing our pride, or suppressing guilt or resentment. I'm talking about the capacity to know, firsthand, how emotional reactions and overwhelming experiences can self-liberate in an instant without any work or effort, leaving us fully empowered to deal with any adverse consequences from a space of love and openness.

SPIRITUAL BYPASSING

I've explained in detail how, in order to purify, deepen, and extend the experience of nondual awareness, we need to take care of our life at every level: the material, social, emotional, and spiritual. Please don't mistake what I'm saying here about always giving priority to unconditioned awareness as an example of what some teachers and psychotherapists are calling "spiritual bypassing" or "bypassing the relative."

When teachers and therapists use the term "spiritual bypassing," they're referring to an engagement with the nondual perspective that disconnects people from their emotions, relationships, and social responsibilities. This can happen if people understand the ultimate level of being only through the language that can be used to reveal it, rather than as a direct experience. Since the ultimate level is often spoken about as a state of egolessness that transcends all moral imperative and goes beyond choice and decision, some nondual traditions talk about relative reality as being illusory.

If people are relating to the ultimate only through a discourse of nonduality, they're seeing only part of the picture, the part that's framed in negations. If they don't have the direct experience of unconditioned awareness, they can infer that there's no finite self, no choice, etc., and that they're relieved of the need to take care of themselves and others at the relative or conditioned level.

The possibility of bypassing the relative is compounded by the fact that some nondual traditions include yogic practices designed to propel people into disidentified states—different types of *samadhis*—in which people aren't even aware of the phenomenal world. These states have nothing to do with unconditioned awareness, or emptiness, *shunyata*, as this is understood and experienced in Buddhism.

We really need to be clear about this. This is why it's very important to work with an experienced teacher. It's unfortunate that some therapists use the phrase "hanging out in emptiness" to refer to practitioners who seem to be disconnected from the world. Emptiness, or shunyata, has a very precise meaning in Buddhism that's unrelated to how people use it in this phrase. I prefer to translate shunyata as openness rather than emptiness, in order to avoid the misunderstanding that it's a state that's separate from the world. As I've explained, the experience of unconditioned awareness automatically reveals the intricacies of our conditioned existence.

It's also important to see that when we're presencing unconditioned awareness, it's impossible to avoid anything. Unconditioned awareness doesn't have the capacity to suppress anything. It's a structureless state. It doesn't have any energy in it. It's not an escape route. It's a state in which we're fully present to everything that's arising. The experience of unconditioned awareness dissolves the barrier between ourselves and others. We become more responsive and responsible to other people because they're no different from us.

THE QUESTION OF PRACTICE

Before we finish, I just want to say a couple of things about spiritual practice. I can still hear some people saying, "We've covered a lot in this book. But I'm still not clear about the place of spiritual practices. I know there will be times when I think I need to be doing something. Is there a way to summarize all of this? Is there a simple practice that synthesizes and integrates everything we've been doing here?"

There is, but before describing it, I'd just like to qualify that the whole question of practice is very delicate from a nondual point of view. We need to realize that *anything* we do to stop or prolong an experience stops us from entering unconditioned awareness. Any attempt to intervene or qualify our experience keeps us identified with our conditioning. If we *try* to reenter an experience of unconditioned awareness through some form of practice, this reinforces the belief that "something is missing."

What we, in fact, need is a practice that acknowledges our *need* to do something when we're struggling, but which also dissolves that need. We need a practice that takes us beyond the need for practice, not because we've given up, but because we've returned to the state where nothing's missing. As long as our practice is located in time, and focused on the future, it can't provide an entry point into the unconditioned.

OBSERVING REACTIONS

If you're feeling a need to develop a spiritual practice, a good place to begin is to observe your reactions. I talked about this in Chapter Six.

The simplest practice is to note whether you like or don't like what's happening to you. Do you want this experience to stop (aversion) or to continue (attachment)? The heart of practice is to tune in to the energy of attraction and aversion as these are manifesting.

The great thing about this practice is that we can do it anytime. We can do it when we're meditating, driving, participating in a business meeting, making love, or standing in line at the supermarket. In this way, we can learn how to integrate the conditioned and the unconditioned, the relative and the ultimate.

The other great virtue of observing attraction and aversion is that this practice links us, in the most direct way possible, to the source of our suffering. The Second Noble Truth of the Buddha is that the source of suffering is grasping. In this way, our suffering can be our most precise teacher because it gives us a direct readout of our attachment and aversion. Our suffering can become our guru or teacher by revealing exactly what we need to be working on.

Observing our reactions in this way immediately gives new depth and subtlety to our perceptions. We begin to perceive a continuous stream of feelings, thoughts, and impulses that function as our automatic guidance system. This continuous stream of experience represents our inner life — our thoughts, imagery, feelings, emotions, and moods — and our awareness of them can function as real-time information about how our body and mind are reacting to their environment and internal processes. We learn how to read this continuous "feed" as indications of our reactivity — our attraction for and repulsion from different events.

When we begin to tune in to our core reactions, we also begin to see the nuances and forms through which these core reactions are expressed. We discover how we try to prolong what we like and to minimize or remove what we don't like. We see how we sometimes try to control our experience and at other times try to let it go. We try to slow things down or speed them up depending on whether we like or dislike what's happening. We see how we try to dilute or intensify our experience in concert with our rejection or desire. We resist and give in, dominate and submit, approve and disapprove.

This practice guides us directly into the paths of ongoing completion and desirelessness (see Chapter Eight). As we make the movement into desirelessness, we find that it's easier and easier to use the keys that instantly liberate the experience of "being someone" who can be "attached or averse to anything."

The moment we enter desirelessness—which is radiant mind—there's nothing to modify or change. Also, once we are relatively free of desire, mental and emotional constructions dissolve by themselves, and unconditioned awareness reveals itself as our ever-present natural state.

"SEEING THROUGH" OUR REACTIONS

Even if we don't use these keys at some point in the process of observing our reactions, we begin to see right through them. What we've been calling "reactions" are no longer experienced as distortions to an effortless way of being. The very notion of distorting our experience loses all meaning. The idea of distorting our experience implies that we could be experiencing something different. This implies that there's something else within or behind our experience that we're distorting. We see that this is impossible. Nothing is hidden; everything is given. There is just suchness (*tathata*).

Thinking that we're practicing doesn't mean we're practicing; it just means that we think we are. And thinking that we're not practicing doesn't mean we're not. And the fact that thinking we're practicing only means that we think we're practicing, doesn't mean that we're not practicing. At this point, there's no way to determine whether we're practicing or not. We're in the state of natural meditation, or the practice of no-practice.

In this practice, we discover that we aren't doing anything different, special, or unique; we're just thinking, as we always do. Prior to this point, we experience practice as a discipline—as the performance of an exercise we are doing as opposed to not doing. Now we experience that there's no practice as a modification of something we could otherwise be doing. We see that we can't modify anything. There's no one to modify reality; and even if there was, we don't have the equipment to do it. Reality is a seamlessly saturated, evanescent sphere of phenomena that has no center or horizon, and is always pristine and inviolate.

From this perspective, either everything is practice or there is no such thing as practice. What we could call practice is effortless; there's no discipline, and practice is indistinguishable from living life. There's nowhere further to go—not because we've arrived somewhere, but because we're exactly where we are at the conditioned level and nowhere at the same time.

The experience I'm describing is completely different from stopping practicing as a decision or as a reaction to the challenge and possible discomfort of becoming aware of our thoughts, feelings, and actions. Stopping presupposes that we could have continued. The act of stopping (or continuing) achieves nothing, because we're still caught up in our fears and hopes about what could, or would, have happened if we had continued (or stopped). If we believe that we need or don't need to practice, we're still trapped by the belief that practice refers to a real and objective activity. We are still inside the construction that we can or can't change our experience by continuing or discontinuing our practice. The experience of transcending practice emerges in the midst of our practice when we discover that we aren't, in fact, doing anything different from what we would otherwise have been doing.

So here we are at a place where we can't stop, because stopping is indistinguishable from continuing. Fortunately, however, writing is a conditioned process, so I can at least stop doing this. Whew!

But first I want to thank you from my heart for taking this journey with me. A journey that's brought us here, to this moment. A journey that's not strictly necessary but beautiful nonetheless. A journey that shows us that we're always, already, exactly where we are, with nowhere to go, and that there's no one to go anywhere. Thank you so much for this.

In some ways, this book has cycled between the conditioned and the ultimate in the same way that you do in your daily life. We've worked at the "result level"—directly experiencing the goal—then we've returned to the experience that "something's missing," and traced many ways to reenter unconditioned awareness. We've built many bridges to show you that you're ultimately free in this and every moment.

Our journey has a contemporary ring to it because we live in the 21st century. But it's the same journey that's been made by hundreds of thousands of nondual masters, yogis, contemplatives, and philosophers throughout the ages. We've joined the contentless wisdom lineage that transcends time, language, history, race, and culture.

I continue to be amazed that, when we rest in unconditioned awareness, we're buddhas, at least temporarily. We're at home in exactly the same state as all the realized masters. They lived in radiant awareness continuously. They awoke into this state at the beginning of every day, and they died into it as well.

We're a long way from being there, but we're on our way. We don't know what we'll encounter on the path to full awakening. Certainly, it will be full of surprises. But we know where we're heading, and that's the important thing.

It's my wish that nondual love and wisdom will grow in your heart, transform all your relationships, and radiate without obstruction throughout the world. If you wish to deepen your experience of unconditioned awareness, I invite you to join any of the Radiant Mind programs that are offered around the world.

I wish you well and hope that we meet in person someday to rest and play in the river of radiant mind together.

CHAPTER THIRTEEN EXERCISE:
AN EVEN SIMPLER PRACTICE

If you want to add some crispness to the process I've just described, you can work with the two thoughts "I like this" and "I don't like this." Begin with the question "Okay, here I am right now. What do I like, or not like, about what I'm experiencing?" If there's nothing good or bad about what's happening, that's great. If you don't like what's happening, start to fill in the blank. Stick with "what's actually happening," and resist the temptation to get into the "becauses." The reasons why we don't like what's happening can be endless: "I don't like this experience of driving to work because it's a waste of time, I could be doing something better, the traffic gets worse each year, I might be late for my meeting, it pollutes the environment, and the price of gas just keeps going up." Etc., etc. Samsara exists in the reasons!

If the reasons are coming on thick and fast, you might let them flow for a while. If the circumstances permit, you could even do some automatic writing (as you did at the end of Chapter Two). When you're done with this, begin to focus on exactly what you don't like: "I don't like the words he's using. I don't like the tone of his voice. I don't like the color of his skin. I don't like his gesticulating. I don't like the feeling in my chest."

At some point, after you've worked through all the particulars, you'll connect with the core structure, "I don't like this," and then you'll lock into the three elements of this structure: "you," "(not) liking," and "this." Perhaps you'll lock into the "this"—what you're experiencing as a gestalt, just this. Or perhaps you'll lock into "not liking." What actually is liking? Where is it? Where does it happen? Or maybe you'll begin to question "who" it is who's not liking. Who are "you" who doesn't like what's happening?

It doesn't matter which of these you look at; if you look clearly at any of the elements, it will dissolve. All that's needed to dissolve any of these elements is to move through the experience of not liking what's happening, until you can see it clearly for what it is—something from your conditioned existence. As soon as you can see through it, you enter unconditioned awareness, into radiant mind.

APPENDIX

RADIANT COMMUNICATION
An Architecture for Effective Collaboration

INTRODUCTION

This book has focused very much on the experience of unconditioned aware-ness, what's sometimes called the absolute. At the level of the absolute, it doesn't matter what we do; nothing can perturb our equanimity and spa-ciousness. But as I've emphasized, in order to enter and rest in the ultimate state of buddha-mind, we need to work at two levels—the conditioned and the unconditioned.

In the spirit of giving you a comprehensive framework for living, I'd like to complete this book with an appendix that focuses on the interpersonal, or collective, dimension of radiant mind. It's really an expansion of learning how to be complete moment by moment as we engage in our daily activities, tak-ing care of ourselves, our families, our communities, and the planet.

I want to give you some very practical skills that will help you in your daily interactions at home and at work. These skills will help keep you up to speed on a day-by-day, week-by-week basis, without feeling rushed or pressured. At the end of each day, you'll feel as though you've done what's needed to be done—no less and no more. This is a wonderful state to work, play, and love in, because you're able to fully engage whatever's at hand, without having your energy depleted and dissipated by needing to get into "fix-up mode."

In this appendix, I'm going to give you an overview of some communica-tion technologies. These technologies are being used by people all over the world to enhance the clarity, compassion, and effectiveness of their commu-nication. What I'm offering here is a set of distinctions and sensitivities that are intimately related to our deepest aspiration to live in a way that is infused by love, compassion, and exquisite care for our world. Before we take a look at how these ways of communicating actually work, I want to make it clear why they are so important.

As soon as we communicate, we've entered the realm of experience and construction, unless we are engaged in "pure speaking" and "pure listening," whereby our communication flows directly from unconditioned awareness. People engaged in spiritual practice can neglect this part of their lives. They imagine that the openness, compassion, and insight that their practice brings will take care of their communication. This is a very common belief. If my heart is open, if my intentions are good, why would I need to engage in a process of learning to communicate? We believe that our connection with unconditioned awareness will take care of everything that happens on the level of human conditioning.

Experience has shown that it doesn't always work this way. A loving heart, good intentions, and a high degree of spiritual awareness do not necessarily make you an effective communicator. Good communication is actually a skill that needs to be studied and practiced on the human level. Because it's not something that we're typically taught as we're growing up, we all carry deep habitual patterns of conditioning into our conversations with other people.

If we are completely honest about it, we'll see very clearly that at the conditioned level, miscommunication is normal. Miscommunication is inevitable for us as long as we're driven by our needs and preferences. It's impossible to communicate, to work, and to relate with other people without producing misunderstandings, because no one is interested in our needs in the same way that we are.

We don't live in other people's minds, and they don't live in ours. The only way I can ever know what you "really" mean is by living inside the extremely complex story of your conditioned experience. And, similarly, you can never, ever know what I really mean when I'm talking from within my conditioned experience. The complexity and ever-evolving nature of who we are makes this impossible.

If anything, miscommunication is the norm. When miscommunication happens, it doesn't mean that something is wrong. In many ways, communication is the continual correction of misunderstandings—the rectification of names, categories, and distinctions. If we think about communication in this way, we're less likely to live in the illusion that misunderstanding and miscommunication shouldn't happen. We learn "great tolerance" at the same time that we seek clarity and understanding.

But we can learn to minimize miscommunication, to anticipate breakdowns in hearing and listening. We can learn to create trust when trust is missing. We can learn to communicate in ways that respect other people's integrity. We can also learn how to create and manage a set of commitments that directly produce more ease and fulfillment in our life.

UNCONDITIONED AWARENESS AS OUR FOUNDATION

Let's take a look at the foundation for this work on communication. You and I are together, and I want to communicate with you about something. In order for this communication to be clear, loving, honest, and effective, certain things are necessary. First of all, I need to be present and open, fully attentive to you, myself, and what's going on between us. The obstacles that stand in the way of that openness are the same ones we've been examining in *Radiant Mind*. If I have fixed ideas about who you are, and who I am, those ideas will get in the way of our conversation. From the beginning of our communication, I need to let go of all the things I think I know about you, because those ideas are based on my past experience, not this fresh and alive moment. We need to be willing to be transformed through our communication.

So this whole way of communicating is actually based on an ongoing connection with the unconditioned ground of our being. This is where learning how to communicate intersects with what we are doing in *Radiant Mind*. If I know how to access unconditioned awareness while we're interacting, it makes all the difference in the world. Otherwise, all I have are my constructed ideas and my fixed positions. And it is these ideas and positions that create all the conflict and confusion in our communication. Take a look at human life. The evidence is everywhere.

TELLING THE TRUTH

Second, I need to be as honest and clear as I can with you about the intentions, needs, and expectations I am holding in relation to this communication. This seems quite obvious. No one would argue with the fact that telling you the truth about what I want and need, and about what is going on for me, will greatly enhance the way that we communicate. Everyone knows this, but the fact is, often we're not totally honest in our communication. This is one of the things we have to face, again and again. In the field of communication, there are big gaps between what we know and how we act. In this sense, communication is very much where our spiritual rubber hits the road.

What is it that prevents us from being more honest with each other? One way of looking at this is that we have hidden agendas. These agendas and motives come from our survival systems—the need to feel safe, to control, to be approved of. There's nothing wrong with these kinds of needs. They are a very natural part of our human conditioning. But if we are driven by them in our communication, it is very difficult for us to be open and honest. We need to be aware of these conditions as they operate in us, and to cultivate a willingness to let go and come from the spaciousness of our unconditioned being. The minute I use my communication to control you, or to gain your approval, I have cut myself off from the freedom to reveal myself as I am.

Our capacity to engage in "pure listening" as we communicate releases these agendas right back into the spaciousness of being. If I can be here, fully and freely, open and receptive to you and whatever you are expressing, this is the open ground of all effective communication. If I lose my connection with this radiant core, then my talk becomes, as St. Paul put it, "like tinkling glass and sounding cymbals." It may sound good, but the real connection between us has been lost.

Communication is life. We are communicating all the time; under, around, and inside the words we speak, something is always being transmitted. A reluctance to deal with the world of communication is actually a reluctance to fully engage in life. On one level, human life is nothing but a river of communication, full of intentions, judgments, promises, agreements, and misunderstandings. We cannot really get away from this aspect of life. We can't just hop out of the river and sit on the bank where everything is clear and dry. We're actually all in this together—tumbling around in this wild river of communication.

The beauty of the following communication technology is that it rests on the foundation of our unconditioned being, and carries us into a profound engagement in life. We can learn to communicate with our whole being, without holding back, and without making ourselves separate. The essential qualities that support this kind of communication are the same ones that support our spiritual practice: openness, honesty, integrity, kindness, and a deep willingness to let go of our judgments and positions.

It's not so easy to sustain this way of being as we communicate. It takes a great deal of practice. Communication is a vast field. There is always more to discover about it. That's why so many people resist this kind of learning. It seems like another discipline that we will have to impose on ourselves. As human beings, we have already adjusted ourselves so much. We've judged and manipulated ourselves in order to get along, to feel safe, to be approved of. What we're really longing for is the chance to just relax and be ourselves.

OUR NATURAL STATE

It's essential for us to understand that this is what the study of communication is really all about. As Suzuki Roshi said, "To express yourself as you are, without any fancy intentional way of adjusting yourself, is the most important thing for your happiness, and the happiness of those around you."

Take a moment to reflect on what happens when we communicate unskillfully. Allow yourself to remember the pain, regret, recrimination, and anguish that can result from this kind of misunderstanding and conflict. Learning how to communicate well can take you to a place where you no longer abandon yourself, where you continually express a deep respect for yourself and for the other person at the same time. This is the real reason why these technologies of communication are so valuable. They radically reduce our human suffering. It's as simple as that.

LIVING WITH COMPLETION

When we create a breakdown or incompletion, we have to either accept the consequences or go back and fix things up. I call this "remedial communication." We all know the suffering that comes when we have communicated without skill and awareness. We know what it feels like to look back and wish that we could somehow obliterate the words that created such a rupture in a relationship. Or we wish that we'd just said some kind words of support and extended our hand to support a friend or stranger—that we hadn't been withholding. If only we'd been more sensitive. Within seconds, these opportunities can pass, and then we're just left with regrets. Of course, sometimes we can go back and repair the misunderstandings and incompletions we have created. But I'm sure you have experienced some seeming disasters from which there was no recovery.

Skillful, honest, loving communication allows us to live and interact without leaving a big wake behind us. And when we can move through life without churning up a lot of drama and reactivity, we are leaving a lot more room for the spaciousness of radiant mind to shine through every aspect of our life. Each interaction is complete. We don't have to go over and over it in our mind, wondering what went wrong, or what we could possibly do to repair the damage. We live with an ongoing sense of completion that is really a priceless gift.

I'd like to share with you now those aspects of these technologies that are easily understood, and which I've found to be of immense value in managing the complex set of commitments that define and determine our social and private lives. These ideas can potentially save you hundreds of hours of "communication repair problems" and perhaps thousands of hours in fulfilling commitments that don't serve you or your spiritual objectives. It can help you to free up time for radiant-mind work, to avert the breakdowns that happen so often in getting routine things done, like organizing a business trip, installing new heating, or agreeing on which movie to see—the things that can derail us for hours or days at a time. The skills I'll be presenting will also help you to negotiate more difficult and sensitive conversations that can help to create and repair relationships with partners, children, and parents. These skills will also help you to build teams, manage conflicts, clarify values, and enhance the quality and reach of your contributions to others. They will also help you in manifesting the opportunity for humanity at large to experience real spiritual freedom.

If you really engage in the kind of learning that happens through these technologies of communication, you will begin to experience what I call "deep learning," or second-order learning. This is not about imposing or adding new behaviors on top of your constructed identity—it's about change that comes from your being, transformation that deconstructs your conditioned identity as it happens.

OBSERVATION WITHOUT JUDGMENT

Marshall Rosenberg, the founder of nonviolent communication, has developed a simple and powerful technology based on a few core principles. The first one is "observation without evaluation or judgment." It's not hard to see how relevant this principle is to our *Radiant Mind* work. Learning how to release all our judgments and evaluations is actually a radical practice that deconstructs our world and our identity.

Rosenberg is very clear that all violence begins with judgment. Watching the stream of our judgments, internal and external, and noticing their effects, is a powerful practice, all by itself. And learning how to communicate without making any kind of judgment allows the deep openness of the heart to permeate all our interactions.

BEING FULLY RESPONSIBLE

Taking responsibility is another principle of nonviolent communication. I am completely responsible for my thoughts and feelings. I am the one who constructs my own experience, moment to moment. You might be the trigger for my feelings, but you are not the cause of them. Most people, when asked, will give lip service to this idea of responsibility. But if we shine the light of awareness on our experience, we'll discover that we are blaming ourselves and each other all the time. To actually live without blaming anyone or anything for our experience is very liberating. It's a bit like being fully grown up. The child inside us has no more room to kick and complain, because there is no one to blame. When we are able to release blame and judgment, we are simply dealing with what is, whatever life brings to us.

Rosenberg speaks about what happens when someone expresses something that challenges or threatens us. This could be just a look, or a torrent of words. It doesn't take a lot to trigger our conditioned responses. When something like this happens, we have four options. The first two involve our conditioned responses. Depending on the whole ancestral stream of our conditioning, we will focus the blame and judgment internally or externally. We either blame ourselves or blame the other person for our own unhappiness or discomfort. Both those responses do nothing except create suffering, separation, and a closed heart.

There are two other options that are always available. We can shine the light of our nonjudging, compassionate awareness on ourselves, and discover what it is that we are wanting or needing right now. Or we can do the same thing in relation to the other person. We can focus on them without any kind of blame or judgment, and find out what their desires or needs are in this situation.

FREEDOM FROM DUTY AND OBLIGATION

Rosenberg makes a wonderful point here. Whenever we act from a sense of duty or obligation, we cut off our access to the freedom and love of our unconditioned being. This is quite a radical understanding, since so many human beings engage in actions based on these conditions of duty and obligation. Rosenberg refers to them as poisons that we use to manipulate ourselves and each other.

The solution here is to stay connected to the flow of compassion and freedom that comes from unconditioned awareness. That flow has nothing to do with constructed ideas of duty and obligation. When I let go of these ideas, I can still ask for what I want or need, but that asking comes from a wide-open space within me. I no longer want to hear your "yes" unless that "yes" is free of duty or obligation. I clearly understand that I have nothing to gain if I make any kind of demand on you. If you give me something out of duty or obligation, what I receive from you has been poisoned. It does not carry the fragrance of love or connection. Because of where it comes from, it carries a sense of coercion and separation, and will only perpetuate those conditions.

THE LANGUAGE-ACTION PARADIGM

Now we are going to take a look at another technology of communication. This architecture draws on the work of Dr. Fernando Flores. In the mid-1980s, Flores produced a brilliant integration of philosophical and pragmatic insights drawn from "existentialism," "speech-act philosophy," and "cognitive biology." His framework is referred to as the "language-action paradigm" for the coordination of action. It's used in fields as diverse as workflow design in transnational corporations and intimacy workshops. It has been adapted to parenting, coaching, and even the design of spiritual practices.

The "language-action paradigm" fits totally with the Buddhist underpinning of *Radiant Mind*. Both frameworks are built on the assumption that our experience of conditioned reality is created through language. Mahayana Buddhists, like post-modernists, say that the world is a text and that everything is brought into existence through linguistic designation. But Asian Buddhists haven't really explained *how* this happens. They haven't brought this down to the conversational level—the medium through which we relate and create.

Flores revealed the mechanics, the architectonics, behind this process with unprecedented precision. His discoveries give real depth to the Buddhist insight that reality is a conversation. His language-action paradigm shows exactly how the different functions of language shape our identity and our experience in the world.

CREATING TRUST

Flores based his work around the understanding of trust. He looked at how we interact, and what it is that we communicate to each other that erodes or builds the trust between us. What Rosenberg calls the space of compassion, Flores identifies as a space of trust, and they are not really very different. Flores focuses on the field of action, and exactly what we need to do in order to establish this basic sense of trust, because without it, things don't really work. What he discovered is that as soon as we engage in action together, we also engage in making promises, agreements, and commitments. The unique focus of his work looks carefully at the nature of these promises and agreements, and discovers how they can support and benefit whatever it is that we want to accomplish.

On the surface, reading about Flores' work can make it seem very dry, almost like listening to a lawyer. So it's important to realize that he is also drawing us into a deep place of honesty and integrity of heart. When we know how to make promises and honor our commitments and agreements with honesty and integrity, we can really begin to collaborate with our fellow human beings. This opens up a whole universe of possibilities.

TYPES OF CONVERSATIONS

Flores distinguishes three types of conversations. These are conversations for:

- Establishing relationships
- Creating inspired possibilities
- Actualizing through collective action

These types of conversations have very different dynamics and produce different outcomes. In order to produce changes that support our well-being with efficiency and minimal frustration, it's very helpful to understand how each of these conversations works and how they relate to each other.

Flores refers to these as "timeless ontological skills." The successful realization of any collective project anywhere at anytime—on Earth by humans or by other intelligent life forms—will depend on being skilled in these conversations. The conversations might be happening at a psychic, mind-to-mind level, but the communication still conforms to the same structure.

I have had the wonderfully good fortune to spend many hours witnessing a famous South Indian saint called Sri Sathya Sai Baba at very close quarters as he went about the business of managing a vast network of ashrams, centers, schools, universities, clinics, hospitals, and other activities, and being responsible for the spiritual welfare of millions of followers. What I've observed is that even though he lives and functions in a very different culture than ours, in order to fulfill his mission, he relies on the skills I will be describing. It seems that the skills put forth by Flores are indeed "timeless and transcultural."

Sai Baba says little, but what he accomplishes is staggering. He is a consummate visionary and communicator, able to effortlessly manifest vast projects. At any one time, he has several multimillion-dollar projects in planning or under construction, is presiding over various spiritual celebrations, and is receiving daily visits by dignitaries. On average, he deals with over 750 communiqués a day. Yet he's never tired, and he's always understanding and loving.

A request to have a conversation with Sai Baba is often made by a gesture. It could be a small movement of a disciple's body indicating that he is keen to talk with Sai Baba. With micro-gestures, Sai Baba accepts, declines, or doesn't commit. If he accepts the request for a conversation, he might be presented with some working documents for a building, the lists of speakers for possible conferences, or the program for a festive event. He might flip through these and put them aside, saying nothing. He might have a brief whispered exchange. Or, he might engage in an animated conversation for five or more minutes.

Even though the atmosphere, transparency, and managerial structure are radically different from what happens in, say, a Western-style committee meeting, the conversations follow the structure I'll describe here. The manifestation of his spiritual mission moves forward through making declarations, speculating, and making and receiving offers and requests. Sai Baba asks for clarity, accepts, commits his resources and sets completion dates, and resolves an unending stream of breakdowns and interruptions in the realization of his vision.

In the following sections, I'll describe the architecture of effective communication. I'll draw on the insights of Flores and Rosenberg. I'll also identify the common ways in which the flow of flawless communication can be interrupted. These ruptures are what we usually call breakdowns, glitches, misunderstandings, and miscommunications. You'll soon be able to recognize where your weaknesses are—where you create incompletions.

When we know how these different conversations work, it's easier to get back on track when we find ourselves in the middle of a breakdown or misunderstanding. When people share a set of distinctions for understanding the structure for effective communication, it becomes much easier to work and live together. We share a language that's specially designed for collaboration, cooperation, and conflict resolution.

This also means that breakdowns can be recognized and dealt with as ruptures in conversations rather than as defects in anyone's personality. We can actually look at what is going on without getting lost in endless cycles of guilt, blame, and recrimination. These communication skills can save us years in the therapist's office.

The whole focus of Flores' work is on identifying the concerns in the world that we are qualified to take care of, and then engaging in a continual process of learning and what he calls "transfiguration"—or radical transformation—so that we can take care of wider, deeper, and more complex areas of concern.

In general terms, there's a progressive movement through these three types of conversations. We usually begin by "getting related" with the other person. In terms of creating a foundation for acting together, this might take five minutes or several years. This depends on the magnitude of our collaboration and the trust and alignment that's needed. Once we feel a connection with someone, it's natural to think about doing things together. We might then begin to speculate about some area of interest or concern where we could combine our resources, love, and expertise. From there, we might move further and actually commit ourselves to working, living, learning, playing, practicing, or loving together.

GETTING RELATED

The bedrock of all collective activity lies in relationships. In the absence of relationships, it's impossible to come together—for work, for love, as a sangha seeking freedom, or simply to have fun.

In order to co-create, we need to be in relationship with the people with whom we will co-create. So there's a specific type of conversation that's designed just to "get related." These conversations move without any predefined purpose or agenda. It's a conversation in which we get to know the other person. We "get related" through a mutual sharing of who they are and who we are. We mutually share the context of our lives—our values, experiences, ideals, interests, aspirations, and expertise.

"Getting related" happens quite casually. It happens in doing things together as well as in talking together. The selection of an appropriate setting is part of the conversation. A meal in a pleasant restaurant or a walk in the mountains can become "a conversation for getting related," in the sense that it's comfortable and pleasant just being with someone in these environments, quite independently of what we're talking about. "Getting related" is a casual and nonintrusive way of sharing the whole tapestry of our life with others, and letting others share themselves with us. It's a nonstrategic form of communication. It has a sense of getting to know the other person quite independently of *doing* anything together. A conversation for getting related involves creating space and letting each other "be," each in our own natural way.

Conversations for establishing a sense of relationship give us the opportunity to establish trust, interest, and a potential for future sharing and collaboration. The conversations in which we get related with people are often the conversations in which we also make judgments about their sincerity. We'll return to this when we look at the question of trust.

RUPTURES IN GETTING RELATED

Conversations for "getting related" can get stuck at the level of "being related" and move no further. People can become habituated to small talk, recycling the same old stories or sharing the minutia of the last week. People can spend decades on the phone or in cafés, sharing last week's episodes as though their life is an event of global importance.

Getting related can also plateau out. "Getting related" becomes "staying related." How many times have you heard friends say, "I don't know why I keep seeing so and so. It's really boring. All they ever talk about is their health, their sports, their cat, their last vacation, their house, on and on. I know if I say anything, it will only hurt them. I'm really sick of it but I don't know what to do." This is a conversation for getting related that has long gone stale. Getting related is a stepping stone. Once we've established a connection with someone, it gives us an opportunity to see if we can create something of mutual value.

Of course, it's appropriate in some relationships to stay connected for many years without needing to move any further. The relationship lives on a plateau and this is appropriate. A good example is the relationship between adult children and parents. We stay in relationship with our children and parents even though we live our separate lives. We stay connected and interested in each other's life even though we are not working or living together. Part of our connection relates to the future, so we are available if and when we are needed for support.

A rupture in establishing a relationship occurs when there's an imbalance in the sharing. One person takes up all the airtime. We might even invite this on ourselves. We encourage the person with whom we're getting related to talk about their life and interests, but we share nothing of ourselves. Or, conversely, we create no space for the person with whom we're communicating to talk about themselves. When we're getting related, it's important to watch the size of our footprint.

CREATING POSSIBILITIES

Once we've become related, it's natural to begin to explore what we might do together. Perhaps we can think about writing a book together, creating a community, seeing if our children would like to play with each other, practicing tai chi together, living together, or perhaps we can just see each other again!

This is where "a conversation for getting related" transforms into "a conversation for exploring possibilities." A conversation for exploring possibilities is designed to move in a particular direction in our personal or professional life. It's a conversation that produces new opportunities. Conversations for creating possibilities can be prompted by challenges and difficulties and also by seeing new opportunities. For example, we might feel that there are a lot of obstacles to making progress in our spiritual practice, so we begin to speculate about what we can do: "Is there another way of approaching spiritual fulfill-ment? Who could I talk to about this?"

Conversations for creating possibilities are also inspired by a vision of what we see is possible for ourselves, our community, or the planet. We might decide, for example, to inquire into how we can balance our spiritual pursuits with our family life, increase our sexual pleasure, find more rewarding em-ployment, or do something about global warming.

Conversations for creating possibilities require what Flores calls a mood of boldness and serenity. The consideration of a future possibility is purposeful—we are not free-associating, letting our ideas run all over the place. These conversations move in a spirit of discovery—a direct and focused way of creating new possibilities. We're free to speculate because we're not committing ourselves to anything. We're free to create a new possibility—to envision something for ourselves and others that doesn't yet exist—and still walk away from it. This may not be our primary intention, but we're still free to do it. At the end of the day, we are free to conclude our conversation with-out producing any rupture or inconvenience, because we haven't said "yes" to the possibility. We haven't begun to commit our resources.

In fact, conversations for creating possibilities move through a number of phases. A conversation that creates a possibility might happen in just a few minutes: "Okay, would you like to meet again to discuss this?" Or the conver-sation can extend over years. This depends in part on the significance of the commitment we make.

We can begin in a mood of unbridled and even audacious speculation, with minimal regard for whether our ideas are practical, reasonable, or sen-sible. We can think and speak outside of what we'd previously thought was possible. We can allow our ideas to flow freely, to move beyond the boundar-ies of our conditioning, in the same way that the nondual perspective invites us to consider that we can be completely healed at the same time that we're physically ill.

At a certain point in a conversation for creating a possibility, we begin to rein in our speculation by asking, "Is this really possible? Do we have the in-terest, commitment, and resources (time, energy, dedication, money, care, and expertise) to bring this to fruition? Do we really want this to happen?" Even here, it's important to realize that we haven't created any commitments. We're creating a "viable possibility" but without committing ourselves to anything.

NONDUAL CONVERSATIONS

I'm not sure where you are with the ideas in this book, but it's possible you're engaging with *Radiant Mind* as a part of your explorations about the nondual approach to human fulfillment. If so, you're in a conversation for possibility right now with this book.

In this book, we've been exploring a unique possibility, namely, that nothing is possible. I hope you're catching the paradox here. Within a conversation for possibility—the possibility of being deeply fulfilled—I've inserted a conversation for impossibility. I'm not telling you to do anything. I'm opening up the possibility that you don't have to do anything. And even more radically, I've opened up the possibility that we cannot do anything. And that we can be complete—in fact, are complete at a level that can't be destroyed—doing nothing.

How does this possibility unfold? Well, first we get connected, and some trust is established. Initially you buy into the idea that there's an ideal, perfect state, and that there might be some things to do to help us get there, or at least get closer to it. Then, at some point, I sense that a paradigm shift is possible. I say, "Actually, I think what we're talking about—being complete—might be possible now." Even though I know it's possible, I might begin by saying it a little tentatively. Then I work my way into it with you. "Yes, I have a feeling we can be complete right now, in this moment. Right now in this moment, I don't think we need anything more. In five minutes we might. But right now this feels complete. What do you think?" You get the sense of how this can open up for you.

So the ultimate conversation for possibility is that nothing is possible. This is the conversation that reveals the unconditioned. We bring ourselves into the here and now through a conversation that dismantles linear time. And in this moment, we always have everything we need. Here, we're completely fulfilled, so there's no need, necessity, or impulse to anticipate or create a future.

These nondual conversations can coexist with all the other conversations we engage in with human beings. They are not mutually exclusive. They are simply a nondual movement within the language-action paradigm. So let's go back to Fernando Flores and creating possibilities at the collective level.

GLITCHES IN CREATING POSSIBILITIES

Conversations for creating possibilities can be interrupted in many ways. Some people simply like the experience of speculating, of letting their minds run wild, producing all sorts of fantasies about making a full-length feature movie when they aren't even in the business. Or fantasizing about living "off the grid" when they don't have any income. People often speculate for the sheer excitement of such conversations. They get off on their emotions and lose sight of the work, time, and dedication that would actually be required to bring a vision to fruition. These are conversations for entertainment or amusement, rather than conversations for creating genuine possibilities. We've all seen how people's interest and enthusiasm in a conversation can deflate like a punctured balloon as soon as we begin to talk about time, money, and commitment, or even just keep notes of a conversation.

A real conversation for creating a possibility isn't just a "fun experience." It concludes with a decision to work toward translating a possible future into a reality, or to not move forward. Either way, though, the conversation is complete. The conversation transforms into a conversation for collective action, or it completes with a decision to not take further action.

Creating a possibility requires the courage and strength to think in a free and unconstrained manner, but it also requires the discipline and maturity to be willing to act if we decide to make our possibility real. If we have *no* intention at any point in our conversation to make our vision real, we're wasting our own and other people's time and energy.

In this regard, the possibilities we invent need to be connected with the general structure of our interests and expertise. They need to be consistent with what Flores calls the "drift" or general direction of our existence. If there's a radical discontinuity or disconnection between our existing set of commitments and a new possibility, we may create enormous difficulties for ourselves. At the very least, we need to factor in the creation of new connections and a lot of learning.

Conversations for creating new possibilities are also ruptured when people feel too constrained by the past. The moment they start to think outside the box, some people become nervous and anxious. They correctly sense that they will need to become a different person in order to realize their vision. This is why Flores says that creating new possibilities needs to be underscored by moods of boldness and serenity. We need the boldness to move forward without worrying too much about all that could go wrong. We need the serenity to accept and live with the consequences of our actions.

I'm sure you've noticed how easy it is for some people to derail speculative conversations by inserting conversations about impossibility into the agenda. How many times have we heard, "That's impossible. We're too incompatible. It will never work. The timing's not right. We don't have enough money. The technology doesn't exist to do this. It's too sophisticated for people to understand. It's too far ahead of its time." When this happens, it's good to remind people that "we're still in speculative mode."

Ruptures can also happen in the transition from speculation (the creation of a possibility) to the generation of actual commitments. If we move too quickly in making commitments, we curtail the free-ranging ideation that is central to all innovation and creativity. If we move too slowly, we can fail to connect our speculations back to our available or projected resources.

COLLECTIVE ACTION

At some point in a conversation that opens up a new possibility, we get around to the question of whether we will try to realize our vision — to bring it forth in us or in the world. The lines between the fields of getting connected, visioning a possibility, and starting to work on it are porous, and the movements between these are fluid and often indistinct. But often even the simplest ways of being together move into some kind of shared activity.

The moment we commit to do something with someone, we enter a very different type of conversation, often called "a conversation for action." Collective action is always based on the creation of a set of commitments that guide us in the manifestation of a previously declared possibility. In the nondual framework, that could be the commitment to live at the "result level," or to realize our natural state. The set of commitments that we generate are fulfilled through "conversations that coordinate action." These are the things we do, and don't do, within ourselves and with others, to realize our visions.

When I say "collective action" or "acting collectively," I don't just mean big-scale initiatives designed to produce large changes in our societies. Going to the corner store to pick up some milk is also a collective action, because our action needs to be minimally coordinated with the shop assistant, the hours that the store is open, the other cars and people on the street, etc. We are never acting in a vacuum.

A large-scale project is made of hundreds, perhaps thousands, of discrete "conversations for action." In fact, the act of being able to buy a loaf of bread at the corner store is also a product of numerous conversations that have coordinated the actions of shop assistants, managers, farmers, owners, distributors, government regulators, tax agents, bankers, and so on.

Societies function and malfunction through an intricate network of interwoven and interdependent conversations for the coordination of action. By and large, the people who are effective and fulfilled are relatively competent in managing conversations for action. Any weakness in the management of these conversations produces frustration, resentment, resignation, anger, and violence.

THE BUILDING BLOCKS FOR EFFECTIVE COLLECTIVE ACTION

In order to engage in a cooperative venture, be it a business project, deepening our experience of radiant mind, or entering a marriage, we need to ask and resolve the following questions:

- With whom will I participate in this venture?
- To whom can I make requests?
- To whom can I make offers?

Sometimes these questions are asked quite consciously. At other times, they are implicit. When we join someone in a love relationship, it's more likely that we "live inside the questions," and the answers come forth in the context of living our life.

A conversation that supports collective action comprises a set of commitments between people that is framed like this:

- A request, which is responded to with a promise
- An offer, which is accepted

Effective, coordinated action is built on the generation and fulfillment of promises and commitments. A commitment is generated every time we agree (make a promise) to fulfill a request, and every time an offer we make is accepted. If I offer you my hand in marriage and you accept, then I promise to marry you. If you decline my offer, then no promise is made.

We can think of a conversation for action as a cycle. It begins with the request (or offer), which, if accepted, generates a promise to fulfill the request (or offer) by a particular time and to a mutually agreed-upon standard. The cycle of a conversation is completed when the person to whom the promise was made declares that they are satisfied that the promise has been fulfilled.

For example, Kevin asks (requests) his partner, Susan, to show him how to meditate. Susan agrees (promises). Susan sits with Kevin and explains to him the practice of "just sitting." She takes action and fulfills her promise. After a week, Kevin says, "Thanks. I'm confident I can do this by myself." He says he's satisfied. The conversation is complete.

MAKING REQUESTS

At this point, you might say, "This is too simplistic. Things just don't work this way." That's true. Much of the time we do not talk in these simple terms of requests, offers, and promises. The word "request" is a single term that covers a variety of actions, which include asking, encouraging, demanding, recommending, suggesting, soliciting, ordering, begging, pleading, urging, and cajoling.

CLEAN REQUESTS VERSUS DEMANDS

The optimal way to coordinate our actions in a group or couple is to make clear requests. Whenever we make demands, we will encounter some kind of resistance. Every being on Earth responds this way instinctively. Deep inside we all feel the pressure and constriction that happens when we lose our basic sense of freedom.

How do we know when we are making demands on another? When we are not ready to hear a "no" in response to our request. A simple way of looking at this is that I am free to ask you for what I need or want, and you are totally free to say "yes" or "no." If I experience resentment or anger when you refuse me, it means I have been making a demand on you. This distinction between asking and requesting versus demanding is one of the core technologies of nonviolent communication.

The virtue of examining these components of a conversation for action—as we're doing—is that it helps us identify *exactly* where we and others create incompletions. As we bring clarity to the creation and management of our commitments, we learn how to remain complete at each stage of our conversation.

For example, if someone seems to be "suggesting" that we do something, we can simply ask, "Is that a request?" If they say, "Yes," then we know where we are. If they say, "Well, not exactly . . . I mean, I was wondering if you'd like to think about combining our skills and running a workshop together." We see that it's not a clear request. In fact, it sounds like they want to speculate about facilitating something together. So we might respond by saying, "I'm certainly open to talking with you about this. When would you like to discuss it?"

Our response is a request. We've moved back into a conversation for action, in order to engage in a speculative conversation about the possibility of working together. We can see here how the natural flow of these conversations moves us in cycles, back and forth between the three different kinds of conversations.

THE TRANSITION FROM "FULFILLING REQUESTS" TO "MAKING OFFERS"

As children and young adults, we're often at the receiving end of a constant stream of requests or even demands: "Put your toys away." "Don't forget to wash behind your ears." "You can't go out unless you finish your homework." "Make sure you use contraceptives." This type of conditioning can continue through adolescence into our adult years. Some people don't grow beyond believing that life consists of fulfilling the requests of a boss and being given some remuneration in return. Our couple relationships can also be built on the same structure: a wife or husband is delegated to the role of fulfilling a spouse's requests for time, attention, agreement, sex, entertainment, nutrition, etc. This is a very limited and self-centered way of experiencing ourselves.

A different experience of ourselves emerges when we begin to see ourselves not as someone who does what others ask of them, but in terms of what we can contribute to others. Surely this is a significant part of what it is to become an adult. Instead of waiting to be told what to do, we ask what we can do for others: "How can I help you?" "Is there something I can do for you?" "It looks like you could use a hand with that." This simple distinction between "fulfilling requests" and "making offers" is a great way for tracking the expansion of our vision from being focused on ourselves to include our relationships with others. Growing and expanding means that we can make more offers, bigger offers, and deeper, more significant offers.

In one of the first conversations I had with Fernando Flores, he asked me a question that I don't think I've been asked before. I was wanting to ask something from him, but he moves fast. He said, "What have you got to offer me?" I thought, "Okay! He obviously doesn't have a problem in getting what he wants or needs. He's in the position where he is receiving a stream of offers every day—offers to give lectures here and there, make an intervention in this company, collaborate on a book, etc. He has to decide what offers he'll accept. So that's a natural first question for him to ask me." I was actually dumbfounded. I didn't have a response. I wasn't thinking in terms of what I could offer him. Flores didn't need anything from me. He was offering me an entirely different perspective. He was asking me to think in terms of what I can offer rather than of what I want.

BEING AN OFFER

I said that a promise or commitment is made for us to do or not do something, the moment we make an offer to someone and they accept it. I might say to my partner, "I promise that I won't flirt with other women." That could be a response to a request that my partner has made. But it could also be an unsolicited offer coming from my own wish to create love and harmony. This is an example of "making an offer."

I'd also like to introduce you to the idea of "being an offer." "Being an offer" is different from "making an offer." We make an offer when we say to our neighbor, "Would you like me to do anything for you while you're on vacation?" Or to a colleague, "Can I help you with anything?" These are specific offers.

But it's also helpful to think of yourself as an offer. What is the offering that you are? Perhaps you're an offering of inspiration for youth. Perhaps you're an offering of meticulous physical care. Perhaps you're an offering of peace and tranquility. Perhaps you are an offering for bringing people together, for networking.

We have probably all experienced being with someone who is living in a place that is full of love, generosity, and integrity. People like this don't need to make offers. They *are* an offer. Their being, their conversations, and their actions can all be experienced as an offer. The way they eat their food, or interact with their secretaries, is an offering for everyone who witnesses them.

RESPONSES

The interesting thing is that there are a limited number of ways to effectively respond to a request or an offer. We can blur the boundaries between these, but if we want to be complete, we also need to be clear. We can:

- Accept
- Decline
- Negotiate
- Commit to commit

Accepting or declining is reasonably straightforward, although *how* we do so directly impacts our identity, and any identity we are wishing to create for the future. It is vital that before we actually respond to a request, we understand and are clear about the conditions of fulfillment for the request.

CONDITIONS OF FULFILLMENT

Every time we make a request or agree to fulfill a request, we must ensure that the conditions of fulfillment are clear. By conditions of fulfillment, we're referring to the conditions—both explicit and assumed—that, if completed, would constitute our request's being satisfactorily fulfilled. The conditions of fulfillment specify the standards, quality, resources, implications, and so on.

"Assumed" conditions of fulfillment hold great potential for conflict and misunderstanding. They should be treated cautiously and with full awareness of the potential breakdown. Why? Because the person fulfilling the request may have quite a different idea of what is required for satisfactory completion.

Many promises need to include an expected completion date. If a "by when" isn't included, it becomes impossible to coordinate action. Imagine trying to oversee the construction of a house if there are no clear completion dates for the foundations, framing, plumbing, electrical, etc.

On the other hand, events that are closely tied to our feelings, emotions, and special karmic connections can't be calendarized. It's difficult to set a "do by" date for falling in love, finding a guru, or gaining full realization! Trying to do this is a recipe for possible disappointment.

FACTS AND INTERPRETATIONS

In order to define "conditions of fulfillment," we need to be clear about the difference between facts and interpretations and assessments. For example, if I tell you that I want you to do a "good" job, "good" is an interpretation. What is "good" for you might be exceptional for me, or it might be really sloppy. It depends on my standards of assessment.

Here, we come back to Marshall Rosenberg's point about observing without evaluation. It's very important to be able to recognize the difference between fact and interpretation, because most people have a strong habit of offering interpretations, assessments, and opinions about nearly everything, as though they were facts. When we say that Swami so-and-so is the greatest living nondual master of the last century, or that the best practice to achieve awakening is the practice of no-practice, these are all interpretations. Interpretations can be very personal (they reflect our own beliefs) or they can be grounded in the social reality. But they can't be true or false. A great deal of confusion is created by believing that interpretations can be true or false.

"Facts," on the other hand, are publically observable phenomena. When we clarify the conditions for fulfilling a promise, we need to ground our interpretation by referring to facts. Instead of saying that I want you to develop and make a top-quality video, I specify that I want a two-camera shoot, with two operators, using high-definition cameras and external microphones going through a mixer, and edited using specific software and output to NTSC and PAL formats. Instead of asking you to make me a fantastic meal, I ask you to make chicken biryani and lemon rice, with a dry red wine and strawberry shortcake for dessert.

PROMISES: ACCEPT OR DECLINE

A promise is the ultimate, effective response to a request. In actual conversations, the promise can be spoken of—and listened to—as an agreement, contract, commitment, guarantee, consent, refusal, or denial. We may promise to do (accept) or not do (decline) something, but without some sort of promise, we cannot generate effective action. A promise is also generated when an offer that someone makes is accepted by the person to whom the offer is made. As soon as the offer is accepted, the person making the offer effectively promises to fulfill that offer. When we promise to "not do" something— that is, we decline—then we effectively close down the conversation for action. This can be useful at times, but if used repeatedly, it will certainly close down future opportunities for collaboration.

The important point to appreciate is that when we make a commitment, when we promise to do something, the person to whom we've made the promise adjusts their life accordingly. They close down other opportunities in order to open themselves to being and working with us. Commitments are not insignificant events. The way we move in the world is primarily a function of the commitments we've made to other people and which others have made to us.

NEGOTIATION

We live in a world where everyone is the center of their universe. It's impossible for people to consistently take care of needs when they have needs of their own. Similarly, it's quite unrealistic to think that we can function in a way that never conflicts with other people's interests and concerns.

So we must be willing to negotiate and know how to do this. When someone makes a request, we often can't do exactly as requested. This is when the skill of counteroffering is vital. Although, there are times when our position in relationship to the person making the request does not allow us to negotiate freely, there are many ways to counteroffer. For example, you may accept the request conditional upon more resources—more time, money, people, and so on. Or you may accept the request conditional upon being relieved of other commitments.

When a counteroffer is accepted by whoever made the initial request, a promise to produce action is established. In other words, we counteroffer in the spirit of establishing a mutually acceptable commitment.

COMMIT TO COMMIT

Sometimes we're not in a position to accept or decline a request when it is made to us. We may need to check our existing commitments or availability of resources to fulfill the request. This is when we "commit to commit." We commit to get back to the person with a clear response (accept, decline, or counteroffer) by a specific time. For example, we may say, "I can't say right now whether I can do this report for you, but I'll get back to you by 9:00 a.m. tomorrow to let you know."

"Committing to commit" gives you some breathing space, but you need to use it wisely. You don't "commit to commit" in order to not think about what has just been requested of you. You "commit to commit" to give yourself time to *feel* how this commitment impacts your life and sits with your other specific and global responsibilities. If you're being asked to commit a lot of resources (time, energy, money), you might want to imagine what your life will be like midway through fulfilling your promise. Is this what you want to be doing? How will you feel? What moods does this work and partnering produce in you? Is this work and partnering consistent with your priorities and values? Is it coherent with your other commitments?

When we develop an interest in the contemplative life, it's very important to not overcommit ourselves to the point where we're stretched and constantly exhausted. We need time and leisure to cultivate unconditioned awareness. "Committing to commit" can give us the time to check if new responsibilities we may enter into support our psychological and spiritual development.

On several occasions, students have asked me if they should accept, or apply for, a promotion. I recommend that they give themselves a week to sit with this possibility, imagining how their life will be in this new situation: "Will it work for my energy level, serenity, and well-being? Does my body want to be in this new environment? What would my body prefer?" Sometimes they come back a year later and say they wish they'd really listened to what their meditation was telling them. They'll often say, "I knew at the time that it probably wasn't the best move, but I felt I couldn't refuse. Now I wish I'd listened to myself, and also to what my body was telling me."

REVOKE

When you make a promise — to yourself or others — your intention to fulfill your promise is given and assumed. The significant thing is that the person to whom the promise is made *changes what they are doing* as a function of your promise. Promises aren't insignificant. If you're unable to keep a commitment, it needs to be clearly revoked.

Revoking a commitment is ideally done as close as possible to when the promise was made. This makes it much easier for whoever made the request to make alternative arrangements and to deal with any breakdown we may have precipitated. It's important when we revoke a promise to give people space to discuss our actions, and to listen openly to any objections they may have regarding our cancellation. Allowing this kind of space can really help to bring things to completion with less conflict and suffering. We need to be aware that revoking a promise is not a small thing on the level of our human conditioning. It has far-reaching implications. It can impact our identity at the same time as it impacts the person to whom the promise had been made.

There is no such thing as perfect planning. We are sometimes forced to revoke our promises in order to take care of other commitments. Doing this clearly and openly is the most responsible way to take care of our commitments. Failing to fulfill a promise, without warning or notice, is a guaranteed way to produce a breakdown in trust.

ACKNOWLEDGING COMPLETION

Conversations for action aren't complete until we formally acknowledge their completion. This is usually done by saying, "Thanks," "Good work," "I'm pleased with the results," and so on. Not only do these declarations signal the end of the conversation; they also maintain the possibility of opening up new conversations in the future. When people feel appreciated, they are more open to future relationships with us. It is vital to appropriately acknowledge others and give them clear feedback.

INTERRUPTIONS TO COLLECTIVE ACTION

Now that we've laid out the structure of a conversation for action, we can easily identify where glitches and ruptures can happen. In order to be able to communicate effectively, we need to have access to all the possible ways of delivering and responding to requests and offers. I'm sure you can identify responses within these conversational cycles that you rarely use, or that you may even strongly resist. For example, many people find it difficult to decline requests.

I know a lot of what I'm saying here must seem quite obvious. It's not exactly rocket science to understand that keeping our commitments helps us create a better life together. But if getting along in this way is really so basic and simple, why is it that the divorce rate in our society is over fifty percent right now?

If we look a little more deeply and honestly, we can see that actually mastering these ways of communicating requires a great deal of integrity. This kind of practice asks us to look clearly and consistently at what is really going on inside us every time we agree to anything or make a promise — to ourselves or the people around us. The lack of integrity in our collective communication at the present time has created widespread conditions of apathy, hopelessness, and despair. Learning how to create real trust in all our relationships is a possibility with profound implications. So let's identify the main areas where ruptures and miscommunications occur within conversations for action.

UNCLEAR COMMITMENTS: MAKING OBLIQUE OFFERS AND REQUESTS

Many communication problems occur because we simply aren't clear when we are making a request or offer. Requests and offers can be sharp and clear, or vague and liquid. A vague or oblique request is one in which we *suggest* that someone *might* do something. Perhaps we say, "Maybe it'd be a good idea to invite your parents." We intend for our suggestion to be received as a request, but we deliver it as a vague suggestion. The person to whom we're communicating may or may not be aware that we are making a request. We can't be sure, because we have not made ourselves clear.

Perhaps we feel uncomfortable delivering a clear request. We might feel that it's too direct or impolite, so we deliver a vague suggestion and *hope* that our partner picks up on it and does what we've intimated. We may spend a lot of time hoping for things that never happen! We could even develop a whole philosophy of life around this.

When we're making an offer to do something, we might say, "I could do such-and-such," perhaps half-hoping that it evaporates into the ether. Our offer is an expression of our "good intentions," but we secretly hope that we won't have to go anywhere with it.

DIFFICULTIES IN DECLINING REQUESTS

For some people, it's nearly impossible to decline a request, particularly in a work environment. People fear that if they decline a request, they'll produce irreparable damage to their career prospects. But it's extremely important to be able to decline requests, to be able to say: "No, I'm sorry. I'd like to help you, but I can't." "I hear you, and my answer is no." "I understand how you feel, but I need to say no."

Of course, there are consequences involved in declining requests. If we do this repeatedly and for obviously self-serving reasons, we are likely to be marginalized and excluded by our families, friends, and communities. If the requests that we decline are integral to our contracts, such as fidelity in our marriage, or doing the work we're paid to do, we could quickly find ourselves on the street, without a job or a spouse.

For this reason, when we decline a request, it's often appropriate and prudent to give reasons and offer an unapologetic explanation: "I have other commitments. I don't have the time to take on anything more." "I don't have the expertise to fulfill that request." "I disagree with the need for us to do that." We can also make suggestions about how to work around the fact that we can't fulfill the request ourselves: "Perhaps Susan would be interested in working with your team on that project."

FAILING TO SPECIFY A COMPLETION TIME

It sounds obvious that when we make or receive a commitment, it needs to include a time for completion. It's impossible to coordinate many activities if we have no idea when we can expect each one to be completed. Yet, how often do we offer to do something—like take a vacation, clean the garage, write a book, or phone a friend—without giving any indication of when this will happen. How often do we say, "Yes, I'll do it," without saying when. Or accept others' offers of support and assistance without asking, "When would you like to do this?" Again, we make assumptions, and our assumptions often lead to disappointment: "I thought we were going to go out for a meal this week!" "Sure, that sounds great. We're going to do it!" "When?" "Soon. I'll call you." We can live in these places of incompletion with people for months or years, and just put up with it.

SPECIFYING A COMPLETION DATE
WHEN IT IS INAPPROPRIATE

As I said earlier, activities that closely depend on the presence of specific moods and emotions can't be orchestrated in the same way as things like setting a date for completing a quotation for a client. Some activities need to be open and fluid. "We have to have sex tonight" has caused innumerable upsets in relationships.

FAILING TO ESTABLISH THE CONDITIONS OF SATISFACTION

One of the most common ways we create dissatisfaction for ourselves and others is failing to be precise about "what needs to be done." We assume that others know what we want done, and that they know and agree with what we intend to do. We assume that we share the same standards. But very often there's a discrepancy between what actually gets done and what we or others expect. We see this all the time. We think we've completed a task to the satisfaction of the person to whom we've made a commitment, only to find them angry or upset. They expected us to do more, or do things differently, consult with other people, use fewer resources, or spend less time, etc. And we had no idea.

What's needed is simply a conversation *within* a conversation for action that specifies the "conditions of satisfaction." We do this for contractual agreements, such as getting our house painted. We specify the type of priming, brand of paint, color, number of coats, whether the trimmings are to be included, etc. We're willing to spend time getting clear with our painters, but not with our colleagues or intimate partners. We can learn to be precise whenever we anticipate unclarity. For example, when we're working with someone new, we can take the time to let them know exactly what it is that we want.

A great deal of frustration and upset can be avoided by spending a little extra time clarifying what we expect when someone commits to do something for us, and similarly, clarifying exactly what we need to do when we make a commitment to someone else.

INABILITY TO REVOKE OR RENEGOTIATE A PROMISE

We can't predict the future, and it's not in our control either. Consequently, even though we have every intention of fulfilling a promise when we make one, circumstances can change. Accidents happen. We get ill. Our priorities change.

While it is important not to revoke a promise or renegotiate the terms of a commitment lightly, we need to be willing to do this when the circumstances require it. Many people have destroyed their marriages rather than renegotiate the terms of their work commitments. And people regularly compromise their health because they're unable or unwilling to broach a conversation in which they explain that they've overcommitted themselves and need to be relieved of some responsibilities.

FAILING TO DECLARE COMPLETION

It's understandable to think that we finish a project when we stop work on it, but if our work is fulfilling a commitment we've made to someone else, we need to communicate that it's finished. This sounds obvious, but it's not uncommon for people to assume someone is still working on a task long after it's been completed: "I assumed you must have had a problem with this. Why didn't you tell me you'd finished? I've been holding off . . ."

FAILING TO ACKNOWLEDGE SATISFACTION

A conversation for action is completed when the person to whom a promise has been made acknowledges completion. If this doesn't happen, it leaves the person who has made the promise incomplete. If they're not thanked or acknowledged in some way for satisfactorily completing a task, they can be left wondering what to do: "Do I need to put more work into this?" "Have I finished yet?" "Can I move on?"

BUILDING TRUST

Let's return to the foundation of Flores' work—building trust. People support us to the extent that they can trust us. And our capacity to create an inspired, radiant field around us depends on others' being able to trust us.

Our inability to know *when* to trust others, and how to *create* trust when it's missing, is a great source of disappointment and suffering for most people. Often we think of trust as a mysterious phenomenon. People talk about it the way they talk about chemistry in a relationship: it's there or it's not. We often hear people say, "I don't know why I can't trust him. It's just something about him. I can't say what it is, but I don't trust him." And, conversely, we sometimes trust people implicitly, to the point where it's impossible for us to imagine their doing anything that would hurt or harm us.

Every day we see how long-standing relationships that have been built on trust can degrade over time, producing immense suffering. And time and again, we see people entering into a relationship or business partnership on a hunch that it's the right thing to do. We also know of cases where people limit their opportunities for intimacy and collaboration because they can't trust anyone.

The first thing to note in the examples listed above is how easy it is to globalize or generalize our assessments about whether or not we can trust someone. It's easy to forget that we can trust someone in one area (being a good father) and not trust them in another (listening to our needs for intimacy or closeness). If we want to collaborate with people, we need to know where we can trust them to fulfill their promises and where we can't. It doesn't help to work with a global assessment.

THE NATURE OF TRUST

So what is trust and how do we create it and nurture it? Flores analyzes trust in a way that gives us a real handle on the experience. Interestingly, he says that most of his learning about trust happened during his three years as a political prisoner under the Pinochet dictatorship in Chile.

When we trust someone, we're making an assessment in four different areas. We're assessing them in terms of their:

- Competence
- Reliability
- Sincerity
- Engagement

Competence signifies that someone has the skill set and knowledge to fulfill promises in a particular area: psychotherapy, financial planning, etc. Reliability signifies that someone can be relied on to do what they say. Their actions are consistent with their words. They follow through on their promises. Sincerity signifies the presence of a correspondence or coherence between what someone says publicly and what their private intentions are. In other words, they operate from a basic level of integrity and honesty. Engagement means that someone is involved in a particular area of our life. They have a genuine interest in who we are, in our fundamental well-being. We can count on them to show up and be fully present. We need to be able to trust someone in all four dimensions in order to have a sound basis for trust. If any one is missing, we shouldn't be surprised when commitments aren't fulfilled.

We also need to be aware of our own behavior. When we make a promise to someone to do something—to co-parent with them, to help them with their computer, to provide them with sound spiritual advice—are we competent, reliable, sincere, and engaged? If any one of these is missing, we should be cautious about making a commitment.

Generally, it isn't too difficult to ascertain if someone is competent and reliable. It's more difficult to determine if someone is sincere and engaged. But it's possible. The less we're invested in personal or self-centered outcomes, the more easily we can read people's intentions. Self-interest always distorts our perceptions of other people.

The ability to build trust with the people in our life opens up tremendous space in which compassion, kindness, and heart wisdom can flourish. Without trust, we encounter constant conflict and the sense of betrayal, no matter how well-intentioned and passionate we may be. When trust is not there, our hearts just close down, and we relate to each other from a place of scarcity and deep separation. The flowering of trust is like a doorway that allows us to move together into a place of unconditioned awareness and love.

A CONTEMPLATION

I want to conclude by offering you an image through which you can experience yourself in this world of relationships and society. The Vajrayana, or Tantric, traditions of Hinduism and Buddhism give us the wonderful image of a mandala. We're familiar with mandalas as aerial views that depict the architectural structure and features of the dharmic environments that manifest around enlightened beings—buddhas and *bodhisattvas*. A mandala depicts the atmospheric, psychic, and holographic creation that flows forth from the radiant mind of awakened beings. A mandala clarifies the multidimensional forces that expedite and facilitate the spiritual evolution of everyone who's privileged to inhabit them, even if only for a few seconds. These are pure or totally radiant mandalas.

THE MANDALA OF OUR EXISTENCE

The concept of a mandala can be applied to any environment that has a center and a horizon. In this way, each of us stands at the center of our own mandala. Every mandala is different, and there are over six billion mandalas on our planet. In a sense, a mandala is the singularity that creates and uncreates our universe moment by moment.

My mandala is populated by my wife, my daughters, my parents, my Radiant Mind students, and my Timeless Wisdom support team. These are the people who figure most prominently in my universe, and to whom I am most accountable. But my mandala is the totality of my experience, so it also includes much more than this, because I'm a citizen of the world and of the universe.

The quality and reach of our mandala as a function of sharing inner peace, harmony, richness, and fulfillment is determined by our access to unconditioned awareness, the love in our heart, and our skills in communication and manifestation. If the communication within a mandala is dishonest, deceitful, disrespectful, sloppy and imprecise, and driven purely by the needs of physical survival or the perpetuation of divisive and egocentric beliefs systems, our mandala will clearly display the results of those communications. It will be fraught with disappointments, insecurity, betrayals, corruptions, and different forms of violence.

If our communication is inspired, creative, respectful, honest, clear, and realistic, then we're capable of producing beautiful structures that serve as foundations and bridges for people to discover harmony, love, well-being, and liberation. Every mandala is different, yet every mandala can serve as an environment that contributes to our collective evolution. There's so much work to be done in creating the conditions that support people in realizing their highest potential that it really doesn't matter where and how we contribute. We're always working within the mandala of our present existence.

DIFFERENT KINDS OF MANDALAS

Some people are in retreat, working exclusively on the mandala of their mind—creating an inner landscape of tender emotions and exquisite feelings of infinite love and boundless joy, coupled with the realization of impermanence and insubstantiality. Your mandala might be focused on building a trusting and powerful relationship with a spiritual teacher. You might be growing a business mandala that nurtures and takes care of its staff and customers. You might be creating a partnership mandala in which you're consciously using the structure and potential of an intimate relationship for growth and evolution. You might be creating a family mandala, learning how to bring harmony to the potentially conflicting demands of work, parenting, and partnering. Or you might be creating several different mandalas, for the different areas of your life.

Whether mandalas are effective or not, the intention of every mandala is to bring people to ultimate fulfillment. This happens through a process of visioning a goal, moving toward that goal, seeing its limitations, revisioning the goal, and so on, until we realize the state where there's nothing more we could conceivably want because we're free of all needs and preferences.

THE GREAT SHARING: FILLING THE FIELD
WITH YOUR OWN PERFECT RADIANCE

Now you're at a special point in your evolution, because you know the experience that's at the end of all your searching, and you're aware of the close connection between how you live your daily life and buddha-mind. You've seen how unconditioned awareness is the ultimate medicine, and how the function of every cultural institution—every religion, every type of political system, every business transaction, and every relationship—can be designed to help us feel complete and whole. Everything you do is ultimately designed to lead to unconditioned awareness, whether you're conscious of this or not.

In this appendix, we've explored the potential for introducing a technology of communication skills into the mandala of our life. In this way, you can cultivate a clearer and more vivid sense of whether your conversations and actions are increasing or decreasing your proximity to unconditioned awareness. You're able to create congruence and alignment between your actions and the structures you build to deepen and share the experience of buddha-nature. You will begin to use the mandala of your existence as a vehicle for bringing love and freedom to your partners, families, friends, colleagues, and communities.

Now that you've experienced the unobstructed nature of radiant mind, and now that you know that this is what everyone's actually looking for, whether they realize it or not, I'm certain that you'll find yourself connecting with others in the unbounded space of pure awareness. As the great bodhisattvas declare, the radiance of the perfectly contentless wisdom of buddha-mind simply can't be obstructed, thwarted, suppressed, or contained. So don't hold back. You can't anyway.

Notes

INTRODUCTION

1. Lex Hixon, "Tilopa's Song to Naropa," in *Mother of the Buddhas: Meditation on the Prajnaparamita Sutra,* (Wheaton, IL: Quest Books, 1993), 247.
As the darkness, even were it to last a thousand years, could not conceal the rising sun, so countless ages of conflict and suffering cannot conceal the innate radiance of Mind.

2. Robert A.F. Thurman, "The Treasury of Wish-Fulfilling Gems," in *Essential Tibetan Buddhism,* (New Delhi, India: HarperCollins, 1996), 175.
From Longchenpa
This reality has names of many different kinds.
It is "the realm " that transcends life and liberation.
And the primally present "natural spontaneity,"
As the "essential realm" obscured by defilement,
As the "ultimate truth," the condition of reality,
As the originally pure "stainless translucency,"
As the "central reality" that dispels extremisms,
As the "transcendent wisdom " beyond fabrications,
As the "indivisible reality" clear-void-purity,
As the "Suchness" reality free of death transitions.
Such names are accepted by the clear-seeing wise.

3. John M. Reynolds, *The Golden Letters: The Tibetan Teachings of Garab Dorje, First Dzogchen Master* (Ithaca, NY: Snow Lion Publications, 1996), 33.

CHAPTER THREE: OBSTACLES TO EXPERIENCING
UNCONDITIONED AWARENESS

1. Lex Hixon, "Tilopa's Song to Naropa," in *Mother of the Buddhas: Meditation on the Prajnaparamita Sutra*, (Wheaton, IL: Quest Books, 1993), 250.

   The noble way of Mahamudra never engages in the drama of imprisonment and release. The sage of Mahamudra has absolutely no distractions, because no war against distractions has ever been declared. This nobility and gentleness alone, this non-violence of thought and action, is the traceless path of all Buddhas. To walk this all-embracing way is the bliss of Buddhahood.

2. Longchen Rabjam, *The Precious Treasury of the Way of Abiding* (Junction City, CA: Padma Publishing, 1998), 39.

   Since effort—which creates causes and effects, whether positive or negative — is unnecessary, immerse yourself in genuine being, resting naturally with nothing needing to be done. The expanse of spontaneous presence entails no deliberate effort, no acceptance or rejection. From now on make no effort, since phenomena already are what they are. Even the enlightenment of all victorious ones of the three times is spontaneously present as a supremely blissful state of natural rest.

3. Lex Hixon, *Mother of the Buddhas: Meditation on the Prajnaparamita Sutra*, (Wheaton, IL: Quest Books, 1993), 65.

   Dear friends, you cannot understand because there is absolutely nothing finite to understand. You are not lacking in refinement of intellect. There is simply nothing separate or substantial in Prajnaparamita to which the intellect can be applied, because perfect Wisdom does not present any graspable or thinkable doctrine and offers no describable method of contemplation.

4. Jennifer Welwood, "Dancing with Form and Emptiness in Intimate Relationship," in *Sacred Mirror: Nondual Wisdom & Psychotherapy*, ed. John J. Prendergast, Peter Fenner, and Sheila Krystal (St. Paul, MN: Paragon House Publishers, 2003), 292.

   Rather than recognizing emptiness as our own nature, we see it as an enemy that we have to avoid or defeat.

CHAPTER FOUR: CONTEMPLATIVE PRACTICE

1. Takpo Tashi Nangyal (trans. and ed. Lobsang P. Lhalungpa), *Mahamudra: The Quintessence of Mind and Meditation* (Boston: Shambhala, 1986), 393.
Because it is devoid of any innate nature, meditation does not exist. The act of meditation is not meditation. Because it is neither substance nor nothingness, meditation cannot be a conceivable reality.
Kalachakra Tantra

2. Keith Dowman, *The Flight of the Garuda: Teachings of the Dzokchen Tradition of Tibetan Buddhism* (Somerville, MA: Wisdom Publications, 1994), 121.
Grasp this paradox my sons and daughters! There is not so much as a mote of dust upon which to meditate, but it is crucial to sustain unwavering attention with presence of mind.
Tibetan master, Shabkar

3. Lex Hixon, "Tilopa's Song to Naropa," in *Mother of the Buddhas: Meditation on the Prajnaparamita Sutra*, (Wheaton, IL: Quest Books, 1993), 248.
To realize the inexpressible truth, do not manipulate mind or body but simply open into transparency with relaxed, natural grace.

CHAPTER FIVE: NONINTERFERENCE AND THE PRACTICE OF NATURAL RELEASE

1. Lao Tzu, *The Tao Te Ching: An English Translation*, 1998 © by Eiichi Shimomissé
http://www.csudh.edu/phenom_studies/laotzu/taoteching.htm
Empty oneself more and more, finally you reach no action.
Where there is no action, nothing is left undone.
Tao Te Ching

2. Miranda Shaw (tr.), "Niguma: Mahamudra as Spontaneous Liberation," in *Passionate Enlightenment*, (Princeton, NJ: Princeton University Press: New edition, 1995), 88.
In a pellucid ocean, bubbles arise and dissolve again.
Just so, thoughts are no different from ultimate reality, so don't find fault, remain at ease.

Whatever arises, whatever occurs, don't grasp — release it on the spot.
Niguma (11th-century female master)

3. Namkhai, Norbu, *Dzog Chen and Zen,* (Oakland, CA: Zhang Zhung Editions, 1984), 30.

When we speak of the path of self-liberation, there is neither a concept of renunciation, because if it is always my energy manifesting, then it can manifest in many different ways; nor is there a concept of transformation, because the principle here is that I find myself in a state of pure presence, of contemplation. If I find myself for an instant in a state of contemplation, then from that point of view, wrath and compassion are one and the same. Good and evil are one and the same. In that condition there is nothing to do; one liberates oneself, because one finds oneself in one's own dimension of energy without escaping and without renouncing anything. This is the principle of self-liberation.

CHAPTER SIX: OBSERVING FIXATIONS

1. Seng-Ts'an, "The Mind of Absolute Truth." In Stephen Mitchell, *The Enlightened Heart: An Anthology of Sacred Poetry.* (New York: Harper Perennial, 1989)

Don't keep searching for the truth, just let go of your opinions.

2. Longchenpa, *The Natural Freedom of Being* (an unpublished translation of the *Rang grol skor gsum*) 1991, 67.

Biased attitudes are the factor which binds one. The meaning of nonduality occurs when you're free of opinions and transcend clinging to extremes. There is no other way to disclose this. You can't see it by looking for it. Nor can you find it though logical analysis. Calling it "this" doesn't reveal it, so in relationship to the natural state don't fetter, or liberate it, with a grasping mind.
Longchenpa

CHAPTER EIGHT: COMPLETING IN THE HERE AND NOW

1. Venerable Shyalpa Rinpoche, "A Path of Honesty," *Shambhala Sun,* May 2003, 34.

[T]he energy that comes out of your primordially pure nature is more valid than anything else.

Shyalpa Rinpoche, contemporary Nyingma lama [2003]

CHAPTER TEN: BROADENING THE RIVER OF LIFE

1. Lama Thubten Yeshe, *Make Your Mind an Ocean* (Boston: Lama Yeshe Wisdom Archives, 1999), 43.
   If you expect your life to be up and down, your mind will be much more peaceful.

2. Howard Raphael Cushnir, *Unconditional Bliss: Finding Happiness in the Face of Hardship* (India: New Age Books, New Ed edition, 2003), 74.
   When we truly hate what's happening, our instinct is to flee from it like a house on fire. But if we can learn to turn around and enter that fire, to let it burn all our resistance away, then we find ourselves arising from the ashes with a new sense of power and freedom.

3. Venerable Shyalpa Rinpoche, "A Path of Honesty," *Shambhala Sun*, May 2003, 34.
   After all, what is so scary about things just as they are? If we see things as they are, at least we know the truth. What should frighten us is denying things as they are.
   Shyalpa Rinpoche, a contemporary Nyingma lama

4. Venerable Shyalpa Rinpoche, "A Path of Honesty," *Shambhala Sun*, May 2003, 34.
   When we ignore the present moment . . . there are consequences: we create karma, we create suffering. If we live this moment only fifty percent, the fifty percent we failed to live will surely cause us difficulties later.

5. Venerable Shyalpa Rinpoche, "A Path of Honesty," *Shambhala Sun*, May 2003, 34.
   "True fearlessness comes from the knowledge that we will never lie to ourselves, that we will never evade a single moment of our lives. We will be fully present for every moment and every consequence." Rinpoche speaks of this "willingness to see things as they are, without having any motive or intention whatsoever to them."

CHAPTER ELEVEN: SERENITY AND "SEEING THROUGH"

1. Lex Hixon, "Tilopa's Song to Naropa," in *Mother of the Buddhas: Meditation on the Prajnaparamita Sutra,* (Wheaton, IL: Quest Books, 1993), 175.

   When the universal panorama is clearly seen to manifest without any objective or subjective supports, viewless knowledge awakens spontaneously. Simply by not reviewing any appearing structures, one establishes the true view of what is. This viewless view is what constitutes the Buddha nature and acts dynamically as the mother of wisdom, revealing whatever is simply as what it is — empty of substantial self-existence, unchartable and uncharacterizable, calmly quiet and already blissfully awakened.

CHAPTER TWELVE: DECONSTRUCTING CONVERSATIONS

1. This is often quoted. There is only one English translation of this Sutra by D.T. Suzuki.

   Reality is not as it seems. Nor is it different.
   Lankavatara Sutra

2. The motto of *The Dot* (Quarterly Newspaper of the Shambhala Mandala): Nothing happerns and we report it.

3. Former website: http://hjem.get2net.dk/civet-cat/mahayana-writings/demonstration-of-buddhahood-sutra.htm

   The Buddha asked, "Manjushri, what should one rely upon for right practice?" "He who practices rightly relies upon nothing." The Buddha asked, "Does he not practice according to the path?" "If he practices in accordance with anything, his practice will be conditioned. A conditioned practice is not one of equality. Why? Because it is not exempt from arising, abiding, and perishing."
   Demonstration of Buddhahood Sutra

4. Adapted from Nagarjuna, (Jay L.Garfield, trs. and com.), *Mulamadhyamakarika: The Fundamental Verses of the Middle Way* (New York, Oxford University Press, 1995), 2.

It is unceasing yet unborn, unannihilated yet not permanent, neither coming into or going out (of existence), without distinction, without identity, relatively arisen and free of conceptual constructions.
Nagarjuna's dedication

CHAPTER THIRTEEN: SOME FINAL LIFT-OFF POINTS"

1. Lex Hixon, *Mother of the Buddhas: Meditation on the Prajnaparamita Sutra*, (Wheaton, IL: Quest Books, 1993), 201.
   Without developing the consummate contemplative art of the bodhisattva — skillful nonchalance and ceaseless concern — no aspirant can remain authentically and passionately dedicated to the boundless task of universal awakening. The perfection of wisdom alone can keep selflessness and love pure and steady under all conditions. Such is the realization of perfect wisdom through the entire body, speech, and mind of the bodhisattva, who is free from controlling, battling, repressing, or extinguishing any form of manifestation.

Recommended Books and Audio

While I hope *Radiant Mind* is reasonably complete and comprehensive, I know that your practice and beyond-practice can be complemented by the words of others. The following is a sampling of texts by ancient and modern Asian masters as well as some books by contemporary Western spiritual teachers including those who teach from a more nondual perspective. I've included a cross-section of books. The list is quite large because I know people have different preferences. For example, I prefer to go back to the ancient texts, especially now that the translations have reached a point of real excellence. Other readers will prefer the works of contemporary teachers, perhaps those who they can see in person. Some books are more strictly nondual, teaching from the result level. Others are more psychological and methodological.

My only caution is not to forget that unconditioned awareness has nothing to do with what you know intellectually. So if you read any of these books or others you come by, read them not so much for what you can understand, but rather with a view to shifting your consciousness into a state that's more spacious and open. You might like to check from time to time. "Why am I reading this right now? Am I just keeping my mind busy, keeping the boredom at bay? Am I looking to confirm that I'm on the right track? Am I intrigued about a different approach to freedom?" The ideal function of nondual reading is to give our minds nothing to think about!

Adamson, Sailor Bob, *What's Wrong with Right Now?* Salisbury, England: Non-Duality Press, 2005.

Adyashanti, *Emptiness Dancing.* Boulder, CO: Sounds True, 2006.

Adyashanti. *True Meditation: Discover the Freedom of Pure Awareness.* Boulder, CO: Sounds True, 2006.

Ardagh, Arjuna. *The Translucent Revolution: How People Just Like You Are Waking Up and Changing the World.* Novato, CA: New World Library, 2005.

Brown, Daniel P. *Pointing Out the Great Way: The Stages of Meditation in Mahamudra.* Somerville, MA: Wisdom Publications, 2006.

Byrom, Thomas, trs. *The Heart of Awareness: A Translation of the Ashtavakra Gita.* Boston: Shambhala, 2001.

Chödrön, Pema. *The Places That Scare You: A Guide to Fearlessness in Difficult Times.* Boston: Shambhala, 2007.

Chödrön, Pema. *True Happiness.* Boulder, CO: Sounds True, 2006.

Chopra, Deepak. *Power, Freedom, and Grace: Living from the Source of Lasting Happiness.* San Rafael, CA: Amber-Allen Publishing, 2006.

Cleary, Thomas. *Zen Essence: The Science of Freedom.* Boston: Shambhala, 1989.

Cohen, Andrew. *Embracing Heaven and Earth.* Lenox, MA: Moksha Press, 2000.

Cushnir, Howard Raphael. *Setting Your Heart on Fire.* New York: Doubleday Broadway, 2004.

Cushnir, Howard Raphael. *Unconditional Bliss: Finding Happiness in the Face of Hardship.* India: New Age Books, 2003.

Dalai Lama, His Holiness the, and Howard C. Cutler. *The Art of Happiness: A Handbook for Living.* New York: Riverhead, 1998.

Dalai Lama, His Holiness the, and Jeffrey Hopkins. *How to See Yourself as You Really Are.* Riverside, NJ: Atria, 2006.

Das, Lama Surya. *Awakening to the Sacred: Creating a Personal Spiritual Life.* New York: Doubleday Broadway, 2000.

Das, Lama Surya. *Letting Go of the Person You Used to Be: Lessons on Change, Loss, and Spiritual Transformation.* New York: Doubleday Broadway, 2004.

Das, Lama Surya. *Natural Radiance: Awakening to Your Great Perfection.* Boulder, CO: Sounds True, 2005.

Fenner, Peter. *The Edge of Certainty: Dilemmas on the Buddhist Path.* Berwick, ME: Nicolas-Hays, 2002.

Fenner, Peter. *The Ontology of the Middle Way.* Dordrecht, Holland: Kluwer, 1991.

Fenner, Peter. *Reasoning into Reality: A Systems–Cybernetics and Therapeutic Interpretation of Middle Path Analysis.* Somerville, MA: Wisdom Publications, 1994.

Gangaji. *The Diamond in Your Pocket: Discovering Your True Radiance.* Boulder, CO: Sounds True, 2005.

Genoud, Charles. *Gesture of Awareness: A Radical Approach to Time, Space, and Movement.* Somerville, MA: Wisdom Publications, 2006.

Guenther, Herbert V, trs., *Ecstatic Spontaneity: Saraha's Three Cycles of Doha.* Berkeley, CA: Asian Humanities Press, 1993.

Gyamtso, Khenpo Tsultrim, *The Sun of Wisdom: Teachings on the Noble Nagarjuna's Fundamental Verses of the Middle Way.* Boston: Shambhala, 2003.

Harrison, Steven. *Being One: Finding Our Self in Relationship.* Boulder, CO: Sentient Publications, 2002.

Harrison, Steven. *Doing Nothing: Coming to the End of the Spiritual Search.* New York: Tarcher, 2002.

Hixon, Lex. *Mother of the Buddhas: Meditation on the Prajnaparamita Sutra.* Wheaton, IL: Quest Books, 1993.

Jourdain, Stephen. *Radical Awakening: Cutting Through the Conditioned Mind.* Inner Carlsbad, CA: Directions Foundation, 2001.

Laozi. *Dao De Jing: The Book of the Way.* Translated by Moss Roberts. Berkeley, CA: University of California Press, 2004.

Leighton, Taigen D., trs., *Cultivating the Empty Field: The Silent Illumination of Zen Master Hongzhi.* San Francisco: North Point Press, 1991.

Longchenpa. *Radical Dzogchen: Old Man Basking in the Sun.* Translated by Keith Dowman. Kathmandu, Nepal: Vajra Books, 2006.

Longchenpa. *You Are the Eyes of the World.* Translated by Kennard Lipman. Ithaca, NY: Snow Lion Publications, 2000.

Long chen rab 'byam pa. *Rang grol skor gsum.* Gangtok, Sikkim: Dodrup Chen Rinpoche, 1974.

Maharshi, Ramana. *Be as You Are: The Teachings of Sri Ramana Maharshi.* Edited by David Godman. New York: Penguin, 1989.

Maharshi, Ramana, *The Spiritual Teaching of Ramana Maharshi.* Boston: Shambhala, 1988.

Manjushrimitra. *Primordial Experience: An Introduction to Dzogs-chen Meditation.* Translated by Kennard Lipman and Namkhai Norbu. Boston: Shambhala, 1987.

Merzel, Dennis G. *The Eye Never Sleeps: Striking to the Heart of Zen.* Boston: Shambhala, 1991.

Milarepa. *Songs on the Spot.* Translated by Nicole Riggs. Eugene, OR: Dharma Cloud, 2003.

Miller, Richard. *Yoga Nidra: The Meditative Heart of Yoga.* Boulder, CO: Sounds True, 2005.

Nagarjuna. *Verses from the Center: A Buddhist Vision of the Sublime.* Translated by Stephen Batchelor. New York: Riverhead, 2001.

Nagarjuna. *The Central Philosophy: Basic Verses.* Translated by Erik Hoogcarpsel. Amsterdam: Olive Press, 2005.

Norbu, Chogyal Namkhai. *The Cycle of Day and Night: Where One Proceeds Along the Path of Primordial Yoga.* Oakland, CA: Zhang Zhung Editions, 1984.

Norbu, Chogyal Namkhai. *Dzogchen Teachings.* Ithaca, NY: Snow Lion Publications, 2006.

Norbu, Chogyal Namkhai. *The Mirror: Advice on the Presence of Awareness.* Barrytown, NY: Station Hill Press, 1996.

Poonja, H.W.L. *Wake Up and Roar.* Boulder, CO: Sounds True, 2007.

Prendergast, John J. and Ken Bradford, eds. *Listening from the Heart of Silence.* St. Paul, MN: Paragon House, 2007.

Prendergast, John J., Peter Fenner, and Sheila Krystal, eds. *Sacred Mirror: Nondual Wisdom & Psychotherapy.* St. Paul, MN: Paragon House, 2003.

Rabjam, Longchen. *The Precious Treasury of the Way of Abiding.* Junction City, CA: Padma Publishing, 1998.

Rabjam, Longchen. *The Precious Treasury of the Basic Space of Phenomena.* Junction City, CA: Padma Publishing, n.d.

Rabjam, Longchen. *A Treasury Trove of Spiritual Transmission.* Junction City, CA: Padma Publishing, n.d.

Reynolds, John M. *Self-Liberation Through Seeing with Naked Awareness.* Barrytown, NY: Station Hill Press, 1989.

Rinpoche, Chokyi Nyima. *Present Fresh Wakefulness: A Meditation Manual on Nonconceptual Wisdom.* n.p.: Rangjung Yeshe Publications, 2002.

Rinpoche, Dubwang. *Fearless Simplicity: The Dzogchen Way of Living Freely in a Complex World.* n.p.: Rangjung Yeshe Publications, 2003.

Rinpoche, Khenchen Thrangu. *A Song for the King: Saraha on Mahamudra Meditation.* Somerville, MA: Wisdom Publications, 2006.

Rinpoche, Khenchen Thrangu. *Everyday Consciousness and Primordial Awareness.* Ithaca, NY: Snow Lion Publications, 2007.

Rinpoche, Lama Zopa. *Transforming Problems into Happiness.* Somerville, MA: Wisdom Publication, 2001.

Rinpoche, Lama Zopa. *Ultimate Healing: The Power of Compassion.* Somerville, MA: Wisdom Publications, 2001.

Rinpoche, Sogyal. *The Tibetan Book of Living and Dying.* n.p.: Rider and Co., 2000.

Rinpoche, Tsoknyi. *Carefree Dignity: Discourses on Training in the Nature of Mind.* n.p.: Rangjung Yeshe Publications, 1998.

Rinpoche, Tulku Urgyen. *As It Is (vol 1 and 2).* n.p.: Rangjung Yeshe Publications, 1999 and 2000.

Rosenberg, Marshall B. *Nonviolent Communication: A Language of Life.* Encinitas, CA: PuddleDance Press, 2003.

Rosenberg, Marshall B. *Nonviolent Communication.* Boulder, CO: Sounds True, 2004.

Sengcan. *Trust in Mind: The Rebellion of Chinese Zen.* Someville, MA: Wisdom Publications, 2005.

Shapiro, Isaac. *It Happens by Itself.* n.p.: Luechow Press, 2001.

Sieler, Alan. *Coaching to the Human Soul: Ontological Coaching and Deep Change.* Newfield Australia: Victoria, 2003.

Thundup, Tulku. *Boundless Healing: Meditation Exercises to Enlighten the Mind and Heal the Body.* Boston: Shambhala, 2001.

Thundup, Tulku. *Buddha Mind: An Anthology of Longchen Rabjam's Writings on Dzogpa Chenpo.* Edited by Harold Talbott. Ithaca, NY: Snow Lion Publications, 1989.

Thundup, Tulku. *The Healing Power of the Mind.* Boston: Shambhala, 1998.

Thurman, Robert. *Infinite Life.* New York: Riverhead, 2005.

Thurman, Robert. *The Inner Revolution.* New York: Riverhead, 1998.

Tolle, Eckhart. *The Power of Now: A Guide to Spiritual Enlightenment.* Novato, CA: New World Library, 2004.

Trungpa, Chögyam. *Cutting Through Spiritual Materialism.* Boston: Shambhala, 1987.

Vesna, B. and Alan Wallace. *A Guide to the Bodhisattva Way of Life (Bodhicaryavatara).* Ithaca, NY: Snow Lion Publications, 1997.

Welwood, John. *Perfect Love, Imperfect Relationships: Healing the Wound of the Heart.* n.p.: Trumpeter, 2007.

Welwood, John. *Toward a Psychology of Awakening: Buddhism, Psychotherapy, and the Path of Personal and Spiritual Transformation.* Boston: Shambhala, 2002.

Wilber, Ken. *The Simple Feeling of Being: Embracing Your True Nature.* Boston: Shambhala, 2004.

Yeshe, Lama Thubten. *Becoming the Compassion Buddha: Tantric Mahamudra for Everyday Life.* Somerville, MA: Wisdom Publications, n.d.

Yeshe, Lama Thubten. *Introduction to Tantra: A Vision of Totality.* Edited by Jonathan Landaw. Somerville, MA: Wisdom, 1987.

Index

completion time for, 248–249
conditions for satisfying, 249
negotiation and, 249–250
revoking, 245–246, 249–250
unclear, 247
communication. *See also*
conversations
commitments and, 245–250
completion and, 225–226
entrainment, 111–112
facts, 243
failures of, 250
integrity and, 247
interpretations, 243
miscommunication, 222–223
negotiation, 244, 249–250
nondual, 109–116, 209
oblique, 247
offers, 240–241, 247
promises, 243–244, 245–246
pure listening, 109–113, 209,
222, 224
pure speaking, 113–114, 222
radiant, 221–255
requests, 239–241; 247–248
responses, 242
silence and, 112
talking about nothing,
114–116
technologies, 221–255
unconditioned awareness and,
223
communities, spiritual (*sanghas*),
209–211, 232
compassion, 116–118, 228

Complete Fulfillment (*Dzogchen*),
2
completion, 79, 80, 217
achieving, 133–142
acknowledging, 246
communication and, 225–226
declaring, 136
failing to declare, 250
in the here and now, 127–145
living with, 225–226
unconditioned awareness and,
128
conditioned existence
acknowledging, 164–166
defining, 160–162
denying, 160–162
conditioned experience
language and, 61–62
understanding, 23–35
conditioned mind, 9–10
conditioning, 10. *See also*
conditioned existence;
conditioned experience;
conditioned mind
connecting with, 64
contemplation as awareness of,
60–61
the future, 141–142
incompletion and, 130–131,
132
transcending, 133–134
conflict, 27–29
between being and doing, 28
beliefs and, 27–28
harmonization of, 24

insight meditation (*vipashyana*),
148
integrity, 247
intense experiences, 208–209
interpretations, 187–190, 243. *See
also* meaning
intimacy, 116–117, 118–119
invincibility, 11

J

jnana yoga, 148
judgments, 77–78
  coexistence and, 31
  conflict and, 28
  observing without, 226–227,
    243
  violence and, 226–227
"just sitting", 64–66, 68–69, 210.
    See also sitting
  adjusting practice, 71–72
  clothing for, 70
  preparing physical
    environment for, 70
  questions about, 72–73
  shared sessions, 73–74
  space for, 70
  support for, 70–71
  temperature for, 70
  timing of, 69–70

K

Kant, Immanuel, 30
karma, 128
karma yoga, 137
Katie, Byron, 134

knowing
  need to know, 44–46
  not knowing, 45, 210–211
koans, 150–152
Krystal, Phyllis, 134

L

lamas, 3
language, 61–62, 228–229
language-action paradigm, 228–
  229
Lankavatara Sutra, 33
Lao Tzu, 4
letting go, 170–171
letting things be
  when nothing is missing,
    80–81
  when something is missing,
    81–83
limitation, 148
listening, 109–113
Longchenpa, 4, 5, 44, 78, 207–208
looking back, 134–136
looking forward, 137–139
lost opportunities, 63
love, 116–117, 118, 121

M

Madhyamaka tradition, 2, 88, 148
Mahamudra tradition, 18, 66
Mahayana tradition, 11, 61, 120,
  148, 175, 228
mandalas, 252–254
  of existence, 253
  kinds of, 253–254

Manjushrimitra, 56

meaning, need to create, 46–47.
    See also interpretations

meditation. *See also*
    contemplation; contemplative
    practice; nonmeditation;
    sitting
    adjusting practice, 71–72
    clothing for, 70
    as conversation, 61–63
    "going beyond", 66–68
    insight meditation
        (*vipashyana*), 148
    "just sitting", 210
    natural, 62
    physical environment for, 70
    questions about, 72–73
    shared sessions, 73–74
    space for, 70
    support for, 70–71
    temperature for, 70
    timing of, 69–70

metaperspectives, 181–182

metapositions, 181–182

Middle Way (*Madhyamaka*), 2,
    88

Milarepa, 4

mind, primordial, 4

mind-to-mind transmission, 114

miscommunication, 222–223

N

nadi (energy pathways), 170

Nagarjuna, 4, 148, 194–195

natural contemplation, 59–60

natural meditation, 62

natural release, 77–85

need for change, systems based
    on, 57

need to know, 44–46

negativity, 24–25

negotiation, 244, 249–250

nirvana, 11

Nisargadatta, 121

nishkama-karma (desireless
    action), 212

no-mind, 4, 11

no one, 120

nondual approach, 66, 77, 80

nondual communication, 109–125,
    235–236

nondual experience, 161–162,
    192–194

nondual perspective, 2

nondual state of consciousness, 10

nondual teaching, 5–7, 16–17,
    18–19

nondual traditions, 2–3, 4–5, 67

nondual work, 3, 17–18
    completeness and, 80
    contemplative practice, 58–59
    unconditioned awareness and,
        16–17

nonduality, 16–17

noninterference, 77–85

nonmeditation, 60, 67

nonseparation, 118

nonviolent communication,
    226–228

not knowing, 45, 210–211

physical environment, 70
physicality, 94, 96
positive experiences, 130–131
possibilities, creating, 233–235,
   236–237
practice, contemplative. *See*
   contemplative practice
practices, 3–4
prajna, 120
Prajnaparamita tradition, 2, 11,
   45–46, 79
prana (energy movements), 170
prasanga-vichara (deconstructive
   analysis), 148
preoccupation with self, 25
presentness, 63–64
primordial mind, 4
problems, 43
promises, 243–244, 245–246. *See
   also* commitment; requests
pure awareness, 4, 11
pure listening, 109–113, 119, 209,
   222, 224
pure speaking, 113–114, 222
purification, ultimate, 190–191
purity, 12, 13–14

R

radiance, in the *Dzogchen*
   tradition, 12
radiant communication, 221–255
radiant mind, 23, 34–35, 217. *See
   also* desirelessness
   evolution of, 23–35
   the future and, 212–214

ineffability of, 34
as personal experience, 34–35
unconditioned awareness and,
   11–12
unconditioned bliss, 34
as union of love and wisdom,
   121
reactions. *See also* responses
   observing, 216–217
   "seeing through", 217–219
reality, 4, 5
   acknowledging, 165–166
   denial of, 160–162
   paradox and, 33–34
reflection, 78
release, 170–171
release, natural, 77–85
requests. *See also* promises
   clean, 239–240
   declining, 247–248
   versus demands, 239–240
   fulfilling, 240–241, 242–243
   impossible, 186–187
   making, 239–240
   oblique, 247
   responses to, 242
resistance, 160–163, 166–167. *See
   also* denial
responses, 242. *See also* reactions
responsibility, 227–228
rigpa (awareness), 147
Rinpoche, Namkhai Norbu, 78–79
Rinpoche, Shyalpa, 161, 166–167
Rinzai Zen, 150
river of life, 159–173

unfindability analysis, 148
unfindability conversations, 187–190
Universal Embrace (*Mahamudra*), 2
unreality, 187–190

V

Vajrayana tradition, 11, 168, 252
violence, 227
vipashyana (clear seeing), 175–184
Vipassana tradition, 147

W

Watts, Alan, 45
Welwood, Jennifer, 47
wisdom
    contentless wisdom, 175
    love and, 121
    of no-wisdom, 175
witness consciousness, 4
work, 26

Y

Yeshe, Lama Thubten, 6
yoga, 137, 148
Yoga tradition, 18

Z

Zen tradition, 2, 11, 19, 56, 114, 147
    koans, 150–152
    Korean Zen, 151–152
    parodies of in Western culture, 193
    Rinzai Zen, 150

About the Author

Peter Fenner, Ph.D., met his root guru, the famed Tibetan lama Thubten Yeshe in 1974. Three years later he was ordained in India as a celibate monk. A condition of his ordination was that he continue to live in the world, with his wife and young daughters.

Peter has studied with many eminent Tibetan masters in Australia, the United States, Nepal, and India including Lama Zopa Rinpoche, Sogyal Rinpoche, Chogyal Namkhai Norbu, Geshe Lhundup Sopa, Traleg Rinpoche, Geshe Thubten Loden, Geshe Ngawang Legden, Zazep Tulku, and Geshe Tringley. He has also studied Zen and Theravada Buddhist practice.

In 1983 he completed a Ph.D. in the philosophical psychology of the Madhyamika tradition of Mahayana Buddhism. He taught Asian religions and philosophies at universities in Australia and the United States for over thirty years. He was a Senior Lecturer at Deakin University for twenty years.

After nine years as a monk, Peter gave back his ordination. This opened the way for an intensive exploration of Western traditions of healing and psychotherapy. In 1986 he began offering therapeutic adaptations of Mahayana wisdom to mental-health professionals. He subsequently founded the Center for Timeless Wisdom (www.wisdom.org), a Californian nonprofit organization. Timeless Wisdom functions internationally to offer the nondual love and wisdom of Mahayana in ways that are relevant and readily accessible to Western needs and lifestyles.

Peter's books include *The Ontology of the Middle Way, Reasoning into Reality, Intrinsic Freedom,* and *The Edge of Certainty.* His psychological essays have appeared in journals such as the *Journal of Contemplative Psychotherapy, Revision, Journal of the International Association for Spiritual Psychiatry, Psychologia, 3e millenaire,* and *Terre du Ciel.*

He has presented his work at Stanford University, Columbia University, University of California, Berkeley, Saybrook College, University of Madison-Wisconsin, JFK University, Spirit Rock, Naropa University, CIIS, Omega Institute, Open Center-Tibet House, Trimurti (France), Les Cormettes (France), Terre du Ceil (France), ZIST (Germany), the Center for Mind-Body Medicine (Israel), the Satya Sai Institute of Higher Learning (India), and others.

In 2002 Peter developed the core nine-month Radiant Mind training, which is now offered in North America, Europe, and Australia. The training is the fruition of his international teaching over the last fifteen years. He also offers individual spiritual counseling to clients.

Peter has a unique capacity for revealing unconditioned awareness. He is known for the precision, intimacy, and humor with which he observes and deconstructs the fixations and fixed frames of reference that block entry to radiant presence.

RADIANT MIND COURSES

Timeless Wisdom offers a three-day introduction to Radiant Mind and a nine-month Radiant Mind Training. The nine-month Radiant Mind Training gives participants a comprehensive opportunity to work directly with Peter in cultivating Radiant Mind over an extended period and learning how to embed this state into their everyday life. The training is based on workshops, teleconferences, individual coaching sessions, and an expanded version of material in this book.

Information about the introductions and trainings can be found at the websites www.wisdom.org and www.radiantmind.net.

About Sounds True

Sounds True was founded in 1985 with a clear vision: to disseminate spiritual wisdom. Located in Boulder, Colorado, Sounds True publishes teaching programs that are designed to educate, uplift, and inspire. We work with many of the leading teachers, thinkers, healers, and visionary artists of our time.

To receive a free catalog of tools and teachings for personal and spiritual transformation, please visit www.soundstrue.com, call us toll-free at 800-333-9185, or write

The Sounds True Catalog
PO Box 8010
Boulder CO 80306